Born in Beijing in 1958, Xinran was a journalist and radio presenter in China. In 1997 she moved to London, where she wrote her best-selling book *The Good Women of China*. Since then she has written a regular column for the *Guardian*, appeared frequently on radio and TV, and published *Sky Burial*, *What the Chinese Don't Eat*, *Message from an Unknown Chinese Mother*, the novel *Miss Chopsticks* and a ground-breaking work of oral history, *China Witness*. Her charity, The Mothers' Bridge of Love, was founded to help disadvantaged Chinese children and to build a bridge of understanding between the West and China.

XINRAN

The remarkable truth of
China's one-child generations

Buy Me The Sky

Translated by Esther Tyldesley

and

David Dobson

LONDON · SYDNEY · AUCKLAND · JOHANNESBURG

10 9 8 7 6 5 4 3 2 1

Rider, an imprint of Ebury Publishing,
20 Vauxhall Bridge Road,
London SW1V 2SA

Rider is part of the Penguin Random House group of companies whose
addresses can be found at global.penguinrandomhouse.com

Copyright © Xinran Xue 2015

Xinran has asserted her right to be identified as the author of this Work in
accordance with the Copyright, Designs and Patents Act 1988

First published by Rider in 2015. This edition published 2016

www.eburypublishing.co.uk

A CIP catalogue record for this book is available from the British Library

ISBN 9781846044731

Printed and bound in Great Britain by Clays Ltd, St Ives PLC

Penguin Random House is committed to a sustainable future for our business,
our readers and our planet. This book is made from Forest Stewardship
Council® certified paper.

MIX
Paper from
responsible sources
FSC® C018179

To my godchildren for their love and kindness, and who are like sisters and brothers to my son Panpan (Yibo)

一个孤独的时代造就了一代孤独的人，

他们在拥有的海洋中孤独地守着自我。

在大陆和海洋的孤岛之间构筑隧道和桥梁，

正是今天中国的独生子女们在做的事情—

An age of loneliness created a generation of lonely people,

Solitary, they keep lonesome watch over their own selves in a sea of plenty.

Building tunnels and bridges between lonely islands and the mainland,

This is what today's only sons and daughters are doing.

Xinran

CONTENTS

INTRODUCTION

E VER SINCE I came to live in Britain in 1997, I have tried my
best to return to China twice a year, in order to keep my 'education' up to date. This is because the immense changes taking place
in China today far, far exceed anything that can be found in school
books or historical records. The evolution of the whole country,
from the stratospheric rise of the economy, to the transformation
of society, and the continual new and surprising developments in
the relationships between people, have all come together to produce
a society that is moving at unprecedented speed. Everything in
China, the people, events and objects have been agitated so much
that it feels as if they are fragmenting at the speed of light. I
know that if I don't keep on top of my 'education', I will find myself
suspended in the space and time of what my son calls 'ancient China'.

Almost every time my son, Panpan, comes back from China,
whether from volunteering in the remote countryside, taking an
ordinary train for twenty hours (he often does this as homework
on China), or visiting friends and family in the city, he always comes
back awash with new questions. Why is there such a great difference
between the cities and the countryside? How can there be decades
of separation between places in a country run by the same rulers?
How can one make sense of the changes that are taking place in
China? Who represents Chinese people today – the white-collar
workers, circling between cities and airports? Or peasants and
migrant workers, travelling on foot in rural villages and jolted
between long-distance bus stations? If China is a communist country,

why do the rural poor have no safety net in childbirth, sickness and death? And if it is a capitalist country, why is the economy run by a single-party government? Does he himself even count as native Chinese? At these times I feel like clapping my hand over his mouth! It is just impossible to find answers that would satisfy him. Truthfully speaking, I don't even know where he *can* find the answers. But I cannot give up seeking them, not just for his sake, but also for myself, as a daughter of China and a Chinese mother.

In the summer of 2010 I returned once more to China to update my 'knowledge of the motherland' and to research this book. I went back to a place that I had not seen in twenty years – Harbin, the capital of China's northernmost province, Heilongjiang. The first time I visited Harbin was in 1991, on a flying visit to research the history of the city's Jewish residents. Both the Jin and Qing dynasties originated in Harbin. In AD 1115 the Jin dynasty set up their capital in what is now Harbin's Acheng district. At the end of the nineteenth century Harbin was still made up of a dozen or so villages clustered together, with a population of only some 30,000. However, this was all about to change, as the city's transport links, trade and population began to expand rapidly. By the time the China Far Eastern Railway was constructed, from 1896 to 1903, connecting Siberia to Vladivostok through Heilongjiang province, Harbin already had the embryonic form of a modern city. By the early twentieth century, it had become an international trading port, with 160,000 foreigners from thirty-three different countries and sixteen consulates.

I have always felt that in the last century of China's history, long before the Reform and Opening-up policy of 1980, Harbin was a gathering place for immigrants. It seemed that out of every ten people, nine were from somewhere else. The city was also a great hub for the children and grandchildren of explorers, for wanderers escaping war or looking for work, and for thousands of escaped convicts in search of shelter. From the end of the Qing dynasty, thousands upon thousands of Jews came to Harbin along the Trans-Siberian Railway, fleeing pogroms in Europe and Russia, making it the largest Jewish community in the Far East. Together with Chinese immigrants from the four corners of the country, Harbin's Jews helped shape a century of the city's history.

The Harbin of 2010, like the rest of China's 600-plus cities, was racing to reinvent itself into a network of skyscrapers, densely populated and surging ahead with commerce, hell-bent on ignoring the character of the settlement and rejecting its traditional style. The same rush for the standardisation of living space was also devouring Harbin's old Russian backdrop and traditions, its old Jewish customs, and the lively, unpretentious workshops and stalls. There was only a handful of places that still carried the imprint of the years: mosques sitting incongruously on the noisy streets, calling out their prayers in proud voices several times a day; the cathedral of St Sophia surrounded on all sides by serried ranks of shopping malls; and Central Street, chock-full of signs using the Western alphabet. Among these man-made constructions, the Songhua River silently witnessed the shifting geography and customs of the city, its riverside culture flowing down the generations. In winter, generations of Harbiners would gather to admire ice-carved lanterns. While in summer, they would take to the river in boats, talking, singing and dancing in a boiling stream of humanity. The Songhua River was the classroom that taught me to understand Harbin.

Strolling quietly and leisurely past its people, watching their words and gestures, occasionally pausing to ask old people respectful questions (even when they found them silly) was a great and genuine pleasure for me. I remember one time in particular seeing something that struck me as entirely new. Six people spanning three generations, all standing around one precious child, watching intently.

Passers-by craned their necks to see and hear the piping tones of a toddler just learning to speak.

'Mummy, buy me the river!' the three-year-old girl said in a lisping voice to her mother.

One of the girl's little hands was clutching her mother's finger, while the other pointed out over the Songhua River. 'Mummy, I want that river, buy me that river!' she said in a determined voice.

The young mother tried to pacify her. 'Sweetie, we can't buy this big river!'

Close behind the mother and daughter, four old people who might have been her grandparents were debating in low voices. 'You can't say that, it's not that you can't afford it, it's that it's not possible to buy it.'

'Don't upset the child, just say we'll buy it when she's grown up. Wouldn't that do?'

'Yes, just tell the little cutie to ask her daddy how to buy a river.'

'*Aiya*, if you say that, won't you be teaching her from an early age to believe in lies?'

'What does the dear little thing know about true and false? Just keep her happy, once she's grown up she won't want to buy any rivers!'

'Be quiet, all of you, listen to what our precious little thing is saying!'

The quietly arguing family suddenly fell silent, as though they were listening to an imperial edict. 'Then I want to buy a star in the sky!' the little girl demanded in her babyish voice.

I did not stop to listen to any more, so I never knew if the little girl had further requests, but I found it impossible to understand those old people's words, and the way they took their little grand-daughter's naïve demands so seriously. That evening, I telephoned a friend, and didn't hold back my feelings on the subject, but to my surprise she didn't agree at all. 'What's so special about that?' she said. 'My four-and-a-half-year-old grandson once kicked up such a fuss about wanting the moon. It went on for days and days, until my daughter-in-law bought a round Japanese paper lampshade for the light in their house, and tricked him with a tale about how the moon had sent her child to our house for him to play with. In order to keep him happy, all the family invited the moon-children to visit, and we ended up buying loads of lanterns. When some visitors from my hometown came over, they thought we were in mourning with all these white lanterns around! There's nothing you can do about it, Xinran. These single-sprout children are more precious than gold.'

'But what if the child brings up owning the sea, or the blue sky?' I didn't know why I was making things so difficult for her.

'Who knows what we'd do . . .' It was as if a black hole, of the kind that Hawking, Thorne, Preskill and their peers are continually debating, formed by the weight of the answers we could not find, had dropped between our two worlds at either end of the telephone line, plunging us both into silence.

In fact, that black hole of silence has already drawn in countless families with only children, all desperately racking their brains for ideas, and this includes me, as a mother of an only child myself. As we bring up our 'one-and-onlies', we spend our days and nights in fear of some one-in-a-million accident. As they grow, our precious 'one-and-onlies' seem to be creating black holes of their own that suck in all the surrounding energy, wearing down us parents, who set out full of vigour, determination and ardour, into exhaustion, but without freeing us from worry. We constantly ask the question, 'Is our "one-and-only" safe and happy?' Together with our children, we have written a 'one-and-only' chapter in China's history books, a black hole of invention and truth – the age of the only children.

After ten or so years of living in the UK, almost all of my Western friends have expressed interest and concern over the phenomenon of China's only children. Western society's speculations and lack of understanding on this issue were highlighted for me when I searched the world's media for information on the subject. Understanding the one-child policy seems to have become a 'marker' of whether someone knows about modern China. It has even become the 'winning hand' of some media people, in their attempt to 'keep up with the fashions of Chinese politics'.

With regard to the history of the one-child policy, a lot of background information can be found in my book *Message from an Unknown Chinese Mother*. So here I will only give a basic reintroduction for readers who are not yet familiar with the policy, and there is also more information in Appendix I.

For a while at the end of the 1950s, China emulated the Soviet Union in encouraging high birth-rate families. In July 1957 Chinese population expert Ma Yinchu published an article in the *People's Daily* newspaper, 'On the New Population', in which he suggested a policy of population control. This directly contradicted the government's policy of strictly limiting abortions and encouraging population growth. Ma paid a heavy price for not toeing the party line, and was punished for many years from the late 1950s. However, come the early 1960s, and the disastrous economic stagnation that followed in its wake, Tianjin, Shanghai, Guangdong and other big cities all proposed population control measures of their own. The turning point came in December 1979 when Vice-Premier Chen Muhua, the first woman to reach that rank, stated that the nation's economic development was lagging behind, and was out of proportion to, the huge growth in population. She then suggested that it would be best if married couples only had one child. By 1981 this suggestion had become a firm duty for Communist Party members, and an unavoidable responsibility for every citizen. However, the promotion of the one-child policy met with resistance from all over China, in ways that the policy-makers had never anticipated, and resulted in several bouts of advance and retreat between rigorous implementation by the government and desperate resistance on the part of the populace. This animosity led to an amendment in 1982, stipulating ten conditions under which people in the countryside could have a second child. After this, resistance from the population calmed somewhat. In April 1984 the term 'population control policy currently in effect' was first coined in official government documents. It was split into three categories: 'residents of towns and cities', which mainly covered large and medium-sized cities, and mainly applied to Han Chinese, where married couples were restricted to one child (multiple births excepted); 'rural areas', where a second child was allowed if the first was a girl (although in practice, many families went on to have three, the policy being difficult to enforce in these regions) and 'ethnic minorities', who were permitted between two and four children. There were some slight variations between the rural provinces as to what was permitted, but there was such a huge difference between city and countryside in terms of living conditions that no one would ever dream of moving to a rural area to have more children.

In post-1949 China *fagui*, which means laws and regulations, refers to rules based not on the law, but on issued government policy. However, those who disobey these rules face sanction under the law. Family planning and the one-child policy are both *fagui*.

Although the one-child rule had been government policy for a long time, it was not until 29 December 2001 that it became enshrined in law. It was put into effect on 1 September 2002 as the Population and Family Planning Law of the People's Republic. After all the years of the one-child policy, this was the first time that it was actually set down in writing as a law. Moreover, the wording of the document was far more relaxed and humanitarian than the terms that had previously been enforced. For example, the twenty-seventh article of the seventh chapter states:

For married couples who agree to have only one child during the course of their lives, the nation will issue a 'One-child Glory Certificate'. A married couple who has been issued such a 'Glory Certificate' will be rewarded as set down in the national regulations, as well as in the regulations of the province, autonomous region or centrally governed city in which they reside. All work units are responsible for implementing the laws, *fagui*, rules and regulations regarding these rewards, and all work units must carry out this policy. If an only child suffers unexpected injury or death, the local People's Government must provide parents the necessary assistance to have another child or adopt. Twins or multiple births will not enjoy the treatment afforded to only children. Those who contravene the one-child policy must pay a 'legally required social fostering or maintenance fee' or see above-quota children confiscated by the government; fee to be determined at provincial level, to take into account average incomes of urban and rural residents.

Over the course of more than twenty years from the start of the one-child policy to near when it was enshrined in law, average birth rates in China fell from 5.44 in 1971 to 1.84 in 1998. These twenty-odd years of birth control resulted in 238 million fewer children in China. By 2012 this number had swelled to approximately 400 million fewer births. One could argue that this is a great contribution to global population control. However, it is harder to put a price on what two generations of Chinese people have had to endure. Countless families financially ruined by fines, incalculable numbers of baby girls abandoned, a catastrophic ageing of the population, and generations of only children who have missed out on close sibling relationships.

The majority of stories in this book come from the first generation of only children affected by the one-child policy, born between 1979 and 1984. Unlike in the West, a 'generation' in this context can be counted in only a few years because change is so rapid.

By around the year 2000 this first generation had all finished studying and were beginning to make their way in the world. By 2002 they had reached the age when Chinese people commonly marry. The time they spent with me corresponded to this point in their lives, when they were entering the world of work and starting to think about getting married. These children have been similar to both my godchildren and my teachers in life. Those who I remember so fondly are mostly now already parents themselves, with careers of their own: a businessman in a multinational corporation, a teacher in an art college, a Chinese-Western media planner, a chef specialising in Japanese food, an architect, a hotel manager, and an academic with a PhD in researching Chinese diaspora. As with the difference between China's 656 cities* and the tens of millions of rural villages, these young people from the same generation are as different as the earth and sky. They travel alongside the 'Emperors and Aristocrats', yet have absolutely none of that sense of superiority. Just as their fathers' generation found things difficult they, too, are struggling for survival: in the vanguard of huge change.

These young people are the same generation as my son, and, as a member of the older generation and a mother, common sense forces me to ask, is it possible for me to understand them? There is an old Chinese saying that the separation between professions is like the separation between mountains; how much more so when one is separated by a generation. Listening to them speak from their hearts, talking with them frankly and without reserve, and striving to understand what has influenced them at their age and in their

---

* The country's sixth national census (May 2014) divided China's 656 cities into four categories: Mega-cities (54): non-agricultural population of above 1 million. Big cities (78 as of the year 2004): non-agricultural population of between 500,000 and 1 million. Middle-sized cities (213 as of 2004): non-agricultural population of between 200,000 and 500,000. Small cities (320 as of 2004): non-agricultural population of below 200,000.

generation have been the three principles by which I have observed their happiness, anger, grief and sorrow, and followed their ideas and desires. As a mother of a Chinese only child myself, instinct propels me to try to understand them, as it is these only children, more than 100 million in number, who will determine the future of China.

When I first set pen to paper for this book, I wondered how I could summarise a whole generation in just a few chapters. Having gone through the records of my previous five books, I found them loaded with scars and grief. So after two years of racking my brain for ideas, I decided to give myself a breather, and became determined to make the main focus of this book about a generation of characters who materially were much better off, and share some of the interesting, sometimes shocking and sometimes amusing, incidents in their lives. And my intention was to act, not as an expert or as a critic, but as a bridge between them and the readers, listening to their views and representing them as they are, so others can make up their own minds.

Then in January 2011, just as I was finishing the first draft of this book, the Yao Jiaxin incident rocked China, causing the following stories, which had started out as light, to take on a more sombre tone.

Late on the night of 20 October 2010, Yao Jiaxin, a twenty-two-year-old student in his third year at the Xi'an Conservatory of Music, ran over a twenty-six-year-old female migrant worker with his car. Not only did he make no attempt to help her, on the contrary, he was so afraid that this woman from the countryside would make trouble for him when he saw her memorising his number plate that he then stabbed her eight times with a knife he used to peel fruit. He killed this mother of a three-year-old child on the spot. Yao then fled in his car to another junction, where he ran over and injured another pedestrian, and it was only then that he was apprehended by a passer-by. However, the local Public Security Bureau released him after only questioning him about the incident at the second junction. Three days later, on the 23rd, he handed himself in to the police, accompanied by his parents. On 11 January 2011 the Xi'an Procuratorate charged him with premeditated murder. On 22 April 2011 the Xi'an Intermediate Level Court found him guilty of premeditated murder, and, amidst intense media scrutiny and internet debate he was sentenced to death, with his political rights stripped. He was also ordered to pay the victim's family 45,498.50 yuan ($6,690) as compensation for their economic loss. On 20 May the sentence was confirmed by the Shaanxi High People's Court.

For a time, it seemed the whole of China was divided into three tribes along theoretical and moral lines. One faction considered the circumstances of Yao's crime were so heinous that if he did not die, it would be tantamount to the death of Chinese law. Another came from a large number of university students, who maintained that the life of an only child who had been put through higher education in the arts was of more intrinsic value than that of an uneducated peasant! The third held that Yao was a victim of an only-child society. His death penalty would also affect the two generations before him because Chinese elders should be looked after by the younger generations in China's traditional pension system.

As journalist Deng Yajun said in the *International Herald Tribune*:

The Yao Jiaxin case shows us many of the strange and grotesque aspects of Chinese society. Originally it was a minor traffic injury, yet he struck the victim eight blows with a knife. Originally the circumstances of the trial were clear and the law could be depended on. Originally it provoked the anger of the masses. Yet some people actually vilified the victim who had died so cruelly and 'rallied to Yao Jiaxin's defence' on the internet . . .

Whether in China's official media or on non-governmental websites, anything that touched on this case was like a stone flung into the water, raising a thousand waves, as a great battle unfolded between five generations of people. The sighing of the grandparents' generation, the repining of the parents' generation, and the fierce debate between three generations of only children (those born after 1970, 1980 and 1990), all of them tussling over the rights and wrongs, and the glory and shame of their own standpoints.

The post-70s generation (the subject of this book) refers to children born between 1970 and 1979, as well as many children born at the start of the 1980s who also refer to themselves as 'post-70s' because their experiences have been similar. Because this generation's parents and grandparents had struggled to fulfil their own potential during the turbulent Cultural Resonation, their 'educational dreams' subtly influenced the upbringing of their children, who accepted the social values of previous generations. They were eager for success, and hoped that their struggles would make up for the lost opportunities of their parents and grandparents.

The post-80s generation, on the other hand, were born in the mid to late 1980s. Due to the extreme changes in China's social values at the time, and their complete incompatibility with traditional family life, many of their parents started to look to the West for a future. This resulted in a generation of children who were adrift, caught between the conflict of old and new ideas within China, and the intense clash between Eastern and Western culture.

The post-90s generation grew up in the 1990s, during all the success of China's Reform and Opening-up policies. It was also the time when digital and information technologies were developing at flying pace. They were born into, and grew up in, a world of 'three screens' – the computer, television and mobile phone – and this had an even more detrimental effect on family relationships. A high-quality, relaxed and comfortable living environment, along with a relatively stable political and economic situation, left this generation uniquely able to take on new things. However, it also moulded their values and standards of behaviour into something radically different from those of traditional China.

Although there is only ten or twenty years' difference between the post-70s, -80s, and -90s generations, the pace of change in Chinese society was so enormous that it created profound divisions between them. These only children are the pathfinders of their generations, and in every decade from the 1970s to the present day, they have been the witnesses and inheritors of all the losses and gains that have taken place in China's families, society and education.

Yao Jiaxin belonged to the second generation of China's only children, the ones caught between old and new. According to media reports, his extreme behaviour, rebelliousness and crushing doubts came from the narrowness of his life situation. Apart from practising the piano and studying, he had no other opportunities to come into contact with society. He did not understand how to deal with people outside the home and classroom. His parents were like gods to him, while the piano was his life. In order to protect his piano-playing hands, he hardly ever dared to use a knife. At home his parents would peel fruit for him, and at school he would ask his classmates to do it. And yet he took up a fruit knife in those delicate pianist's hands and stabbed to death a woman he had already injured.

China's sociologists maintain that from an early age only children are cosseted by their parents, doted on by friends and relatives, and drilled and trained at school, so much so that they never have the opportunity to take on responsibility. The material and spiritual burdens, that should be theirs to bear, are 'kindly' taken away by the people around them, leaving them without a 'self' of their own. For this reason, their behaviour in difficult situations falls back into base intuition, fight or flight mode. After all, a person without a 'self' is barely different from a wild animal. In this sense, Yao Jiaxin is a victim of China's one-child families.

I think that Yao Jiaxin's parents, like the majority of parents of only children in China, poured all their hearts and hopes for life into young Yao, believing that this was parental love. However, only children of this generation were burdened with the lives and responsibilities of their brothers and sisters who would never be born. They enjoyed all the material gifts and spiritual love and care that should have been shared with their unborn brothers and sisters. For this reason, they lacked practice in communication, friendship, sharing, helping others and being helped in return, forbearance and all the other basic interpersonal skills one learns growing up. It seemed as if the whole world belonged only to them. This generation of only children suffered from a lack of all those shared experiences that come from having siblings. They were always alone in their comings and goings, and, as such, character problems and a lack of humanity were bound to emerge. And the parents of these only children, having only one precious sprout, spent what seemed like all their time shaking with terror as they watched over their lone shoot, 'afraid that it would shatter in their hands, and melt in their mouths!'. Any accident that happened to an only child would mean the parents would have lost everything. For the sake of their only child, those parents reached the point of 'setting their own lives at naught'. In this situation, what kind of life was left to Yao Jiaxin's parents in the aftermath of the calamity? It was not an accident, but a disgrace, a source of self-reproach, a remorse, a sharp pain that nobody will ever be able to share with them. Would they ever be able to forget the little three-year-old son of the victim? Their failed child-rearing and love had stolen a child's mother for ever, as well as their own beloved son.

In May 2011, when Yao Jiaxin's sentence was confirmed, I was interested to know how the interviewees in this book saw the controversy.

I therefore sent them a written question, begging them to help me understand.

How do you view the Yao Jiaxin incident? Why is Chinese society debating him (a post-80s man) so fiercely?

The majority of them did not send me their replies until after Yao's execution on 7 June 2011. Reading between the lines, I not only saw their burgeoning maturity, but also recognised feelings of responsibility towards Chinese society as a whole, and their own attitudes to popular sentiment and morality. I have attached their individual replies at the end of their chapters, as their stories may help you to understand their points of view.

I admit I was surprised, and sometimes deeply shocked, by their replies but it was through their answers that I really became aware of just how difficult it was for them to live their lives as so many 'suns', 'emperors' and 'tyrants'.

The ten or so only children described in this book are all peers, all from the same generation, all born in the same country. At the same time, they are also from totally different backgrounds, and grew up through various periods of enormous change in China's remarkable development. When I look at their beliefs, values, survival skills, even the words they use, I am surprised by how different they are one from another – yet, in the eyes of ordinary Chinese people, they are all lumped together as 'the only-child generation'. However, I believe that, by the time you get to the end of this book, you will perhaps, like me, have been moved by each of them. In fact, not one among them is tied down by the consensus of the times. Not one of them feels limited by the segregation imposed upon their generation. There is a naturalness in their hearts that is refreshing.

Yes, this is a book about China's first generation of only children.

However, as you progress through the chapters, you will also see that it traces the course of the rapid changes that have taken place in Chinese society. To understand the Chinese only children of today is an invaluable resource to understanding not only China's future, but also how it interacts with the rest of the world. Why should we take heed of and try to understand the voice of this generation? Because the tomorrow we share with them is as priceless as the bright blue sky.

DU ZHUANG | 1

B Y THE end of the 1970s, the first group of 6.1 million children had been issued with only-child certificates by the Chinese government. These were to become the first generation of only children in China's unique history. Because of the Cultural Revolution and China's other, frequent political movements, many of their parents' and grandparents' marriages had been driven by politics and the need to survive. There were many cases of people denied the chance of an education due to their families having been made political scapegoats, forced to the countryside for re-education, married there and then returned to the city. Or of intellectuals and illiterate peasants coming together in marriage as no other choice was available to them. Or of husbands and wives forced to live apart on opposite banks of the Yangtze River or in opposite corners of the country. All of these were commonplace.

The children of these families were products of China's final age of extreme politics, at a time when family and social education were still bound up within closed-off traditions and campaigns of political terror. Their textbooks did not mention a word about China's real history after 1950. They experienced earth-shaking changes every day, snatching after definitions of right and wrong as best they could. As children, this first one-child generation had, to some extent, endured years of material deprivation, and through the quarrels and grudges between their parents they garnered but few faint hints about the past. All they had to accompany them through their lonely days and nights were overworked, exhausted parents, homes like empty nests, and the belief that if they were not spending their time in study or practice then they were bad children. Very many of these children became the ropes binding political marriages together, the only pretext for their parents to tolerate each other, and an analgesic for the pain of marriage. There were many such painful and humiliating cases to be found among my colleagues in the Chinese media, children who directly witnessed their parents' extramarital affairs, or even became embroiled, acting out roles from a perfect holiday family for the grandparents and wider family. Their level of understanding and filial obedience towards their parents left me startled, moved and uncomprehending.

In my many years as a journalist, I did come across some love stories from the 1970s, although not many. Du Zhuang's parents were one such couple.

In the early 1990s, even after nearly twenty years of Reform and Opening-up, so many things in China remained to be done. There was still no open cultural scene, with pop concerts, nightclubs and discos regarded as a few 'novelties from the West'. All media programming remained strictly controlled by the Communist Party. However, one group of people in the media were not willing to act simply as a mouthpiece for the party. They saw that radio and television were just entering a transitional period from state to independent management, and made use of this. As journalists, they used their special powers to experiment with a few new cultural activities on the radio. At that time, apart from my evening programme for women I was also one of those in charge of planning cultural programmes at my radio station. My responsibility was to find ways, within the limits of what was 'permitted', to produce more commercial programmes, so that the station could develop and survive. Part of my plan for 1991 was a new programme for choosing and judging soft drinks through public vote. We arranged for soft drink manufacturers from all of China's provincial capitals (over thirty in total) to take part, and organised three groups – listeners, experts and the media – to vote for their most popular beverage. At the time, drinks such as beer and fresh fruit juice had not yet entered mainstream culture, and people had to admire them from a distance as 'sophisticated and Western'. Ordinary people considered them to be part of 'elegant capitalist bar culture', and few believed that soft drinks could feature in China's culinary 'weather'. I hoped that this programme would broaden people's knowledge of soft drinks, and help the industry to expand in the domestic market. Du Zhuang's father was one of the first pioneering captains of industry to be given the task of running a soft drinks factory as a Chinese–overseas joint venture with foreign capital. He was a man of outstanding achievements, and for many years had been considered one of the nation's top ten businessmen. Through our radio station's 'Tastiest Soft Drinks Nationwide' poll, we became good friends.

Not long afterwards, Du Zhuang's father asked me to help him apply for a driving licence from the Traffic Control Office. At that time in China, people with a car of their own were as rare as phoenix feathers and unicorn horns, but I had held a driving licence since 1989 (I may also have been one of the first women in China to ride a motorbike!). The Public Security Bureau was then in charge of traffic management and I was on good terms with the organisation as I had previously helped them with public awareness programmes on road safety for rural areas and primary school children. The upshot of this was that I could help a few friends through the back door, by simplifying the political checks and paperwork that had to be got out of the way before they could officially apply for a licence. I had never really been able to understand why everything in China, from the most trivial to important issue, was tangled up in politics. However, I reminded myself that it was not that long ago since children as young as three had had to declare their parents' political status on entering kindergarten.

On the road to the Traffic Office with Du Zhuang's father, I fell back into my old habit of asking questions, and quizzed him on his family and society in general.

'You hold an important position, and you're very busy, yet you want to learn to drive. Why don't you just get a chauffeur to do the driving for you?'

'I want my wife to see me driving a car.'

His reply was most unexpected, as at that time in Chinese society it was a rare thing indeed to hear a big man utter words like these.

'When you say you want your wife to see you driving a car, what do you mean exactly?'

'You probably don't know this, but my wife is a peasant from the Shandong countryside. I was sent there during the Cultural Revolution, and as I was one of the Five Black Categories that were politically ostracised, everyone looked down their noses at me, anybody could pick on me. My wife's father was the head of the Big Brigade, and he treated me very well. He moved me from the communal fields to teaching in the primary school, and married his eldest daughter to me. My wife's an honest, unsophisticated country woman, who's had no education to speak of, and from an early age she did all the housework and looked after her little brothers and sisters; she's been through a lot. I brought her with me when I came back to the city. She had never left the countryside before, so life in a big city was like landing on another planet for her. She's very adaptable though, and in no time found a job as an entry-level manager for a women's clothes company. She's very ambitious and highly competitive; she even hopes I'll be the first captain of industry to learn to drive, so that her colleagues can see me come to pick her up in my car.'

I had met his wife before, and she seemed a good, honest, kind-hearted and frank woman, always dressed in red and black. Her favourite topic of conversation was where the cheapest goods were to be found. Close second was her husband, and how he could do anything. He always brought his wife along at public appearances, something that very few Chinese men do. Normally, Chinese men do not attend banquets with their wives, instead taking a secretary, a lover or a girl who they refer to as a student.

'Does the difference in education between you two affect your feelings towards her? Does it ever cause conflict?'

At this question, he gave me a serious look and fell silent for a moment. Then, gazing out of the window, he said calmly, 'Yes, sometimes it's very hard, especially in terms of our temperaments and interests. But I believe marriage is a responsibility, a contract between two lives. Once you have entered into that contract with another person, you shouldn't break it. I don't want to do anything that will make her family feel that I've let them down. I owe them a debt of gratitude, I want to give her a happy life.'

To think that there are still such men in China! How I sighed to myself upon hearing these words as keeping a mistress had already started to become 'fashionable' among Chinese men, and having a lover was nothing out of the ordinary at all. There were even a few bars and karaoke clubs where large numbers of female workers, recently laid off from their jobs, would congregate. Sometimes even their husbands kept them company as they plied their trade.

'Then how can you make your wife happy?' I said. 'The difference between the city and the countryside is like that between the earth and sky. The culture, all the different social classes in city life, the stylish clothes, how do you know that you can make her happy?'

'To tell you the truth, Xinran, at the moment she still hasn't fully got into city culture. The only way I can make her happy is by giving our child a good education. Country women take more pride in their man than anything else in the world, and after their husband comes their son. To a country woman a son who brings glory to the ancestors and the family is the biggest source of satisfaction in her whole life.'

Now, twenty years after that conversation, under the guidance and loving protection of her husband, Du Zhuang's mother has become a successful businesswoman in her own right. Not only that, but after her retirement she took up the piano and ballroom dancing, and goes to weekly ballet classes to keep herself in shape. She enjoys a standard of living to which many city women can only aspire.

I have a lot of friends in China to whom I can open my heart, but not many like Du Zhuang's parents. They give me encouragement and hope that the distortions of history and the cruelty of politics have not yet strangled the feelings and loyalty that Chinese people share. Because of my admiration for their sincere love, a sort of family feeling has evolved as part of our friendship, and these days many people assume that they are my older sister and brother-in-law.

Since I wrote *The Good Women of China* (published in 2002), I have observed an endless stream of China's good women, but barely a handful of good men. Over the last ten years I have interviewed or come into contact with over a hundred bosses, men of letters, politicians, peasants and workers, but very seldom have I heard any of them say their wives are good women or that they deserve to be loved and cherished. Du Zhuang's father has often appeared to me between the lines of my writing. Here at least was a good man who regarded his wife's happiness as his duty.

In 1999, when I had finished my book and gone back to China, I heard from my friends that a major rectification campaign was under way against Chinese–foreign joint ventures. Many leading businessmen had already been imprisoned, and it looked uncomfortably like Du Zhuang's father would be hard put to avoid a similar fate. I immediately telephoned his home, and he told me that while his foreign business partner was protecting him for the moment, there was no guarantee that he would not be in prison sometime soon. China's economy was feeling its way blindly into unfamiliar territory, and lacked the oversight and protection of an independent civil legal system. Apart from bringing criminal charges, no one was sure what the authorities could or would do. Finally he sobbed down the phone, 'If I go to prison I'll manage, but I'm worried that my wife won't be able to bear it, and my son's still at university – I'm afraid he'll be dragged down with me!'

'Is there any way I can help you?'

'Nobody can help. I know we don't have the old system of punishment any more, where entire families were executed because of the crimes of one member, but we do still have punishment by association, and blood guilt is still deeply embedded in Chinese consciousness. The boy isn't yet twenty; whether he will be able to come through this disaster and stand on his own two feet is a matter for fate now.'

Six months later on my return to China I visited the couple again, and was shocked by what I saw. Du Zhuang's father was reduced to skin and bones, and his wife was dreadfully pale and drawn. Both of them lived in fear of a knock on the door, and whenever the bell rang they thought it was someone coming to take them away.

I remembered what he had once told me, about the safety, health and happiness of their son being right at the heart of their family, so I said to them, 'I tell you what, my son has just gone off to boarding school in England. I still have a bit of energy left over, so send your son to London to study abroad; that way you can both rest easy, at least you won't be living in fear for your son.'

And so in the autumn of 2000, the year he turned twenty-one, their son Du Zhuang became part of our family life in London. He also became the key to unlocking the doors of my interest in China's first generation of only children, and the beginning of my serious attention to the subject.

The day of his arrival came, and I made my way to Heathrow airport to pick up Du Zhuang. This was before Chinese students had started flooding into the UK in the way they do now, and a tall, skinny Chinese youth standing at the airport exit was quite noticeable. Du Zhuang, thin, frail and as insubstantial as plywood, was pushing his suitcase with one hand, and talking to his mother on the phone with the other. He was not looking around for anyone, but instead was listening with single-minded attention to the phone. His expression was serious, almost devout, as if receiving an edict from the emperor. It was only when I was standing right in front of him that he finally stopped and looked at me with a smile. In those days Chinese people did not hug or exchange pecks on the cheek, and shaking hands was for grown-ups only. Clearly Du Zhuang saw me as part of his parents' generation, and did not dare to make any such rash moves.

Just five seconds after I had found him, Du Zhuang passed his mobile phone to me, saying, 'My mother's been waiting to speak to you!'

Over the phone, it seemed as if Du Zhuang's mother had jumped right out in front of me. I will never, ever, forget her first words, shouted at me down the phone: 'Xinran, my son's in your hands now! Remember to help him to open his suitcase, he can't do anything . . .'

She had said something else to me, but I couldn't remember it as I was totally stupefied by her words.

'Xinran, did you hear me? You absolutely must help him open his suitcase! He doesn't know how to deal with it! Hello? Xinran?'

I stood there in a daze, not knowing how to reply, and ended up just repeating what she had said back to her to be certain that I had not misheard: 'Big sister, you want me to open his suitcase for him? Which suitcase?'

Du Zhuang's mother was clearly irritated by my confusion. 'His suitcases, his luggage, he doesn't know how to open a suitcase, I packed everything for him!'

I was even more confused, 'He doesn't know how? But they're all his own things?'

'Yes, yes, yes! They're all his things, everything in the case is his own stuff!'

'Oh, is there something in the case you're worried might get broken?'

'Nooo! He doesn't know what's packed in the cases, and he doesn't know how to hang up his clothes, so you'll have to open everything for him, OK? Say you will! I handed him over to you, remember?'

It took me almost a decade spent with many Chinese only children before I fully understood the full implication of those three sentences!

Before I left China for the UK, I only knew that at some unknown point only children had become a focus for society, and had been given numerous pet names like 'little suns', 'little emperors' and so on. It was almost as if these children were seen as a different type of being, but I had no idea how they went about being emperors and suns. My only son Panpan was ten years younger than Du Zhuang, and in our family he was just the Pole Star at the very most.

On the way back from the airport I asked Du Zhuang, 'Your mother says you don't know how to open a suitcase or hang up your clothes, is that true?'

Back then Du Zhuang was just a big kid, introverted and shy. He lowered his head and muttered something in agreement.

'Why?'

'I don't know either.'

'But you've graduated from university, haven't you? How did you keep all your clothes in order at university?'

'My mum would come to the dormitory every week and tidy up for me.'

'She used to go to your university dormitory and put away your clothes? What, every weekend?'

When I heard this I could not make head nor tail of it: a mother clearing up her son's clothes in a university dormitory?

Du Zhuang saw my astonishment, but seemed baffled as well. 'Isn't that what all mothers do?'

I was starting to feel scared. His mother wasn't expecting me to tidy up his clothes for him every weekend . . . surely not?

Later on that evening, his mother confirmed my worst fears. Every weekend Du Zhuang was at university, she would descend upon his dormitory to organise things for him. She would change his bed, bring him fresh clothes and enough snacks to see him through the week, including several big dishes such as slow-cooked goose, roast duck and hearty stews. Her comings and goings often left all six of his dorm mates feeling awkward. Sometimes she would come charging in without even knocking, regardless of whether they were dressed. Seeing that they were embarrassed, she would say, 'What's the problem? I'm a mother! What mother hasn't seen those things of yours?'

Du Zhuang was the first only child I helped after coming to live in the West. I had no idea or experience about the best way to be of use to him, and acted purely on instinct. Before Du Zhuang arrived, I thought that, like Panpan, who came to the UK aged eleven, any Chinese person coming to the UK to live and study would have three main hurdles to overcome: language, which would give them freedom; good eating and drinking habits for health; and making local friends, which would define their future lives in the country. Language could not be picked up in a day, and for friends they would have to wait for opportunities to arise, but eating and drinking habits could start from day one. So I decided to take Du Zhuang to a pub called the Black Lion for roast chicken, a meal that most Chinese people can cope with.

Just as we were about to go in to the bar, a horrified expression came over Du Zhuang's face. 'I'm not sure that this is a good idea.'

'What's wrong with it? I don't understand.'

'I shouldn't be going to this sort of place,' he said hesitantly.

'Why shouldn't you be going to a pub? What sort of place do you think you should be going to, then?'

My ideas were plainly out of alignment with his notions of good and bad, which had been formed by a Chinese education. When I saw how uncomfortable it was making him, I had no choice but to take him back home, get two large chicken drumsticks out of the fridge, and roast them for him. I did not give him any chopsticks. 'You've come to the West, now you're in Rome you should do as the Romans do, so start practising with a knife and fork.' Poor Du Zhuang! That really was an exhausting meal for him; his face was coated in sweat, the knife and fork in his hands were a pair of tools that refused to obey his commands. But, like most Chinese children nowadays, he uttered not a word of complaint, nor a word of thanks (you just never know what they like and what they hate). Looking back on it now, I really put him on the spot that day. He had just come off a twelve-hour flight, and I dropped him into the jabbering world of English, and forced him into his 'Western cultural training' before he had any chance to recover.

That night I could not sleep. First, I was quite uneasy, as I had no idea how to help this young man acclimatise to an utterly alien world. Second, his mother had repeatedly phoned me from China wanting to know all the details of her son's ten hours in the UK. She had left me with instructions and explanations: her son was delicate because he was a fussy eater, with little interest in food, so I had to think of ways to tempt his appetite. He didn't dare to speak English because of his character, which made him shy away from people. I had to help him to get to know more people. When I asked her about his ability to live independently and organise his own life, she replied, 'What does a child of twenty understand?'

I objected strongly to this. Chinese parents never believe that their children can grow up, or that they can take charge of their own future. Confucius did not believe it 2,000 years ago, and neither do parents nowadays, not even in this age of information technology. It seems to be ingrained in Chinese culture.

However, subsequent events proved to me that Du Zhuang's mother was right and I was wrong. A few days later I went up to his room for a 'visit', and found the table, floor and every available surface covered in clothes and socks.

I asked him casually, 'Why haven't you hung up your clothes in the wardrobe?'

'Hang up? In the wardrobe? How do I do that?' he asked me in bewilderment.

I saw then that Du Zhuang really did not have the first clue about how to organise his own clothes. In his twenty years of growing up, had he never learned these basic skills at home? To be sure, in the past wardrobes had been rare and treasured items in ordinary house-holds, with only senior family members using them. Children's clothes were stacked in piles on simple shelves. But Du Zhuang's parents were very modern. If Du Zhuang had never organised his own wardrobe at home, how was he going to do it in England?

Every couple of days I would make Du Zhuang a Chinese meal to take the edge off his pining for his mother's cooking. One evening he mentioned that he fancied potato slivers in vinegar, so I bought two potatoes and told him, 'I'm busy editing my book, chop the potatoes into slivers and steep them in water, then I'll make them for you this evening.'

After about twenty minutes, hearing no sound or movement from the kitchen, I went to see what was happening. Du Zhuang was looming over the kitchen counter, knife in one hand, potato in the other, staring into space.

'Du Zhuang, what are you doing?'

'I'm wondering how to turn this spherical potato into slivers . . .'

At this I lost my temper. 'If you don't start by chopping it up, how are you ever going to turn it into slivers?'

'How do I do that?' he said, perplexed.

I got more annoyed. 'You're really telling me that you've never done any work in the kitchen, at your age?'

'No, at home the only thing I did apart from eating and sleeping was homework, nobody made me cook anything.'

'You managed to make it through university, you might just give it a try! Think, how would you turn a round potato into slivers? Can you cut it into slivers directly? Or do you first have to cut it into another shape?'

He mulled this over for ages. 'I don't know, strips? Or slices? I only studied economics at university.'

'Then just pick up the knife and give it a try. First cut the potato into strips or slices or chunks, and then see what the easiest way of cutting them into slivers is.' By this time I thought that my eyes must be radiating sparks.

He stood there, earnestly repeating, 'Cut the potato into strips, slices or chunks, then cut into slivers.'

I really had no time to spend going over these most basic of cooking skills with him, so I returned to my editing. Several minutes later, I heard a very slow noise coming from the kitchen – he had started to cut the potato! However, that slow, measured chopping sound continued unceasing for a very long time; twenty minutes later it was still going! How could he possibly be taking so long? I went to check on him again, and did not know whether to laugh or cry at the scene that greeted me. The kitchen counter was very low, and Du Zhuang was kneeling beside it. As I hadn't told him about slicing in batches, he was holding down a slice of potato with one hand, his eyes very close to the slice, carefully cutting it up, one sliver at a time! I took a photograph of him there and then. 'This photo I'm definitely going to show your family, how you finally grew up when you came to London aged twenty!'

In order to help Panpan and Du Zhuang understand the British countryside, we would sometimes accept friends' invitations to spend the weekend at their holiday cottages. One time we spent a long weekend at a friend's house on the south coast. Soon after we settled in, Du Zhuang dived into their office, and we all thought he had got hooked on some computer game. On Monday morning, our friend's part-time secretary arrived. She had only been in the office a couple of minutes when she started shouting, 'Who's been messing with my desktop? Where have all my files gone?'

We were all scared stiff by her violent outburst, but nobody knew what she was talking about. How could we have inadvertently moved her desktop files and messed up her system?

As we stood staring at each other in bewilderment, Du Zhuang very nervously announced, 'I tidied up her desktop for her; it was too chaotic, there was no logic to the way it was arranged at all!'

'You? You touched somebody else's work computer? Tidied up her files? What did you think you were doing? How did you tidy them up? Do you understand her business? How can you know anything about the logic behind her work? Aren't you afraid of being accused of invading someone's personal privacy? That's a crime, you know!'

Faced with reproaches in seven or eight different voices and in two different languages, Du Zhuang seemed bewildered and kept on repeating, 'I meant well, I just wanted to help her quietly!'

True enough, we Chinese do believe in the virtues of the old story of seven fairy maidens visiting the mortal world and performing good deeds, and the morality of the revolutionary soldier Lei Feng, who did good deeds without leaving his name. Moreover, we have never really got to grips with Western cultures' customs of etiquette and concepts of self and privacy. We are a confident race, and we teach our children these ancient codes of behaviour. Many overseas Chinese are full of well-meant, kindly advice for Westerners, through which they hope to convince them about their ideas of right and wrong, their methods for maintaining good health, and family education at home. I do not think that Du Zhuang was alone in not understanding what he had done; his mother would not have understood either, nor perhaps would lots of us who have spent *many* years living in the West!

After this incident, Du Zhuang said in an aggrieved tone, 'When I went to my father's office, nobody would say anything to me, no matter what I did to their things!'

I asked him, 'Is the world your home?'

At that moment, I could really see the sun and emperor that people spoke of.

The first time Du Zhuang met Toby, who is now my husband, was shortly after Toby had injured himself falling from a horse in Argentina, and had been repatriated back to London. Before going to the airport to collect him, I repeatedly impressed upon Du Zhuang that Toby was seriously hurt, and that he should mind his manners when he met him, so as not to make Westerners think that young Chinese people are heartless and ungrateful. However, I neglected to point out to him the differences between Chinese and Western culture on meeting someone for the first time.

As soon as Toby and I got home, Du Zhuang greeted us warmly, and in his halting English proceeded to give a textbook example of how Chinese people express their concern and good wishes. 'Hello, I'm Du Zhuang, you really have taken a terrible fall! Tut tut, your eyes are as black as a panda's! Tell me, does it hurt dreadfully?'

As soon as I realised that Du Zhuang hadn't the slightest clue about polite greetings in the West, I nipped behind Toby's back and gestured for him to say no more. But to my surprise, he totally failed to catch on. 'Yes, I heard you broke your shoulder, no wonder your lower back is all swollen up like a bear!'

I looked on helplessly as Toby blazed with fury at Du Zhuang's 'good wishes', and hurriedly got him settled into bed to rest. Toby, who was in a lot of pain, said angrily, 'Why are young Chinese people so cruel, making fun of my suffering?' I knew this was not a good moment to explain the cultural differences; what he needed was rest and painkillers.

I returned to the living room with a heavy heart, yet Du Zhuang was sitting there, plainly very excited. 'How did I do, I put on a good show, didn't I? I've never shown that much concern even to my mum and dad!'

I looked at him. From his expectant gaze I could tell that he was waiting for me to praise him, but he had never given a thought as to how best to help me tend to Toby in his injured state. I really did not know what to say for the best. Was this a generation of young Chinese people totally bereft of the nurturing influence of close family relationships and feelings, with no awareness of our common problems in society, to the extent that they were both self-centred but also hollow inside? Their basic knowledge of daily life seemed copied and recorded from books, films and the classroom. The way they expressed their feelings was, in many cases, an imitation. As for entering into other people's joys and sorrows, perhaps, to them, it was like coming into contact with an alien?

After spending several weeks coming to an initial understanding of Du Zhuang, I came to an arrangement with his parents that before he started his Master's course he would spend one year studying language. During this time he would live in a British household, where he could immerse himself in the language and get used to British society and culture. Of course, he would still come back to my home on weekends and holidays, to speak Chinese, get his fill of

Chinese food and discuss how he was doing with Chinese and Western culture.

We ended up finding an elderly lady in west London who took in students. Her kindness, knowledge and proper English were a priceless treasure for Du Zhuang as he learned about Western society. We agreed on three rules: he would eat three meals a day with the old lady; every day he would come up with a subject to talk about, with at least three questions; and he should take care of his own laundry. Perhaps this sounds ridiculous. To a Chinese only child just turned twenty-one, however, this is no small challenge. To put aside ideas of their own uniqueness and importance, and follow other people's wishes is a concept that barely existed for them when they were growing up.

The day we were helping Du Zhuang move into the old lady's house, his mother phoned just as we were opening the door to his room. Over the past few weeks, she had followed her son's progress closely, so that she could issue her instructions at precisely the right moment. Sometimes I found myself wondering if she possessed some kind of sixth sense. How else could she keep track of her son's movements so accurately from thousands of miles away and in another country?

On the phone his mother was not speaking, but shouting: 'Xinran, whatever you do, don't let him hang up his clothes for himself, he'll hang them upside down and back to front; he doesn't even know whether a coat hanger should go in from the collar or the sleeve!'

I was in a mischievous mood that day, and wanted to tease his mother for her determination to attend to everything personally, matters great and small. 'Sister, you don't really believe your son that incapable, do you? I'm sitting here today watching him open his cases, hang up his clothes and put away his own things!'

'You don't believe me? You'll soon find out how ridiculous he is! By tomorrow he won't be able to find any clothes to put on!'

'His room is only the size of a shoebox, he'll be able to find his clothes even if he has to turn everything upside down. I'm more worried that if he puts things away neatly as I would, if I take that first step for him, then at the next step, how is he going to be able to think to find his clothes himself?'

'*Aiya*, Du Zhuang, thinking? You need to put the clothes together for him in sets, otherwise he'll just throw them all together any old how! You really don't understand, kids today aren't a bit like in our day, when we did everything ourselves!'

'But if you always do it for him, how is he ever going to get the chance to learn? Besides, he can't always have his mother following on his heels. Anyway—'

At this point, Du Zhuang's mother interrupted me. An aggressive tone had entered her voice. 'I understand all those fancy principles! But I just can't stop worrying about him. I've spent over twenty years worrying every day; the instant I can't see him or touch him, how can I not worry? What mother's heart wouldn't ache if her son was cold or hungry?'

'But all the same, we have to help them grow up, right? Otherwise how are they ever going to find a wife? I just don't believe that he'd go out wearing two thick padded jackets and shorts. Besides, if he gets cold a few times it'll teach him that there's a link between clothes and the weather.'

That day she spent over an hour debating these points with me on the phone. She refused to let up until her son had given her a detailed report of how he had organised his belongings, by which time it was already two in the morning in China. I did not dare hang up the phone, as I told Du Zhuang, 'I know the fears a mother has for her only child; we spend every moment in fear that our one-and-only might get hurt through some million-to-one unlucky accident.'

And so, Du Zhuang ended up shuttling between the old lady's

home and ours. A great change came over him during this time, one that none of us would have predicted.

First of all, Du Zhuang's appetite seemed to spring to life, and almost all his fussy eating habits disappeared.

The first weekend he came back to ours, although it only felt as if he had been away three days, he was like a ravenous wolf. Before we sat down for the main meal, he had devoured everything in the fridge that would fit in his mouth, down to the stale bread! Pleased and surprised, I asked him where this new-found appetite had come from. He said that he had eaten everything the old lady put in front of him, out of good manners. However much she gave him was how much he ate, as he did not know if he was allowed to ask for more. On top of this, his language skills were not up to the task, so he often did not understand when the old lady talked about food. Still, there was some Western food, mainly cold and sweet dishes, that he just could not get used to. The old lady would ask him questions, and when he did not understand he would invariably answer, 'OK, it's fine.' There were also no corner shops near where he lived, so he would often be famished at night. Chinese dishes he had never before given a thought to would parade themselves in front of him in his dreams. Now he was back at my place, he was determined to eat his fill!

Very soon, however, I discovered that Du Zhuang's new appetite was like a bottomless pit. Every weekend, when I would go shopping for Panpan and Du Zhuang, it was like providing for a family of seven or eight. Incredible as it sounds, Du Zhuang could eat half a goose all by himself, or enough roast meat to feed three or four people. Besides this, he was also constantly snacking between meals. Once, before one of his weekend visits, he mentioned on the phone how much he missed braised pig's trotters. Where was I going to find pig's trotters in London? All my know-it-all friends shook their heads, saying there was no way they'd ever heard of such a thing in

London. However, my colleagues at the School of Oriental and African Studies all said, 'Of course there are!' Following their directions, I managed to buy eight big fat pig's trotters at Brixton market in south London.

On Saturday, when Du Zhuang came home and smelled the braised pig's trotters, he was very excited. I told him that they needed to stew on a low heat until the following day, and that they were extra rations for him to take back with him to the old lady's. That night, I thought I heard faint sounds coming from the kitchen, but dismissed them as just the neighbour's cat come to visit us again. Who would have thought it, but when I got up early the next morning to check on the trotters, I lifted the lid and was amazed. There were only two trotters left in the pot . . . Where had the other six gone? Surely not . . . I could not believe that Du Zhuang had eaten them all, they were the fattest trotters imaginable, from huge fat pigs! How could one person . . . I really couldn't believe that he had done it, but there was no trace of anyone breaking into the house. By the time Du Zhuang got up, I couldn't wait to find out if he knew anything about the trotters.

As soon as I opened my mouth and said, 'Du Zhuang, good morning! Do you know, the braised pig's trotters—'

'Stop right there, don't even mention the "p" word!' he interrupted testily.

I did not understand, and continued, 'Some of the pig's trotters have gone missing, I don't know—'

'Stop it! Don't say another thing, I can't handle that "p" word just now,' he said in a very earnest voice.

First I was bewildered, then thunderstruck. 'What? Why can't I say . . . Good God, no, it can't be!'

Du Zhuang clutched his stomach and nodded his head – his taste buds had got the better of his reason. During the night, he had crawled out of bed and quietly devoured six big, fat pig's trotters!

For a very long time after that, Du Zhuang did not let any of his friends mention the 'p' word!

Much later, after he left us to start his Master's course outside London, whenever my husband and I saw enticing supermarket displays of delicious foods, we would always get nostalgic, as without Du Zhuang, there would be no way we could possibly finish such a feast.

When his parents came to visit him about six months after his arrival in Britain, they couldn't believe their eyes. Their thin, frail son had metamorphosed into a great strapping lad with a back as wide as a tiger and a belly like a bear!

His mother asked me, 'Xinran, I thought of everything in the world, brought it for him, and cooked it for him, but nothing I did was able to awaken Du Zhuang's appetite. How on earth did you manage to feed him up like this?'

'I starved him out,' I said.

'How is that possible?' His mother flat-out refused to believe it.

Actually, many children's interest in life and food is squashed by parents who pander to their every whim. Common sense tells us that where aspirations and longings are concerned, distance makes the heart grow fonder. But as parents, we do not have the heart to make our only children wait and yearn for things. Time passes, and our unrestrained over-indulgence ends up limiting our children's ability to reach out for life, and curtails their interest in natural society around them. This tendency is particularly pronounced in one-child families.

Independent living changed Du Zhuang in another way too. For the first time in his life he became aware of his own ignorance.

At the end of the year, Du Zhuang celebrated his twenty-first birthday. In the UK, twenty-one is one of life's milestones. From this age onwards, a person is fully admitted into society, and treated as an adult. To celebrate, we threw him a 'coming-of-age dinner', at which we explained to him the Western idea of twenty-one being the start of adulthood. We told him that we hoped he would be able to challenge his closed-off personality, and climb out of the deep and constricting 'abyss of awareness' formed by his Chinese conveyor belt-style education, so that he could learn how to think and ask questions for himself. Du Zhuang did not seem particularly inspired by all this, but still meekly nodded his acquiescence to this 'edification from the elders'. Chinese people generally believe this to be proper behaviour in a good child, student or employee. But I believe that for a person to have vitality, their ideas must first have vitality. Only then will they be able to communicate with others in a flexible and lively manner, and only then can they have physical vitality. China's centralised, monolithic education system is like an amoeba reproducing: it curbs the liveliness of youth, and hothouses for excessive knowledge at the expense of practical ability. What is this sense of isolation and alienation, experienced by tens of thousands of Chinese students in the West, but an after-effect of this 'abyss of knowledge'?

In order to stimulate Du Zhuang's interest in contact with others, and to get him thinking more about society, I helped him plan out a few topics of conversation that he could use with his landlady and classmates. Several weeks later, his thirst for human contact, and embarrassment at his ignorance, awoke in Du Zhuang a spiritual hunger. I took this opportunity to encourage him to read a children's encyclopedia. First, he could read around topics that interested him and gradually improve his reading skills. Second, it allowed him to fill in a few gaps in his knowledge of history and society. Third, it made him practise how to think about issues, and forge links and comparisons between them. Over the course of three months, Du Zhuang diligently read his way right through the *Oxford Children's Encyclopedia*, something that makes me proud and touches my heart to this day. That huge volume opened up endless new vistas of pleasure for Du Zhuang. He started to enjoy thinking and questioning, to the point that debating became one of his hobbies, and he was impossible to stop once he got going! I ended up bearing the brunt of this, and was his adversary innumerable times. He would argue with me until we were both red in the face. Du Zhuang, who had once been shy and retiring, politely acquiescing to everything, was now up and running, and never looked back. He had stood up on his own two feet, climbed out of that abyss, and started to live with his head held high.

From then on our conversations started to become more adult in nature. Why is Chinese history as Westerners know it so utterly different from what we learn? Why does China, as such a huge and populous nation, have so little voice in the world? What is democracy, truly? Could Western democratic beliefs be incorporated into China? Is the Western economic model out of date, and would the West consider taking the Chinese economy as a model?

However, just when I thought I had steered Du Zhuang into learning how to pack the luggage of his own life, his new flight led him into a pain I had not anticipated, one that followed his emotional awakening. He had run headlong into a clash of values and a collision between Chinese and Western cultures.

One afternoon in Du Zhuang's first spring in the UK, I came home from teaching at the university to find him sitting anxious and fretful on the sofa. His face was flushed bright red, his ten fingers knotted, and his toes clasping together as if they were comforting each other.

'Du Zhuang, today's a weekday, how come you're back? Aren't you feeling well?' I asked him in a deliberately casual tone as I took off my coat. I thought that if I made a big fuss I might make him too embarrassed to spit out whatever was bothering him, and scare him off.

'It's . . . it's nothing,' he stammered, as though he did not know what to do with his tongue.

'Are you ill? Or has something happened?' I sat on the sofa opposite him, leafing through some students' homework, trying to assume a relaxed air while I got to the bottom of his problem.

'I'm not feeling ill at all, I just can't go out on the street today,' he whispered.

When I heard these words I was baffled. I looked at him and asked, 'Why can't you go out on the street?'

He shot me a glance, then hurriedly hid his gaze behind his interlocked fingers, saying, 'The Western girls on the streets of London wear so little, they jiggle all over the place when they walk. My heart thumps at the sight, as if it's about to jump out of my mouth! All the blood in my body comes roaring to my head, and I feel like my skull is going to explode!'

When I heard Du Zhuang utter these words, I honestly had no idea what to say to him.

True, before 2000, very few Chinese girls wore spaghetti tops or short strappy dresses, and those who did were mainly confined to the two big international cities of Beijing and Shanghai. Even I found myself feeling a bit embarrassed at the sight of British and European girls going about all bare-backed and low-cut when I was teaching at London University. How much more so must it be for a Chinese boy like Du Zhuang who had never seen the 'free women of the world'. But how was I to help him? Although we were not contemporaries, I too came from a culture where 'one mention of sex and people change colour'. At the time, it was forbidden for our books, media and art to touch upon 'yellow' sexual content. Moreover, sex education in China was not made compulsory in primary schools until 2002, so both of us had missed the boat there.

I remember that before my son Panpan started school in the UK in April 2000 a teacher asked him if he had received any sex education, and not understanding English he just raised his hand and waited for me to translate. I went totally red in the face, as I had never even broached the subject of sex with him before. In Chinese culture, and in the times I had lived through, it was a word that we just couldn't bring ourselves to say. I ended up having to admit truthfully that there was no sex education in Chinese primary schools.

The teacher replied, 'Then we can't take this child. British children start sex education from age ten; if he hasn't had any sex education by his age, we have no way to guarantee his safety in this regard. We don't have any Chinese teachers, so there's nothing we can do to help. I suggest that you bring your child up to speed as soon as possible and then come back and enrol him.'

I was out of my mind with worry. I should say here that my own knowledge of sex only came after marriage and was based on practical experience. How was I possibly going to get my head around the concepts and ways of teaching a boy sex education? I was a single mother at the time too, but how could I allow a child to be held back from starting school because of his mother's ignorance? In the end a British friend rescued me from my predicament. One day, his three sons took Panpan into their bedroom and gave him a lesson in sex education. I was puzzled as to how this was going to go, as none of the boys could speak Chinese. How were they going to explain things to Panpan? The eldest son replied, 'That was a live-ammo exercise – all four of us boys just took our trousers off!'

However, Du Zhuang was not my son, so was I really justified in handing him over to British friends for 'combat exercises', with or without 'live ammunition'? Toby suggested that Du Zhuang should go out and get some experience in mixing with girls. He said it was a necessary skill that Du Zhuang should be perfecting by diligent practice. I spoke to Du Zhuang's mother over the phone about what her son was going through, again at Toby's suggestion, in the hope that his parents might do some quick decision-making for their child. Instead, Du Zhuang's mother said, 'Don't you go teaching the apple of my eye wicked ways!'

The weather got hotter and hotter, the girls on the street wore less and less, and Du Zhuang became more and more tormented. However, his mother's advice became increasingly horrifying. Apparently, if he was just the tiniest bit careless for a moment, he would be devoured by sex! As before, I did not feel I would go against her wishes.

Seeing this, Toby eventually said that if practical lessons were out of the question, then why not try books? Maybe Panpan would be able to help him? With this in mind, we took Du Zhuang off to our country place at Stourhead, and deliberately left a copy of *Africa Adorned* on the coffee table. This was a large picture book about African culture, designed and promoted by Toby, which included a fair number of nude photos. We hoped to make use of Panpan's weekend visit, and give the boys the chance to take a look and chat about the differences between men and women as they leafed through it. Later on that day, as Toby and I were returning home from a stroll through the fields, we saw the two boys looking at the book. Toby said to me quietly, 'I first talked a bit about the book to them, then they came and joined in. We deliberately turned to one of the pages with nudes, and I talked about the human body from the perspective of a photographer. Just look at how they've reacted; as soon as they were able to start expressing their opinions it was all fine.' That day, Toby did all the talking, and Du Zhuang and Panpan barely opened their mouths. However, several days later, Du Zhuang seemed to have got over his fear of going outside, and even gradually started to talk about girls.

Toby's influence on Du Zhuang over this period was profound. He encouraged Du Zhuang to read and think, and to go out and get to know people, including going to nightclubs to dance with girls, and going to all manner of student parties. Toby's idea was that at parties people had a bit of close contact, which would give Du Zhuang the opportunity to get to know about Western culture step by step.

One weekend, Du Zhuang told us he was going to an overnight party, held by some of the European students in his class. Toby said that it would help him to understand his European classmates outside the classroom better, and that this was the kind of thing that young people should be doing. However, when Du Zhuang came back it was barely midnight. I asked him, 'How come you're home so early? I thought it was going to be an all-night party?' He gave me one of his looks, apparently not knowing where to begin. After quite a long pause, he blurted out that there was a very rich student in his class, whose relatives had a big house in London, and that was where they held the party. 'There was a Spanish classmate of mine wearing these incredibly skimpy clothes, all transparent material. When we danced *disco* together, it was as if her shaking chest was calling out to me! I really couldn't stand it, I was afraid I'd lose control!'

I knew what he meant by 'lose control'. Du Zhuang's forebears had been controlled by the personal wishes of emperors over many dynasties. The two generations before him were controlled by the family values formed in unique and turbulent times. What was considered good and bad had become very unpredictable in that political stranglehold. Elements of Confucius and Mencius still remained in people's lives, but there were also Red communist beliefs, which crept imperceptibly into their thoughts through daily political study. I thought that the loss of control that Du Zhuang spoke of was a fear of going against the teachings of his parents, and a fear of losing a morality that he had once held dear.

Nonetheless, the very thing that Du Zhuang was afraid of was inevitably taking place in his life in the UK. It was not just a matter of men and women going too far, or a change in his habits. It was also a deep questioning of, and disappointment in, a family that he had once been so proud of, and a father he once worshipped.

Du Zhuang was born in the countryside, and when he moved with his parents to the big city, he was already seven years old. He told me that his first impression of the city was the buses. Those big cars that could hold so many people, bigger and faster than a tractor, even! He remembered how the morning after he moved to the city, he had noisily demanded to see the big cars. He walked up to a parked bus, raised his head and carefully examined the enormous object in front of him, staring until he toppled over backwards! To him, the city was synonymous with smooth, broad streets, a world away from the dirt tracks of the countryside, where he had jolted along on his father's bicycle until his bottom ached. Although everything was bigger and further away in the city, sitting on the back of his father's bicycle for the hour-long journey to and from school each day was still a great treat. He would stare contentedly at the colourful streets, and at all the streams of different people with their individual expressions. His father did not usually talk while riding, and would only occasionally ask him about school, his voice often swallowed by the roaring traffic.

Although later on he got a car, Du Zhuang never forgot these journeys to and from school with his father. Particularly on rainy days, the two of them would sing songs together all the way, their voices drowning out the sound of the rain. In those days Du Zhuang used to wish it would rain every day, so he could sing songs with his father! As he got older, Du Zhuang began to feel that his father was spending less and less time with him. He was gradually becoming less of a father and more of a public figure. Even Du Zhuang's university often invited his father to give guest lectures. Gradually his father became a god in Du Zhuang's eyes, his life enveloped in the shining halo of his classmates' admiration. He seldom mentioned his mother, and when he did it was in a small, helpless voice.

After Du Zhuang came to study in the UK, I remained in constant contact with his parents by telephone. I am not sure how it came about, for I was close in age to his mother, and had received a more formal education, but I could never get the better of her in our debates about life. My theories always seemed like exotic greenhouse plants, and not nearly as fresh as her hardy, outdoor white cabbages!

When his parents came to visit Du Zhuang accompanied them on a sightseeing tour of Europe. One day I received an agonising phone call from him in France. 'Xinran, I don't know how to say this, but over the past few days the adoration I used to feel for my father has been shattered. I used to believe that he was a god-like figure, a great economist, a highly respected entrepreneur, one of China's leading businessmen. But in Western civilised society he seems so uncultured. He slurps his food when he eats in restaurants, and when he smokes a cigarette he bares his teeth, all stained yellow. He brays with laughter on the street, with never a thought for how it might look. I took the chance to call you while they're off shopping in a department store. How can they understand so little? My mother's been trawling the streets for brand names, when in fact all her brands are tacky in Westerners' eyes! I really can't hold my head up high when I'm with her, it's agony. I don't want to spend the rest of the European tour with them, I want to come back to London tomorrow!'

When I heard these words I was stunned. For a moment I did not know what to say. How could Du Zhuang's attitude towards the parents he had previously been so proud of turn completely upside down in the space of just six months? In his eyes and heart, had they now been transformed into country bumpkins who were causing him to lose face? I realised straight away that he could not drop everything and come home. He also could not let his parents know about this sudden change of heart on which 'the dust had yet to settle'. This would be a blow that no parent would be able to face – that their only son, the son that they had toiled so hard to raise, was rejecting them!

'Du Zhuang, now you listen to me,' I said in a tone that brooked no argument. 'You're twenty-one now, nobody can force you to do anything, but, even if just for the sake of repaying the debt you owe your parents for raising you, you absolutely must see this European trip with them through to the end. Otherwise you'll be sure to regret it in the future. As for your feelings, I think I understand what you're going through, but this isn't the time to discuss it. You mustn't keep your parents waiting around in Paris while you sneak away to make long phone calls. Wait until you get back and we'll talk it over then.'

'Well . . . well . . . OK then,' Du Zhuang reluctantly agreed on the other end of the phone.

After they came back from Europe, we had a long discussion by the banks of the Thames.

'What brought about this sudden change in you?' I wanted to hear his thoughts.

'Um, it's just that the difference is too great.' He seemed not to know where to begin.

'What is the difference, then? The difference between Chinese and Western culture? *Come on*, this is a feeling that everyone from the East gets when they come to the West. Why do you feel that your pain is greater than that of other people?' As I spoke, I noticed that the tide was changing direction on the Thames – a strong tide was pouring water from the sea back up the river, even as it flowed day and night towards its goal.

Du Zhuang was watching the river too. 'What's the difference? They're not cultured and refined like Toby is. They don't take pleasure in daily life the way you do. And they don't have the respect for ordinary people that Westerners do. I'd never noticed this before, but now I'm living independently in the West and can observe and think independently, the space and distance has given me a fuller picture of my parents. But with this more complete picture, I now recognise that my father's god-like image is actually just a social halo perched on his head. Take away that halo, and he's no different from any other Chinese father. Just like one of those ripples on the Thames, occasionally appearing then vanishing again among countless waves.' He sighed as he spoke. 'I used to worship my father, but now . . . how can I not be in pain? Xinran, can you understand this?'

Could I understand? I thought I could – his god-like father was a Chinese clay figurine. When it met the waters of the Thames, its substance washed away! In a similar manner, a great many Chinese people discover after they come to the West that their national pride starts to dissolve in the vibrant, colourful world outside. Actually, Westerners who go to live in China suffer similar pangs. The modernity in which they take such pride seems so naïve next to China's thousands of years of civilisation. But I did not say any of this to Du Zhuang. What he needed right then was not an academic discussion on the progress of globalisation, but someone to guide him in understanding his Chinese mother and father. 'I think I understand what you're going through. But I think that what you believe to be the fuller picture is in fact not complete at all. The father and mother you saw were actually a flat two-dimensional surface seen at a distance. You could not see the history behind the picture, nor the society that formed its side faces. Six months of British education has shown you a fact: your parents, who in China are among the elite, the aristocracy, seem like Chinese peasants on Beijing's Wangfujing shopping street as they walk along the Champs-Elysées, isn't that right? But how many Chinese parents have the ability to set foot on those bustling Western streets?

'In China where you were born, 90 per cent of the population are living either in the countryside or came from there not long ago. Several thousand years of agrarian culture have formed some "special characteristics" in Chinese behaviour and customs, and these can sometimes make us feel awkward, or even lose face, am

I right? But you know, every country in the world has a similar agrarian culture in their not-too-distant past, and similar "uncivilised behaviour" that today has been transformed. Now you're studying abroad in Europe, but a hundred years ago Dickens had plenty to say about noisy peasant markets, and Maupassant's works are full of the unpleasant habits and backward customs of France's lower and middle classes.

'And your mother, who in twenty years went from being a peasant woman, carrying goods on a pole in the fields, to the official she is today. Who can just hop on a plane to Europe to see her son studying abroad, what a change in her life that's been, and how fast it's all happened! It's like your mother still has a deep furrow on her shoulder from the weight of the pole she carried for over a decade, and it's not going to be smoothed away just because your English is getting more fluent daily. How can she keep up with the struggles of life in a Chinese city, and be the way you want her to be as well, no different from any other Western woman, living among the twenty-six letters of the English alphabet? When she started out she didn't talk like a city person, and only knew how to read a smattering of words, let alone knew anything about city life or urban civilisation. When she came from the countryside to the city, wasn't she just the same as you when you came to the UK from China? But your mother fought her way through it all. She's given your father a peaceful, happy family, and given you a Chinese and Western education. She's even become a member of the local politburo. How many women from the countryside can stand in front of city folk, living strong and independent lives, the way your mother does?

'And that's not to say anything about your father. In society, he's a successful entrepreneur, but very few people see his qualities as a family man. After the Cultural Revolution, how many educated young people sent down to the countryside discarded their country wives when they came back to the city? But not your father. Not only did he not discard your mother, carrying pole and all, he made it his mission to help her to lead a strong, independent and happy life for all the city folk to see. Moreover, his feelings of responsibility towards your mother and her happiness led him to help all her sisters to come to the city and travel the world. He also helped give all their children in the countryside a good education. In China, or even the world, how many men, how many husbands, give their wives this kind of love and responsibility?'

The more I spoke the more impassioned I became, and the surging waves of the Thames as the tide turned seemed to add their strength to my words. 'What is nobility? Position? Wealth and fame? As I see it, how can someone who doesn't even love their own family be noble? How can they be worthy of a good reputation? Just because you've absorbed so-called Western civilisation, can you no longer see the nobility of your Chinese parents, and your peasant mother's greatness? What is education for? What is culture and civilisation? Every place has its own unique culture to go with it! Those people living in the desert, the mountains or the coast, with no education, still have the culture of their region. Our education is meant to help us understand different cultures. Civilisation means having respect for all cultures and being able to learn from them. Nobility is a giving heart and tolerance. By this logic, between you and your father, who is more cultured? Who is more civilised? Who is more noble?'

Du Zhuang wept when he heard me say this. I knew that these tears would water his parched Chinese soul and his feelings towards his family, which had come perilously close to withering away.

Later on, Du Zhuang told me that this discussion had been like a reforging, which had forced him to think long and hard, until gradually his dust-covered parents began to shine once more.

However, when he came to re-identify with his parents' values, he once again became influenced by the family's embrace in his daily life. Even three years later when he went back to China to begin his career, start a family and buy a flat, he still hadn't managed to extricate himself from his parents' all-encompassing and smothering love.

I later heard that when Du Zhuang got married, the two only-child families got together and bought them a 180-square-metre flat, with three bedrooms and two sitting rooms. Du Zhuang's mother took full charge of supervising every aspect of decorating their new home, using as a blueprint her experience of what was most fashionable in her part of the countryside, as well as international 'perfect homes' she had seen in Chinese magazines. But she didn't stop here. Every weekend she would think nothing of cooking a week's worth of main meals for the couple at her Shandong home, then driving them all the way to Beijing, in order to make certain that her son was eating properly!

I once paid a visit to Du Zhuang's 'little' newlyweds' home. Although their names were swamped in a long line of doorbells within the sea of Beijing's countless new-build complexes, as soon as I went through their individual door, this 'old fogey'* returning from being 'sent down to the west'† was stunned by the opulence of the flat. In the hallway stood ornate, expensive display cabinets full of gold and silver treasures, just like in a boutique. All manner of labour-saving gadgets gave the kitchen an ultra-modern, almost magical appearance. The main living

---

* *Laoxiu* 老朽: roughly translates as 'old fogey'. A modest expression that older Chinese people use to refer to themselves, meaning that they are old and no longer of any use.

† Sent down to the west, *yangchadui* 洋插队: *Chadui* was a Cultural Revolution term for educated young people who were sent down to the countryside. After the Reform and Opening-up movement of the 1980s, Chinese people often compared the hardships of studying or working overseas as *yangchadui*, or 'overseas *chadui*'.

room, which was almost one hundred square metres, had been
done up with a stereo system and screen like a small cinema.
One alcove was filled with dozens of silk-stuffed quilts and other
bedding – wedding gifts from relatives. Standing outside the
bedroom, listening to their proud tour, I thought of how much
a Westerner I had become. All the bedding was of a five-star
hotel standard, but why on earth would they want to live in a
home like a hotel? At least there was one area not 'perfect'. They
had piled high their pretty semi-circular balcony with unused
furniture, turning it into a storage space.

The bits and pieces littering the bathroom floor reminded me
strongly of peasant households I had seen, where things were left
lying on the floor as they had never been forced to tidy them away
for lack of space. When I suggested tentatively that I would like to
eat a meal that the young couple had cooked themselves, the two
of them exchanged glances, and said awkwardly, as if in one voice,
'In the six months we've been married we haven't once cooked a
meal.' At this, I decided to make their first meal in their new home
with them, each of us contributing one dish. When I opened their
kitchen cabinets I was dazzled by dozens of sets of cooking pots,
costly kitchen utensils, and every conceivable gadget for preparing
food, enough to open a restaurant! However, when I went in search
of herbs and spices, I discovered that they had all been put with the
toilet cleaning things. I asked them why they had arranged them
that way, and Du Zhuang's pretty, elegant and gentle wife said in
surprise, 'They're all bottles, right?' Before we cooked she modestly
asked me several questions: 'Is it the oil that goes in first when
cooking? Or is it the heat first? Or the salt? With rice, is it the rice
or water that goes in first?'

Du Zhuang told me that the two of them hardly had any opportunity to cook, as both sets of in-laws took turns to send over food.
Sometimes there weren't enough mealtimes to eat it all.

I asked him, 'Why don't you suggest to your parents that you might try cooking for yourselves?'

He retorted, 'In only-child families like ours? How could we? They're afraid of us touching the hob or even using knives! Didn't you say we should respect our parents? We have to accept their love and concern to keep them happy, otherwise they'll get all panicky and keep phoning to see what we're up to. My mother says that Chinese people care a lot about filial piety, and that filial piety means doing whatever they say in order to be a dutiful child. To tell you the truth, after I came back to China all the independence I learned from Western culture was soon twisted right back to where it started by the "status quo" of Chinese family life.'

What Du Zhuang said was quite true. We often find it very hard to get used to changing times and cultures.

In 2006 Du Zhuang went to America to work for a multinational company that made household goods, with responsibility for opening up the Asian market. Just before he set off I suggested that once he arrived in America he should send a few cards to thank all those who helped him when he was in Britain. However, Du Zhuang said, 'But didn't I thank them when I left the UK? Why would I want to thank them again?' Well, what about the Chinese saying about a drop of kindness being repaid with a well of hope? But I did not argue the point. He was an adult now, and should have his own set of values. After that there was no contact between us for a long time, and we did not disturb his world just because we missed him. Perhaps he had found his sun again – an awareness that was all his own. In a person's own solar system there can be only one sun in the sky; of what use would any other light source be?

But, like any mother who longs for the day when her child will understand all the toil and sacrifice she has been through for their sake, every time I threw away an old calendar to replace it with a new one, I would always pray for my son, for Du Zhuang and for all the other only children in China. At the same time I would comfort myself: that the new year might bring them the awareness so precious in human life, an understanding of the place for gratitude in life, because of all sources of happiness, gratitude is the most egalitarian, knowing no gap between rich and poor.

Just as I was coming close to abandoning all hope of hearing from Du Zhuang, in March 2011 I unexpectedly received a phone call from him. 'Xinran, today I became a father! I have a daughter!' His voice held that mixture of intense emotion and exhaustion that is perhaps common to all first-time parents. When I put down the phone I was overcome with emotion. Had that big kid whose mother used to do everything for him actually become a father? And was that naïve little wife of his really now a mother? Would this pair of big kids be able to hold up the sky for their own child? Would their own parents be able to stop worrying about their 'still not grown up' son and daughter enduring the perils of parenthood?

After three uneasy months, my worries were dispelled by two photographs of the baby and a text message. The baby was so chubby that her little round cheeks squeezed up against her small mouth until there was nowhere else for them to go but to bulge out even more. Her smiling, embracing parents looked full of health and confidence. Du Zhuang told me that, unlike many Chinese couples of their age, they had not asked their parents for help. Instead, they had trawled through books and the internet for the basics on child-rearing. Parenting classes in their American suburb were also a great help. He said that both he and his wife consider it a mark of maturity to be able to repay their parents' nurturing with a healthy independence.

This reminded me of something that Du Zhuang once said to me: 'We are different from other people, we have no brothers and sisters to talk about and share our parents with, or share family space with. We have to work through our feelings and insights into our parents and come to an understanding all by ourselves. Can other people ever really understand the loneliness and struggles of people like us, who will grow old with no other family members of our generation, caught between one extreme and the other, and hurting ourselves and others as we collide? In the family, we are like the sun and moon all rolled into one, and are given no time or space to grow by ourselves . . . Everybody is instinctively watching us with the eyes of tradition, and judging our generation, we who were born and grew up alone.'

Spending time with Du Zhuang and getting to know him really got me thinking about his generation, and the question of how China's first group of only children will deal with that unprecedented transformation of the family when they come to have only children of their own. From Du Zhuang's first words to me in 2001, to now, over a decade later, I am still trying to get my bearings amid the complex maze of *baguazhen*.*

———————

How do you view the Yao Jiaxin incident? Why is Chinese society debating him (a post-80s man) so fiercely?

This incident itself is one of many reflections of the general belief of Chinese society that moral standards in modern China are deteriorating. His death penalty is a great tragedy for Yao Jiaxin who committed such an appalling crime, as well as for the public who influenced the imposition of the death sentence. Both are equally tragic.

The heated debate reflects the public dissatisfaction about the

* *Baguazhen* is an ancient Chinese divination system that uses the I Ching trigrams to navigate a safe path through the myriad uncertainties of life.

inequality widely existing in our society, the deep-rooted question over our education system, as well as the rights or wrongs of the death penalty itself. There is also the question of Deng's famous policy: Let part of the Chinese become rich first, which will lead everyone to become rich. When will we see the second part being delivered? Can our society afford to focus only on being rich?

2 | GOLDEN SWALLOW

A T 2.28 on the afternoon of 12 May 2008, a terrible earthquake hit Wenchuan county in eastern China's Sichuan province, leaving almost 80,000 people dead. During the arduous and painfully slow rescue process, people were left stunned by a scene that emerged from the rubble. A young mother was found holding up a lump of concrete weighing almost 1,000 pounds. She had used her body as a wedge for a day and a night to protect her baby, who was crying with hunger beneath her. When the mother and baby arrived in hospital, the doctors were moved to tears by what they found. The baby was unharmed, and after a drink of milk fell into a contented sleep, but the mother would never stand up straight again. Her back had been permanently crushed out of shape, leaving her frozen in the act of protecting her child. Her very flesh and bones had been reforged by her love for her child.

For a long time after hearing this story I felt a deep sense of unease. Had not all the mothers I encountered in my twenty years as a reporter also been reforged by love for their children? From countryside peasants to professional city women, the nurturing of those tiny bundles of cells would start a kind of de-thawing and remoulding process that gathered speed through the weeks and months of pregnancy. This process continued after birth, as they willingly wore themselves down out of love for their children, who consumed all their time, energy and emotions. Mothers of only children in particular, once girlish timid fauns, were transformed into parents who would face down wolves and fight to the death to protect their children. But as for the children who grew up in these emotional waters, could they ever understand their mothers' transformation and sacrifice?

Many people believe that the Yao Jiaxin incident was just a 'one-off'. In reality, Chinese society is under an almost constant barrage of tragedies played out by only children. On the evening of 31 March 2011 a boy just returned from studying in Japan stabbed his mother eight times simply because she had refused to give him any more money. The boy, called Wang Jiajing, told the police that he had met his mother at the airport, and asked for more money. The mother replied angrily, 'I can't give you any more money. You've been studying in Japan for five years, you've never had a job, your school fees and living expenses came to more than 300,000 yuan ($44,000) a year. All this came from savings that we parents have worked our fingers to the bone to scrape together. If you come after us for more money it really will be the end of us.' As soon as Wang heard this he exploded with rage, took two knives from his bag, and rushed at his mother, stabbing repeatedly. Many Chinese people sighed with exasperation and sadness for this mother, who survived the ordeal. How could her love and care have been rewarded by such hatred and violence?

Traditional Chinese culture respects five types of human relations. The first and foremost is 'father and sons are bound by blood' (this also extends to mothers and children). As in ancient times, a child who harms their parents is deemed to have committed the worst possible crime. However, time and again today we see tragic and cruel incidents. Chinese society and families are in crisis. The current emphasis on grades and academic achievement overlooks the importance of basic morality, and has led many only children to see gratitude and kindness as something rotten and outdated.

Why do some Chinese only children turn against all natural laws and human nature, and act with such hostility to their parents, to whom they owe such a debt of gratitude? In New Zealand, I met a young Chinese girl who provided me with some answers.

I went to New Zealand for the first time in 2002 to launch my book, *The Good Women of China*. My husband Toby and I checked into our hotel in the afternoon, after a twenty-three-hour night flight and stopover. By this time my body clock had been thrown into total disarray, and I was not looking forward to a third night so close on the heels of the last two! We decided to take refuge in a couple of glasses of sake and a bite to eat in the hotel's sushi restaurant to help us cope with our third night in the space of thirty hours. It was about six o'clock in the evening, an hour or two before local dinnertime, so the place was deserted and gloriously peaceful. We had just taken our seats when I noticed a woman who appeared to be the manager giving the waitress a severe dressing-down. Both women looked Asian, and the waitress was in floods of tears. I guessed from their appearances, and use of English instead of Japanese, Chinese or Korean, that the manager was probably Japanese, and the waitress Chinese. They did not notice us creep in and we did not disturb them, but sat quietly at a table near the entrance waiting for them to finish. The waitress was nodding her head, listening meekly, with tears cascading down her face. I looked at her for a while, thinking to myself, if only her mother could see this, how her heart would ache! After four or five minutes I had had enough. Even if you break the law and the police have to get involved, regardless how great the mistake, you cannot endlessly scold a young girl! I rapped on the table with my chopsticks, to show that there was a customer waiting.

When she heard the noise, the manager's expression changed immediately, and with a typical Japanese lady's stooped gait and little steps, came over to us and asked demurely, 'What would sir and madam like?'

I asked in English, 'I'm sorry to disturb you both, but what are your opening hours please? If you're open, can we have a meal?'

'We are part of the hotel, and open twenty-four hours a day,' she replied deferentially, a totally different person from a moment ago. To my surprise, she then signalled the waitress to come and take our order.

'Are you Chinese?' I asked the waitress tentatively in Mandarin.

She looked at us with an embarrassed expression. 'Yes, I am.'

'When do you get off work?'

She did not understand why I was asking this, and replied dubiously, 'The shifts change at ten o'clock.'

'I've come from London, and only just arrived at the hotel today. I'm trying to get over my jet lag and have nothing to do this evening. If it's OK with you, can we have a chat?'

The girl looked at me. She did not say yes or no, just walked away uncertainly.

From then on, until we settled the bill, we were only served by the ultra-respectful manager, and did not see the waitress again. At nine o'clock in the evening I took a long shower, my usual way to relieve tiredness. I said to Toby, who was reading in bed, that I couldn't settle and wanted to go down and wait for the waitress. If I could persuade her to talk to me, perhaps I could help her. If she was unwilling, I would come back and read a book. I knew it was not easy for Chinese children to be away from home, especially this generation, many of whom are only children, and have no experience of living independently.

At about ten past ten, the girl emerged from the restaurant. Out of uniform, her beautiful hair hung loose around her shoulders, and she was dressed in a fashionable Barbour jacket. Only her large backpack identified her as a student. When she noticed me sitting waiting for her on the sofa in the foyer she seemed surprised. She approached shyly, and said in a quiet voice, 'You're really waiting for me?'

'Of course, that's what we agreed.' I shifted along in my seat, and motioned for her to sit down beside me.

She sat down, saying rather apologetically, 'When we met earlier I thought you were just feeling sorry for me, and saying whatever came into your head.'

I helped her off with her backpack. 'If I'm not far wrong, I'm about the same age as your mother, which makes you the same generation as my son. Although we come from different times, and probably have totally different ways of making friends, I think I can at least lend an ear to what you have to say, and maybe take the edge off the gloomy cloud you seem to be under.' I knew my words might seem a bit odd and upfront to her, but I believed she could feel the sincerity in my voice.

She blinked a pair of huge, long-lashed, questioning eyes at me. 'What do you want to know?'

'Tell me whatever you like. Your name, what happened today, how you ended up in New Zealand, where you come from in China . . .' I gestured around the cavernous lobby, as if the space had been specially laid out for her to fill with her story.

When she heard me say this, her eyes turned pink with unshed tears, and her red, glistening lips came together briefly in a pout. 'I'm Golden Swallow, at least my mother and father hoped that I would be a gold-coloured swallow. It's so embarrassing that you saw me humiliated like that today.' She pursed her lips again, as if something was trying to break free. 'I feel very hard done by. I treat the manager like my mother, but she's often as fierce with me as you saw today.'

I found this surprising. 'You look upon her as your mother? Are you an orphan? Did you grow up with only your father?'

'No, no. I have a real mother and father of my own, but I hate them, especially my mother!' As Golden Swallow spoke, waves of bitter resentment came welling up in her eyes.

'You hate your mother? Why?' I found it very hard to match the charming, soft Golden Swallow in front of me with her harsh words.

'If it's not from the harm she did me then how come I find it so difficult to live life today?' At this, the floodgates of Golden Swallow's heart came crashing open. 'I've already graduated from university, soon I'll be twenty-four years old. But I left China having never done three of the most basic things. I'd never been in a kitchen, I'd never touched a knife and I'd never ordered a meal in a restaurant!'

How could this be? It was almost impossible for me believe. 'You're a graduate, but you've never done any of those three things? How on earth did you get through university?'

At the time, student life in China was still quite limited. Students with money would take their main meal of the day in a restaurant outside the university, while students with limited means would eat in the university cafeteria. Very poor students would hide an electric hob in their dormitory to cook instant noodles, made only slightly more palatable by a pack of pickled vegetables. However, no matter what their circumstances, they should all at the very least be able to order a meal from a menu, or boil up noodles in a kitchen!

Golden Swallow clearly noticed the disbelief on my face. 'You have to believe me, I'm telling the truth. My father's deputy mayor and my mother's a Communist Party official in my home city where I went to university. Mummy and Daddy thought the university cafeteria was unhygienic and the food disgusting. So for three years I had breakfast at home. Every lunchtime Daddy's chauffeur would pick me up and either take me home to eat or to a restaurant.'

'OK, but then how did you get to the evening homework sessions at university? Or get together with your classmates?' I was still having trouble imagining university life like this.

'After supper the chauffeur would drive me to university for evening study then bring me back at half past ten. Getting together with classmates? My parents never allowed me to go out at night. They said only young people whose parents didn't know how to bring them up properly went out at night.' Golden Swallow said all this in a tone that suggested that this was just 'the way things were', mixed with surprise that it had never even occurred to me.

'OK, but what about when you ate out with them, are you saying that you never ordered your own meal in a restaurant? And you never went into the kitchen at home?' I still could not see what she actually meant by her words. It was not that I did not understand her language, but rather it seemed as if we came from such different times and ways of life.

'Mummy says there's fire in kitchens, and knives with sharp blades, both very dangerous. Every time I went out with family or friends for a meal, they would always be the ones who did the ordering. I did try ordering my own food once, but before I'd finished reading the menu, my mother said, "You don't understand at all, you don't know how to order properly." After a few times I stopped arguing and ate whatever they ordered. Luckily everything they ordered was stuff I liked. It wasn't until I came to Auckland that I realised I didn't have a clue about how to order in a restaurant. It wasn't just that I struggled to read the English, it was that I had never even heard of many of the foods and spices.'

'If your parents wrapped you in cotton wool with their love, then how could they bear to let you study abroad, so far out of their reach?'

'Chinese people like to keep up with the Joneses, they're always comparing themselves to others. They compare houses, cars, watches, mobile phones, cameras, even their children. As soon as parents meet, they start comparing their kids' schools and grades. In the last few years they've moved on to which parents send their children abroad to study, and which country is the best. For my mother, saving face is far more important than her husband or me. When she saw in our local paper that New Zealand has the longest-running hotel management course in the world, she had my dad look into it. His people at the mayor's office did a bit of research on Chinese websites, and discovered that there was something to it. So six months ago my parents sent me over through an agency. It was only after I arrived in New Zealand that I realised that the best place for hotel management is on the other side of the world, in Switzerland. Actually, this little island doesn't have any history to speak of, let alone world-class hotel management courses.'

Golden Swallow had put it very neatly. Chinese only-child families are preoccupied with just three things: making money, cosying up to government contacts for protection, and making outrageous comparisons between their children. I think about 80 per cent of Chinese only-child families aspire to sending their children to the best universities abroad for 're-education'. Favourites include Oxford, Cambridge and Imperial College in the UK; and Harvard, Yale and Princeton in America. The gossip on internet chat rooms is that more cultured families send their children to Britain, whereas less cultured nouveau-riche families invariably pack their children off to America. A smaller number of families, with little international knowledge or funds, think that the important point is just being abroad, as it is all the same kind of place.

Golden Swallow's tone was typical of Chinese young people today. 'What's the big deal? I know a lot more than just this place. It's not as if you can't find it all on Google!' Having spent a bit of time in one foreign country, they think the rest of the world is exactly the same as the 'Western culture' and 'foreigners' they saw in that one place. It is not only their combination of ignorance and fearlessness that leaves people aghast, they also often bring back to their friends and families in China 'knowledge of foreign customs' which not even foreigners themselves know about! Ever since the 1990s, the almost limitless variety of the outside world has been described by countless young Chinese students as 'a deep, narrow well of Western culture'.

However, there was something about Golden Swallow that was a bit different from her know-it-all contemporaries. 'The scenery in New Zealand is really very beautiful, why would all those film-makers come here otherwise? So I don't regret coming to New Zealand at all, there're bound to be good hotel management courses here. The agency in China was all talk, full of fine promises and over-the-top enthusiasm, but went pretty quiet as soon as I got here! They set us up in a glorified dormitory, threw in a few bits and pieces to get us going then "put us out to pasture"! By the end of the first week, almost half of the students who came out with me had left. We then discovered that the hotel management college wasn't really a college at all, but a language school. The enrolment documents they gave us, which were not easy to come by, turned out to be valid only for the language school. They would only let us start the Master's course when they had earned enough money from us!

'The other thing was that most of us had no idea how to live independently. Our dormitories were nothing like the agency had advertised to our parents, with staff to cook and clean for us. We had to do all our own cooking, washing and cleaning, but we didn't know the first thing about how to look after ourselves. We didn't even know how to buy things in an English-language supermarket. For the first few days we lived off fast food to keep hunger at bay. By the fourth day we couldn't stomach any more of this curious but disgusting food, we all missed Chinese food so much. It wasn't just our Chinese stomachs that couldn't bear any more of those weird flavours, but the four or five hours' time difference had thrown our body clocks out of kilter. In those early days, we took turns to have a good cry by day, and at night we all clung together and wept! How did I make it through? Simply because I was determined not to give in. I'd already left home, why would I want to go back? Could I really not live by myself? My mother also phoned me several times a day, and got me to send her photos of everyday life.'

'You can take photos on your phone and send them to her?' At that time I did not even know that mobile phones could take pictures.

'We all have the newest camera phones. When we don't know what to do, we phone home. We take pictures of things we don't understand, and send them home for answers. Because I'd never gone shopping by myself back in China, I would often phone my mother from the supermarket. The first time I went into a supermarket in New Zealand, I didn't recognise any of the English names, and had never seen any of the fruit and vegetables on the shelves. I remember that it took me three hours to cook my first meal, which was some spinach dish. Mummy directed me every step of the way, from what to buy in the next-door supermarket, to how to prepare and cook it, all the way to getting it into my mouth.'

'You spent three hours on the phone to your mother just to cook a single dish?' It sounded like something out of a Chinese *xiangsheng* comedy double-act.

'Mummy asked me what I wanted to eat, and I said spinach soup, and a spinach and egg stir-fry. So she sent me a photo of some spinach, and I went looking for it in the big supermarket next to the dormitory. She told me I had to buy the best spinach. I asked her which that was and she said, "the most expensive kind". So I bought the most expensive spinach I could find, and a box of eggs with a picture of a chicken on the front. When I got back to the dormitory kitchen, Mummy told me to wash the spinach then cut it into pieces, and to mind my fingers when chopping. I had a go and told her it was really hard. "Maybe it's not the right knife for the job," she said. "Try another." But still I couldn't make it chop. "How can it not be possible to cut spinach?" she said. I replied that perhaps New Zealand spinach was different from ours.

'She told me to take another picture, and said that it looked the same as Chinese spinach. "How can it be so hard to cut?" She then had me take a picture of the knife. "Ah, you need to use the thin sharp side of the blade to cut, you can't use the thick back of the knife." It was only then I realised that I'd been using the wrong side. The cooker was different to my mother's, and she didn't know how to work it. I couldn't understand the English instructions either. She ended up losing her temper, and cursing me for a fool over the phone. After three hours the food was finally done. I took a bite and it was dry and tasteless. Only then did she ask me if I'd added oil and salt. I replied crossly, "Nobody told me, how was I supposed to know?"'

Golden Swallow paused for a moment and shot me a brief glance. She seemed to be making up her mind whether to continue. 'Do you know, Xinran, after that three-hour phone call, my first reaction was that I hated my mother! It was the way she kept on blaming me for everything, saying I couldn't do this and didn't understand that. It wasn't that she was resentful about me no longer being the precious little girl she once held in her arms, and I wasn't angry at her for saying nasty things to me for the first time, it was because she had treated me as a pet for twenty-three years. Even after all this time, I still can't live like a normal human being. She's had me in a gilded cage for over twenty years! I've grown wings, but lack the ability to fly. What's that if not a pet? I swore there and then that I would prove to her that I'm not the useless little girl she was cursing. I'm not a feeble-minded, incapable idiot making them lose face. True, most of the other girls have gone home, back to their comfy little nests, but the day will come when they will wake up. They'll realise that they lost face and all their self-respect in New Zealand. When I was growing up, my parents constantly indoctrinated me with their notions of self-respect. But I intend to live a life of real self-respect. I'll show them who I am!'

Her words were like a boulder crashing into the large empty foyer. My vision and hearing wavered for a moment with the shock waves, and my heart felt as if it were caving in. I fought to restrain myself as distress and anger washed over me. How could any mother bear to hear these words? Her mother had spent twenty-three years raising Golden Swallow as a pet, and now her beloved child felt she could not even live like a normal human being!

I was left speechless, not knowing what to think.

We sat there in silence, surrounded by the reverberations from her words as they came crashing down to earth. Everything around us stood still. At that moment all the guests in the hotel lobby seemed to disappear.

I do not remember how long we sat there. It was not until her manager went tripping past that I realised it must be very late. Golden Swallow should be getting home.

'I'm sorry, have we been talking too long? You should go home. Do you have work or classes again tomorrow?'

'It's no problem, I only live in the staff quarters next door.'

'Oh? You're in staff quarters? You work for the hotel? In that case, why are you still working in the sushi restaurant?'

'Just to stay alive!' Golden Swallow shot me an unreadable look.

To tell the truth, at that moment I did not know how to continue our conversation, my only option was to follow her lead. 'Just to stay alive? Because there is food and a bed here for you? You know that Westerners say there's no such thing as a free lunch?'

'I'm still studying English at the language school, and they have an internship arrangement with the hotel. I know that my English is way too bad to get into a proper university to study hotel management. At this rate I'll be lucky even to get a training certificate from the hotel, but if I do then at least I'll be on their system. It didn't take long to switch to a course on basic hotel management. That solved my day-to-day living difficulties, as I could stay in staff quarters on full board and lodging. They're teaching us all kinds of random stuff, but, to be blunt, both sides get something out of it; we're their unpaid interns. I heard not long ago that when our training year is up we can apply for an entry-level management position, but you also need a certain amount of work experience.

'I met a girl at a student party who was very good to me. She introduced me to the manager of the Japanese restaurant in the hotel. Now I work there two days a week, and it doesn't affect my training in the hotel. I'm now in my fourth week. For the first week I really didn't have the first clue about kitchens, since, as I told you, I'd never even been into my own at home. My colleagues tried to explain to me, "This is where we prepare the food, these are the cooking implements for main and side dishes, over there is where we select and clean the vegetables, that's where we put the dry goods." But the more I heard the worse my head went into a spin! In the end I found an illustrated dictionary, but although it had very detailed descriptions of all the items, I still didn't understand what they were all for! At times like that I would curse my mother to the heavens. My manager told me, "Normal people take an hour or two to catch on, and understand how the kitchen works by the end of the first week. By the second week they understand how the whole restaurant runs."

'But even four weeks in, I still don't get what she is trying to tell me. I've tried having a frank talk with her, but she said it's nothing to do with my bad English, it's that I can't do anything at all! I told her that if the others do five hours, I'll do eight, for no extra pay. She replied, "The thing is, it's not about what you learn or not, or how much you do for free. The more you do, the more of a mess you make the restaurant!" Take yesterday for example, it was past three o'clock and already time for me to leave, but I wanted to stay behind and learn about place settings for dinner. My manager told me to practise in the restaurant, as there was nobody about. Late dinner is generally gold-rush time for the hotel. But it's also different to the flow of customers in normal restaurants on the street, as mealtimes ebb and flow depending on check-in times and who is in the hotel. At the weekends it's all holidaymakers, and in the week it's business people. They order different kinds of food, so it's also about preparation.

'When the manager explained this to me a million questions came bubbling up in my mind. I interrupted her, and asked why we arranged place settings the way we did. Unluckily for me, just as I was asking the question, I managed somehow to break a china sake set. At this, the manager totally lost it and said, "Careless again! What's going on in that head of yours? How many things have you already broken this month? And always questions, questions and more questions." She then gave me a severe telling-off. I felt very hard done by, I had treated her like my mother, so why was she being so fierce with me? You were there, you couldn't bear to watch either, could you?'

'Did she dock your wages today?' I asked in concern.

'Why would she dock my wages?' Golden Swallow asked in a puzzled voice.

'Because you damaged hotel property.' I didn't think this warranted an explanation.

'No, I never, did I? Oh. But she's usually so good to me, much better than my mother is,' Golden Swallow said very seriously.

'Um . . . why do you regard her as your mother?'

'Because she teaches me how to do things and how to be a person.'

'Then . . . what's the difference between a mother and a manager? Are they interchangeable? Will you look after your manager as you would your mother when she gets old?'

Golden Swallow's pretty eyes grew huge as I asked her this; even her lips, which had been thinned by hurt and distress, puffed out at my question. 'I see her as a mother because only a mother can really understand me in this world, care for me and forgive me, right? But why would I have to support my manager in her declining years? At the end of the day, she's not . . .' Golden Swallow's argument ground to a halt at this gap in her logic.

'Then, do you think I am kind?' I was trying to make a path for her through her confusion.

'Of course!'

'Why?'

'You felt sorry for me and listened, and tried to cheer me up.'

I gazed through her eyes into a world of uncertainty and said, 'You know, your manager is ten times kinder than me, a hundred times! If I were the boss of that restaurant, I would never have taken you on in the first place. The people working for me would need to be able to bring in money. Managers need their employees to work hard and bring in customers, using their knowledge and professionalism. Someone with no experience who wants to enter a company to learn is treating the place as a school, and they should pay tuition fees for that, right? Your ignorance has made a mess of her business and damaged her property, but she is still paying you the regular rate. Not only is she not asking you to pay her back, she's even helping you out with advice and patience, isn't that right? She's turned her own restaurant into a school for you. That's true kindness. Golden Swallow, remember, you only have one mother in this world, no matter whether she's rich or poor, intelligent or incompetent, nobody can replace her gift of life or care for you. We should also always treat other people as equals. We have no right to take up their time or demand that they mollycoddle us. We should thank people for whatever they give us. If you're looking for a mother, you should try having a proper talk with your own. If you don't feel that she's taught you anything useful, you can't use other people to replace her. Family isn't something that can be exchanged. A mother isn't someone you can accept or reject at will.'

Golden Swallow seemed completely bowled over by my outburst. 'Xinran, are you really meaner than my manager?'

I nodded, saying nothing. What the little girl in front of me needed right now was not an indulgent auntie to wipe away her tears and loudly curse the world on her behalf, but a kick up the backside to snap her out of her childishness. She needed to stand on her own two feet in the world, and understand the concept of gratitude to friends and family. I hoped this kick of mine would penetrate to the bone, and spur her on to follow her heart.

After a moment's silence, Golden Swallow looked at me earnestly, and speaking her thoughts aloud said, 'If that's the way things are then my manager isn't really that bad at all. Even though she's told me off countless times, I've broken so many things, and she's never docked my pay. I suppose she could sack me, couldn't she? Then . . . why is she going to all this trouble to teach me? Why?'

On hearing these words, I felt a glimmer of light shine into the darkness of all we had been unable to express. I opened that door a little more to let in more illumination. 'Because she's kind, she feels sorry for you, and she's exasperated that you aren't being all that you can be!'

Golden Swallow's face, long and drawn with hurt and self-pity, suddenly came back to life, a girlish happiness sparkling in her eyes. 'That's amazing! If you look at it in that way, I'm actually pretty *lucky* to have a manager like this.'

The fog surrounding my heart suddenly dispersed under the beam of her realisation, and our conversation took a brighter turn. 'In the trinity of modern Chinese values: family, school and society, there's a lesson you only children have missed, which is how to value the people, events and objects around you. It isn't a mathematical formula like $1 + 1 = 2$, or a chemical equation, or vectors in physics, but rather an understanding of the respect between people at home and in society. If you never learned this at home, then you have no idea how hard it may have been for your mother, or what your father sacrificed, or what other people lost or gained as a result of your existence. You can't learn everything from books, society isn't just what fits into your father's palm, and you can't let your life be dictated by your mother. To be honest, I also don't think it's fair for you to push all the responsibility onto your parents.'

Golden Swallow seemed a bit upset at my lecture. 'Then . . . my mother not teaching me to cook, and not letting me order food, was that the right thing to do?'

I understood why she was playing dumb to justify herself like this. It was human instinct, that self-protection mechanism we all pick up on the road of life: *It's not my fault!*

'Let's think it through together. Why would they spoil you like this? How many children did your grandmother have?'

'My granny had lots of children.'

'Can your mother do housework?'

'Yes, she's very good at it.'

'Can your uncles and your aunts do housework?'

'Yes, they're all very capable, in and out of the house.'

'You should ask your granny some time why your mother, aunts and uncles are all so capable. The majority of the older generation gave their own beloved children all the good things they longed for most themselves. But sometimes, along with the things they thought were best, they also did things that weren't in their children's best interests, and this is particularly marked in only-child families. However, I think that using family members' faults to explain away one's own lack of ability is selfish escapism, like a shot in the arm. People who lack willpower or ability sometimes use drugs to find spiritual release, but it often results in terrible pain to their friends and family. Using family members' past mistakes to excuse one's own weakness and laziness, or not being ashamed to sponge off other people's hard work, isn't this really the same thing?

'I have a lot of respect for your willpower, Golden Swallow. You have the courage to challenge your ignorance and lack of ability, and the will to live by your own efforts. But this alone isn't enough to make you free and happy, as you'll never be able to totally escape your mother and father. Only when you let your parents see that their darling little girl has stood up, and has created a new world for the new millennium all by herself, only then will your happiness be complete, from inside to out. Only then will you live your future in true freedom, because your family is an an inseparable part of your life.'

At that moment, the pouting, doe-eyed little girl of a few hours earlier suddenly matured. 'Do you know, Xinran, I haven't phoned my mother for several weeks now. I changed my SIM card, swore that I wouldn't call her for three months, and not go home for three years. I did all this so that she would understand how much I hate her. I also wanted to use this pain as a warning to myself. I am not my parents' pet, I am an independent person, and I am going to learn to live like a real human being.'

'Forget hate, learn how to love and you'll be free and happy,' I gently murmured in Golden Swallow's ear as we shared a parting embrace.

The next day I left a card for Golden Swallow at the front desk with three questions: *Why did your mother spoil you like this? Would your manager treat her children like this? How will you raise your own children in the future?*

I came back to New Zealand the following year, and was fortunate enough to stay at the same hotel. I could barely believe my eyes when I saw Golden Swallow at the front desk! When I approached to check in, she did not recognise me. A young man greeted me cordially, but I said, 'I'm sorry, can I ask that young lady to book me in please?'

'Of course,' he said. I suppose he thought I wanted to register in Chinese.

Out of respect for him, I explained, 'It's because she left a very deep impression on me the first time I was here.'

The young man tried to correct me. 'I'm not sure that's possible, this Chinese girl has only just started working on the front desk.'

I said very proudly, 'Last year when I saw her, she was only doing work experience here. I'm surprised that she's on the front desk already.'

'Oh, yes, Chinese girls are good at what they do.' I could hear that he was being serious.

At that moment, Golden Swallow recognised me, and shouted loudly, 'Wow . . . Teacher Xinran, it's you, you've come back this year!'

'Golden Swallow, this is such a surprise! You're already at the front desk?' We put our arms around each other and embraced over the counter.

Golden Swallow was in high spirits. 'I've only just started. I'll check you in, OK?'

'Young lady, it can't have been easy for you to get to the front desk in a year!'

Golden Swallow, dressed in hotel uniform, took the passport from my hands, saying, 'I haven't officially started yet, it's just a trial period. I've got another three months before I'm made permanent, and then it's only running errands. I have to finish university before I can become a manager.'

As I watched her go professionally through my paperwork, I was unable to avert my gaze. My mind was leafing over the pages and chapters of her experiences last year, stuck together with the tears and tribulations of life. My heart was full of admiration for this young lady who could make her words reality. Golden Swallow really had come through it all, and made good on her promise to herself. But what about her mother? I was hoping very much that she would fill me in on the events of the last year, and while I checked in we agreed to meet for a long chat once her shift finished.

That evening our drinks party ended very late, and added to my jet lag, so by the time I got back to the hotel I was completely exhausted. However, as I walked through the grand lobby, a girl dressed like a student was sitting on the same sofa on which I had spoken to Golden Swallow a year earlier – she was waiting for me. I knew I had to hear this girl's story!

In outward appearance, the Golden Swallow sitting beside me had been completely transformed, the startled rabbit of a year before being replaced by a relaxed and confident, professional woman. However, I never thought that our reunion would be such a continuation of last year's story.

Golden Swallow told me that since the last time we met, she had neither been home nor called her mother. These words were a heavy blow to my heart. What it must feel like for a mother who was afraid her little girl would cut her fingers if she cooked to be so harshly rejected like this! Golden Swallow had warned all her friends that she would never speak to them again if they told her mother where she was. However, her mother apparently knew that Golden Swallow was working in the hotel, and had persuaded one of the other employees to contact her on her behalf. Golden Swallow had told the go-between that the day her mother found her would be the day she lost her daughter for ever. She was determined not to see her parents again until she had set herself up in a career. Her mother was too scared of losing her to attempt any further contact, and had since kept her distance. Golden Swallow wanted her parents to see that she had grown up all by herself, that their daughter was not a pet.

As I listened to her talk, spasmodic sobs threatened to burst from my throat. I felt as if I were experiencing her mother's unspeakable pain.

Golden Swallow continued: 'Teacher Xinran, after you left, I started to learn how to get on with my Japanese manager. After a while, she really did stop shouting at me. I did double the work of the others, and learned to apologise for everything, no matter who was to blame. Later on, not only did my English improve, but I even made some suggestions on how to improve the cooking and customer service. My manager began to look upon me in a new light, and recommended me to the hotel. The hotel management said that as I had no official qualifications, I could not become an employee. However, they let me take part on some occasions, like receptions for foreigners. I worked harder than anyone else, arrived early and left late. Gradually, people started to think well of me, and after a while they made an exception and let me intern with their deliveries logging system. Very quickly, I discovered problems in their record-keeping, so I offered to help them improve it. They seemed to realise that I had a talent for management, so let me take part in a market research project on customer flow and pricing levels in the hotel. I learned so much on that project and made quite a few friends. Not long ago, I got my level 1 hospitality qualification, and the hotel immediately moved me up to the front desk for a trial period. My plan is to combine work and study, and try for the hotel's fast-track management programme. I want to plan my own life, do the things I want to do, and not just go along with my parents' plans. Are there any boys who fancy me? I don't know, I don't want a boyfriend right now, I need to find myself first. New Zealand is a country of immigrants, I can live here easily.'

'Perhaps you could write to your parents about these plans of yours?' I still wanted to try to put her in touch with her feelings as a daughter.

'*Aiyo!*' Golden Swallow let out a shout. 'Who writes letters in this day and age? It's so old-fashioned! Teacher Xinran, nowadays we all use mobile phones and email, stuff like that. I understand that you still want to talk me round, you want me to get in touch with my family. I'll tell you the truth: I'm not going to get in touch with them until I'm a line manager. They gave me life, and I should give them a result in return, I am still their daughter. I want to let them know that I've stood on my own two feet in my adult life, that I'm a success, and that it's all my own hard work. I want to prove them wrong, that I haven't become a cripple, despite all they've done to me!'

Through Golden Swallow's heated language, a vision of her mother's face floated up in front of me. The little girl who arrived through great pain after nine months of pregnancy, the precious baby she clasped to her bosom and nurtured day by day, had suddenly gone missing. The disbelief of the first day, the worries of the second, the madness of the third, and the fourth . . .? I did not dare think any further.

On my third visit to New Zealand, I stayed at the same hotel, but Golden Swallow was not there. The staff told me she was now at university, and gave me her phone number. I dialled and got through. On the end of the line was obviously the Golden Swallow that I knew, but her tone had become strange to me. Her former enthusiasm had cooled with maturity. 'Teacher Xinran, it's great that you're here again. Unfortunately I'm really busy, in a mad rush with an essay, so I won't be able to come and visit you this time.'

'I see. Is there someone you're sharing your life with now, someone to share your happiness?'

'Er . . . I have a boyfriend, he's a New Zealander.'

'Have you told your parents this news?'

'Not yet, no, I'm going to wait until we decide to get married before I tell them.'

'Have your feelings towards your parents changed in any way?'

'Not yet. I don't know why, but these days I find myself wanting to see them less and less. Let's talk about something else. I might go to Europe. My boyfriend spent several years there. He says that New Zealand is too small; just like a drop of water, it could evaporate at any moment! My future's not going to be squeezed into this little island.'

We did not spend long on the phone that day. Golden Swallow was on the way to becoming a woman and walking towards her own future. However, behind her she was still dragging a long, black shadow. How could her mother and father live in this shade?

From that time on, I started asking media friends to help me locate Golden Swallow's mother and father. I wanted to explore their own feelings about the disappearance and hostility of their only child in case I could help Golden Swallow further. In China, where everything is changing, finding people and making enquiries is no easy task. However, it turned out not to be too difficult to locate her parents; the hard part was persuading them to let me talk to them over the phone.

In 2007 I finally managed this though, by this time, they had divorced.

Golden Swallow's mother told me on the phone that since her daughter had severed contact she had fallen into a deep depression and started having delusions. She did not want to see anyone or do anything. She felt that she had bled her heart dry over her whole life, yet could not even keep hold of her only daughter. Her father was a bit more open. He believed that his wife had over-indulged his daughter before she left China, so she had no space to grow by herself. After she went abroad, he felt that his daughter had been 'corrupted by the West'.

I separately asked both of them the same questions. 'Do you still worry about your daughter? What are your thoughts on her future now? If one day Golden Swallow returns, what would you do for her? And what do you hope she would do for you?' Their replies sent chills down my spine.

The mother, who was now bedridden, said, 'How could anyone be so brutal? Even a lapdog feels grateful to its owner. I might have been bad in many ways, and done a multitude of things that I shouldn't, but does it justify her treating us like this? I've lost hope of ever seeing my daughter again, it's as if I never gave birth to or raised her.'

Her father, the deputy mayor, said, 'I never expected that much of her in the first place, how could a girl amount to much anyway? She's gone off to university, will pick up some foreign gilding then come back and get married. That's her whole life, isn't it? If she doesn't want to acknowledge us, it's all the same to me, that's daughters for you, just like water down the drain.'

Golden Swallow did not contact me again after 2007. Perhaps she no longer wished to re-live the history that we had shared? Perhaps she thought that she had left the dark shadow of her family behind her? Or had she just drawn a line under the struggles of growing up? But I still wanted to know whether she had gone home to see her mother. Every time I went back to New Zealand, I would wish her well. I hoped that some day I might bump into her in a crowd, or see her in a hotel. I even hoped to see her become a mother, because that journey would help her understand her own mother.

I used to think that mothers and daughters were as closely linked as the earth and sky. When the sky darkened the earth would grow dim. When there was a sandstorm on earth, the sky would become gloomy. That children and families were like a river and its banks; if the river ran dry the banks would become ugly, with no scenery or purpose. I thought back to Golden Swallow: 'I hated my mother. She treated me as a pet for twenty-three years. Even after all this time, I still can't live like a normal human being.' Her words seemed proof that my belief was like the moon reflected in a lake, or like flowers in a mirror.

I do not know how Golden Swallow would have replied to my question, but this was her mother's answer which she sent me in a letter.

Xinran, on the phone you asked me my views on the Yao Jiaxin incident. Is it possible to understand the man himself? I have thought a great deal about this, because my daughter, Golden Swallow, has perhaps been even more cruel than Yao Jiaxin; she drove eight knives into her mother's heart! That migrant mother knows no pain now, maybe the son she left behind will suffer when he grows up, or perhaps he'll grow up in an age that doesn't know pain. But I am still alive, and every day I'm stabbed by my daughter's eight knives, over and over again. It's Yao Jiaxin's mother I think about the most in this whole business, she is a woman living in purgatory.

On the internet I saw the last letter written by Yao Jiaxin to his parents; real or fake, it's heartbreaking. I'm sending you a copy, you can take it as my reply.

Dear Mother, and Father too I suppose, always trying to be cool but actually a phenomenal pain in the arse, how are you these days?

Not as fragrant as a flower, not as tall as a tree, I'm a convict that even Martians have heard of.

In jail, my limp and feeble body is like mud and dross, ready to be shattered with one stroke of a knife, filthily scattered on a damp wooden plank bed. There's no more bright ceilings, or soft, thick sprung mattresses, or that tender, white, lush girl that I used to enjoy. With eight savage blows of a knife, in a single night I transformed all those things into an embarrassingly frail soap bubble. This fragile bubble is loaded down with sorrow and pity. There's no more tasty steamed bread for me, fancy or plain. I am a condemned criminal who can't even get himself half a twist of deep-fried doughnut to eat. In front of the iron window, the ice-cold bars waver before my dazzled eyes. Beyond them a bewitching night sky, forever emitting cold light and sprinkled with stars. Restrained by a pair of handcuffs and an iron door, it all takes on an exceptional cold beauty, fading in and out of existence.

When I was eight years old you made me learn the piano. When I was eighteen you forced me into a famous university. When I was twenty you pulled strings and worked your connections to plan the rest of my life. Even on trivial matters like falling in love, getting married and having kids, you still had to shove your oar in. You wouldn't let me associate with a peony, you would only let me marry a water-lily . . . the reason was that water-lilies were water flowers and peonies were for the land.

They say that in the north is Flying Car Li, wicked son of the official Li Gang.* To the west there is an army officer's son, Eight Stabs Yao. In this age of correctness, your methods weren't illegal as such, but you sure weren't thinking straight when you used your wrong ideas to create a wrong 'un like me. Who was all this for? Was it so that in the future the pair of you wouldn't have to worry about food and clothes? Or in order to show off to the world that you have the same reproductive abilities as everyone else? Or for continuity, to have someone to 'keep the incense burning' for you? For all those years, you flagrantly 'pulled out a knife' in an attempt to inoculate me. Today, I, in full public view, pulled out a knife and with it struck eight blows. Not only did I kill off your whole life's glory and political achievements, I also snuffed out the 'incense fires' that burned so brightly in your hearts. That guy Li Gang was in the north facing east, and his sun was in the ascendant. When he blinked his left eye, the Governor of Hebei Province came out to cover up for him, when he blinked his right eye, the central government came out to protect him. When Li

* The Li Gang Incident took place on the evening of 16 October 2010. A black Volkswagen Magotan knocked over two young women in Hebei University campus, leaving one dead and the other severely injured. The driver did not stop, but drove on and dropped off his girlfriend at the dormitory. He was detained by students and security guards on his way back, but failed to show any concern for the injured. His attitude was cool, indifferent, then aggressive. He shouted, 'Report me if you dare, my dad's Li Gang!' The boy's name was Li Qiming and he was sentenced to six years in jail on 30 January 2011. His father was Li Gang, deputy head of Baoding city's Public Security Bureau. As soon as the story came to light, it became a hot topic among Chinese netizens and the media. 'My dad's Li Gang' became one of the top catchphrases on the internet, used to describe only children who break the law but have powerful protection.

Gang blinked both eyes together, the former Japanese premier Junichiro Koizumi prostrated himself in worship of China in the wake of the tsunami. What am I compared to Li Gang? I'm not worth a single teardrop from the eye of his son, Flying Car Li. And compared with Li Gang, what is your own powerful military background worth, Father? All you know is earning and counting money all day long. Everything you do by day and all your dreams at night just ape those corrupt officials. Picking up girls and dancing and all that, how can you have lost even the most basic self-knowledge? You couldn't even recognise your own reflection in a pool of your own piss.

All I wanted to do was chat to girls, fall in love maybe, but you made me play the piano or take vitamins to keep my calcium levels up. Many times I really wanted to interrupt you to say, 'You're the ones who should be keeping your brain oxygen levels up.' Actually, I know you're not short of oxygen, you're just the same as all the corrupt officials and unethical businessmen. What you're missing is virtue and morality. I remember one time I was just doing the fashionable thing, fooling about a bit with what they call 'naked chatting on the net'. As soon as my dad, the former official, found out, he immediately went on a thunderous rampage. His eyes bulged and stuck out like a toad just out of the water, blustering that he was going to pack me off to web addict rehab. He was cruel and inhuman to me. I only had one reply for him: 'Naked chatting is hardly sex, it's just an escape for the heart and soul.' Seeing that Dad didn't react, I explained again: 'It's like eating, I was just leafing through a menu, but you and Mum eat a slap-up supper every night and that's how you got yourselves an unfilial son like me.'

Mum, Dad, other people's kids are all outstanding young people, gentle and refined, educated and reasonable, steeped in books and culture. They understand how to respect the old, cherish the young and love life. They know how to spare a thought for others and give selflessly to society, and they know how to move with the times. But from when I was young you filled my head with famous universities and passing the civil service exams. For the rest, you neither asked nor cared. Those other parents' loving care was like a caress, those moments where parents kneel down and sit with their children. All those little gestures of how to be human, I never got any of this. Quite the reverse: you were as cold as a freezer with me, educating and controlling me with your extreme strictness, with your so-called super-strict education. All of it was built on military methods that are unscientific and inhumane.

There's a story I remember that goes like this. A mother turned a blind eye to the fact that her son had been pilfering little bits and pieces from a young age. He progressed from sneaking and thieving to murder and arson. Before his execution the son's last request was to drink a last mouthful of his mother's milk . . . Suddenly red blood flowed, the mother let out a scream of agony, and the son went away with his mouth full on the road to the next world. Perhaps you'll say I have no one but myself to blame. Maybe you'll say this is a failure of education, the school's responsibility. But what I'm asking is, if you can't sweep clean a room, how can you clean up the world? Any excuse is pushing away responsibility, a sign of shamelessness. Mum, Dad, we have a 'flying car' in the north and 'eight stabs' in the west, isn't this sounding alarm bells for Chinese family values? I think you understand.

A man can only die once, it's been that way since ancient times. And don't be too heartbroken, living on this patch of dirt with no fairness, no justice, no humanity, where filth and corruption run riot, that is Yao Eight Knives' eternal tragedy. Lightly I go, leaving behind a pile of bones. I will never again hurt another human being. Contain your grief and carry on with life as best you can. See you in hell, Mum and Dad!

'('–My death draws near, this tragic symbol is all I have to leave to my parents!

(Oral testimony: Yao Jiaxin; edited by Zhou Lubao)

Golden Swallow's mother continued: 'Xinran, I think that all of us parents of only children should read this child's words. If only we could teach our children what love is before they learn how to hurt people with knives . . . But as parents of these children, at a time like this of "breaking down the old and building up the new", how do we know what kind of love they need? While everyone is so busy chasing after their own dreams, we are losing our only children. Who can understand our pain?'

As I read this final letter from Yao Jiaxin to his parents, I was saddened. It was the writing of both a genius and an emotional cripple. A child ruined by 'mainstream education', unrealistic competition and social climbing. I reread, again and again, the letter that Golden Swallow's mother had written. Yes, I thought, who indeed can empathise with the love and pain of Chinese mothers with only children?

WING | 3

'I HATED my mother. She treated me as a pet for twenty-three years. Even after all this time, I still can't live like a normal human being!' Golden Swallow's words had gradually changed from the voice of one girl's heart into a rising chorus of shouts from China's only children. At first their parents were perplexed, then hurt, then righteously indignant.

China's first group of only children were all born between 1979 and 1984. Their parents generally subscribe to the same viewpoint: 'We suffered hardships, and we won't let our children go through the same thing.' They were willing to undergo hardship and exhaustion, but were determined that in the future their children would have the same opportunities as everyone else. However, it often turned out that their children did not live the happy, satisfied lives their parents wished. According to an official report* into 6.1 million only-child households, estrangement and conflicts between parents and children exist in almost half. These are the biggest worries for only children, and have influenced Chinese families and society in ways that are impossible to ignore. But why are the parents shouldering all the blame? Why has nobody realised that parents are struggling under the burden of a social policy without precedent in the world? No mothers and fathers know how to be a parent when their first child is born. Their parenting skills increase day by day as the child grows. It is only once the second child is born that they

* www.xinhuanet.com 25 August 2004.

learn to refine their parenting skills. But parents of only children never get this opportunity. They rely on other only-child families to help them 'seek out a cure'. However, as when consulting a doctor, hardly anyone remembers that they too get sick, old and die. Society is forever debating the loneliness of only children, yet they seldom consider the parents' isolation and helplessness.

I sent Golden Swallow's 'famous words' to several parents of only children who I had been in touch with for many years, though I sent them anonymously. They reacted angrily: 'Is the mother keeping her child as a pet, or is the child keeping her parents as slaves, to be at her beck and call with every wave of her hand?!'

The relationship between mother and child, that most treasured of all relationships, has in the eyes of some only children metamorphosed into the mutual recriminations of pet and slave. Why? How many sons and daughters are crying and shouting 'why' at their mothers and fathers? Their parents are asking themselves the same question, over and over again during sleepless nights.

I think one of the main reasons we have created families so different to previous generations is that we have lost the traditional support network of the extended family. The parents of today's only children grew up in large families. There was poverty and overcrowding, but very little opportunity for loneliness. They grew up in a noisy, cheerful environment, full of close family feelings and squabbles with their brothers and sisters. Even in the cities, where the work unit was 'society', these units were often as close as families. But in this age of only children and Reform and Opening-up policies, city life is no longer dominated by the empire of the work unit. The people have been divided up along economic lines into forests of box flats and skyscrapers. There is less contact between people, who often do not even know their next-door neighbours. This isolation is even more pronounced for only children, each living in their little well, unaware of what is going on outside the window.

I think many parents were like me when their children were small. They tried to make up for the lack of extended family by teaching them about what family means. I went to endless pains to explain to my son the difference between family and other relationships, from ancient times to today, from China to the West, and from all sorts of different angles. However, they all grew up so fast in this modern digital world that they never experienced the family home as a place to relax and set their hearts at ease. A place where they could be themselves, a branch to perch on when weary of flying, a safe harbour to drop anchor and rest from the storms of the ocean outside.

For my son and other only children, brought up in families with no brothers or sisters to dilute their parents' attention, they were painfully aware of their parents' scrutiny every second of their lives. Home became a prison, with their parents as the bars, constantly protecting them and correcting their every move. Only children, seemingly much more than children with siblings, yearn to break away from the family and their parents' control. Even if they do not know whether the light beckoning them from outside is heaven or hell, they still yearn for the freedom of flying the nest. And parents also know that when their children grow up they should learn to fly. However, their endless worry and suffocating love all too often leave their beloveds incapable of flight. A bird cannot carry its cage when it flies! And as for those who manage to fly, many have no direction. Relentless and unrealistic competition causes many Chinese only children to flap laboriously through the broad streets and narrow alleys of Europe and America, dragging behind them the gilded cages of their parents' riches and worries. The space in between them interlaced with countless threads, one end tied to the cage, the other knotted to the parents' hearts, neither end free.

Before we met in London in 2008, Wing's mother and I had only exchanged a few polite telephone calls. Her daughter was a volunteer in my charity, Mothers' Bridge of Love (MBL). As with many Chinese only-child volunteers, their families would often telephone to 'verify' information received from their children. Actually, they were also hoping to find a roof to shelter their child from the wind and rain. With the passing of time, friendships often grew up between us. These parents also helped to keep me up to date on China's rapid development and its consequences. We were members of the 'only-child club' too, and our conversations would always come back to our little treasures. Wing's mother lived in Beijing, where I was born, so we naturally had more to say to each other than other people.

In autumn 2008 Wing's parents came to London to see their daughter. I invited them for a stroll in Kensington Gardens. It was my custom at MBL always to find time to spend with volunteers' mothers who had come all this way. Partly to express my respect and thanks for the volunteers, and partly in the hope that I could comfort those anxious mothers. I have always believed that mothers' hearts are linked. It was also a good opportunity to learn about their children's develop-ment, as they set themselves up in careers, marriage and adulthood.

That day, with yellow-gold leaves beneath our feet, we walked slowly in the park as autumn colours reached their height. We chatted about our lives in Beijing, my perceptions of China through Western news, and of course Wing, who we both cared about. Wing's father followed behind us two women in silence. He was a retired mechanical engineer, and apart from saying hello at meeting and goodbye at parting we barely had any other communication. Many Westerners would describe this as Chinese male reserve, but I had often seen men with their tongues wagging freely at the banqueting table, going on and on interminably. Wing's mother had the air of a consummate teacher, which could only have come from being a true product of generations of teachers in her family and years of teaching herself, page by page and class by class.

I cannot recall exactly what we were talking about, but for no particular reason the conversation petered out into silence. When I think back, that silence was more chilling than an angry shout.

Wing's mother suddenly stopped, turned and said to me, 'Do you know, Xinran, Wing hasn't been home to see us once in the four years since she left, and her phone is always "out of battery".'

'Is that so? Surely not, I'm in touch with her on my mobile practically every week, her mobile . . .' I suddenly realised that I might have made a big mistake, but it was too late.

Wing's mother looked at me with a stunned, frozen expression. 'You can get hold of her any time, but I, her mother, cannot, is that how it is?'

'I, I don't know.' I did not know how to answer her, for it had honestly never occurred to me that Wing was capable of treating her parents like this.

Wing's mother stared at the open expanse of park in the distance and said, almost to herself, 'Ever since Wing was a little girl, we never had any reason to criticise her. She obeyed everyone in the family and never overstepped the mark by so much as a millimetre. She grew up on a line between two points, home and school. Her entire living space, apart from the bed she slept on, consisted of her school desk and the dining table. She hardly ever went outside to play, and barely had any friends. I sometimes tried to persuade her to go out, but she never did. My husband and I thought we were blessed, our daughter had never given us any reason to worry in her whole life! When she graduated from secondary school, her father hoped she would study computers, so she went to the best university in China to read computer studies.

'In fact, she had always excelled at literature, liked reading books and writing poems, but she never gave any sign of wanting to study arts subjects. At the time, our friends were all overwhelmed with the trials and tribulations of only-child families, but our daughter grew up in line with our plans every step of the way, never giving us a moment's unease. My husband said that she was like the fuse box in our house, silently ensuring power and security for the whole family! When she mentioned that she would like to go overseas to study and see the world after university, we agreed without a moment's hesitation. Besides, she had passed the entrance exam for a Master's degree in the Asian Research Centre of the UK's best university. The child had always had a liking for arts subjects, how could we refuse? Living in a globalised age, if we didn't let her go she wouldn't have a complete education. That would mean as parents we did not give her the best possible start in life. However, as soon as Wing left our home in Beijing, I realised that she had taken the family fuse with her, plunging our world into darkness.'

'I don't know what to say.' I had hardly been able to follow her words, my head was full of images of her perfect daughter.

Wing's mother ignored me. 'Xinran, do you think that Wing is a good girl?'

'I should say so; compared to many Chinese girls I know she's outstanding. She's a genius with computers and I'm always impressed with her knowledge of literature. Nobody in our office compares to her! Besides, I like that classical beauty you see in her from time to time.' My praise of Wing was sincere.

Wing's mother stared at me, her eyes like piercing arrows. She said slowly and deliberately, 'Do you know something? Since Wing first came to Britain she hasn't written us a single letter, nor of her own volition given us a single phone call. It's only on the last day of the month that we can ever get through to her, no matter what tone we take with her, or even if we beg, she doesn't pay a blind bit of notice. I don't understand how the good girl who grew up by our side, our daughter who was closer than close to us, could be so unfeeling!' Tears poured down her face in a torrent. I could see that this had been a very long time in the brewing.

To tell the truth, it was very hard for me to believe what she said. The Wing I had spent time with was a cultured, charming and timid girl. How could she be so cold and inflict such pain on her mother?

I could not get any words out. With great difficulty, I finally took a breath and asked, 'Why do you think your daughter is so unfeeling?'

'For a girl to leave home for so many years and not spare a thought to ask about her parents, does that not seem cold to you? We're not uneducated peasants, we've never oppressed her for being a girl. We not only gave her life, we gave her all the life and education she ever wanted. But now it's as if she's discarded us without a backward look!' Wing's mother was getting increasingly furious and emotional, while her father was standing a long way back, as if we were nothing to do with him.

'I was really hoping that through you, MBL or a social meeting like this she would come back to us. I know that perhaps she will never live with us again, but I hoped that she would come back to us as our beloved daughter.'

Wing's mother's words made me think of my radio programme in China, *Words on the Night Breeze*. Letters and phone calls for help flooded into the programme from every corner of China, from country and city women. Exactly how many women I helped I do not know, but I remember that in those eight years two women in particular phoned me in absolute despair. Afterwards they felt I had not helped them, and ended up taking their own lives. From that time on I started to doubt myself, even to hate myself for not having the strength to match my ambitions. I desperately hoped for another chance to make up for my feelings of uselessness. It was not just about helping others any more, it was also a way to save myself. I hoped that I would be able to free myself from those heavy self-reproaches by doing good deeds.

After my chat with Wing's mother, I started to pay more attention to Wing, who often came to the MBL office to help out.

Wing joined MBL as a volunteer two years after it was set up in 2004. The first time she came to the MBL office at Orme Court in London I was pleasantly surprised. A pocket-sized, shy Chinese girl, hair piled up elegantly on her head and held in place with a pretty red chopstick, she came sweeping in dressed in the dark colours of China's south-western ethnic minorities. In the half-hour interview, I was impressed by her independent understanding of modern China and her skill with computers. I also discovered that she spent her limited holidays hiking, a thing that is very rare, not only among Chinese women, but among all that generation of young Chinese people. I sensed too that combination of ignorance, powerlessness and aloofness that so typifies only children, and makes life such a challenge for them.

Wing's arrival very soon made life a lot easier at the MBL office. Her fluent English and Chinese, and her casually assured web skills meant that she very quickly took over the running of the website. It was inspiring to see our website of several hundred pages renewed and expanded under Wing's wise management. However, during all her time with us she never expressed any feelings or discussed her hopes for the future. It was as if she did not need to communicate with anybody else, she was a universe unto herself.

In order to complete the task Wing's mother had set for me, I started seeking out opportunities to get closer to Wing. She was fond of reading and I had a small library in my home, set up specially for Chinese students, so I often asked her to 'house sit' for me. I invited her for weekends with the family and trips to the countryside, in order to get to know her better and to let her see my family life.

Wing appeared to be very self-assured and careful, both in her personal and professional life. When she was in the office anything seemed possible. However, she was fearful of contact with strangers. No matter who came in, she would give them the briefest of glances and a word or two of greeting before scurrying back to her corner. Her smile always seemed to be tinged with embarrassment, as if she were constantly asking, 'Is this all right? Have I done something wrong?' When listening to her talk about work, I had to shut out all other sounds in order to make out the quiet buzzing of this little bee! But when she recited poetry or spoke English, her voice carried to every corner of the office. I have noticed over the years that when extermely talkative Chinese people speak English, their voices often go very quiet, but with Wing it was the very opposite. Her voice carried when she was on the dependable ground of classical literature or when speaking a foreign language. Perhaps she had little contact with others when she was growing up? Perhaps always feeling that she was in the wrong had left her no space to express herself? Or perhaps she had done little else but recite poetry in the classroom?

I tried to explore this with Wing on one occasion. She gave me a hurried glance, lowered her head and said quietly, 'I grew up in a world with the sound turned down. My father never said very much, so as not to interfere with my studies and sleep. In class the teachers didn't let us talk, and with classmates if I said the wrong thing I'd get hit.'

Oh, my poor little girl! When I heard this I wept inside. I wished I could fold her in my arms and let her yell at me to her heart's content. Chinese people say that silence is golden, meaning that one should talk less nonsense and think before one speaks, to avoid causing offence or getting into trouble. But that does not mean we should strip away children's ability to speak their mind.

I wanted to help her live at the top of her voice, and a secret determination arose in my heart. 'Why is it that your voice is so clear when you recite classical poems and speak English?'

'I know my classical poetry so I'm not afraid of being laughed at. And when I speak English, well, I'm Chinese. Nobody will blame me if my words are incorrect,' Wing said very seriously.

I really wished Wing's mother could have overheard that conversation.

Many parents have found comfort and pride in their perfect daughters, without ever realising the high price paid by the child. It is not just a sacrifice made while growing up, but a lifelong warping of the personality. This practice is actually also part of the Chinese national character. We have used the notion of silence being golden to shackle children's lively minds. Times have changed, but these shackles have remained, like so many old customs, in our subconscious. Carried forward by their own momentum, they are transmitted hidden to each new generation, who in turn fasten them blindly on their children's spirit and freedom. This is particularly cruel in families with only children, who have no brothers and sisters with whom to share this silent burden of loneliness and helplessness.

I asked Wing if she wanted to learn my voice training method. She knew I must have mastered at least the basics of elocution from my many years in radio, so she agreed. We took two and a half hours out of her weekly volunteering time to practise three skills: volume control, the feel for language and sentences, and the logic of narrative. We would sit in opposite corners of the office, a good six metres apart, and discuss the news. First face to face then back to back, we would try our best to make the other hear clearly, understand and remember what was said. After several months it was possible to distinguish Wing's voice across a noisy crowd. At least in the office people no longer had to crane their necks to catch her words. However, the timidity and self-abasement in her body language were still present.

In order to help her fully release her potential and self-belief, I suggested that she chair a big cultural event that MBL was holding in London. Wing agreed to give it a try. On the day, I watched as Wing walked elegantly onto the stage in front of 150 people. She gave an impressive and dignified welcoming speech in ringing tones. Tears flowed from my heart to my cheeks . . . 'Thank you, Wing! Thank you, thank you!' I said quietly again and again. It was as if Wing's heart had suddenly taken flight and begun to soar!

After the event, Wing said that while standing on stage speaking, a strange feeling came over her, as if her life had changed onto another channel.

'What was the feeling?' I asked. I did not understand at the time, but subsequent events made me savour her words in retrospect.

A few days later, several girls in the office took advantage of the absence of any men to discuss what each of them knew about the other gender. I blundered unaware into the room and the twittering sparrows promptly fell silent. I felt rather embarrassed, unsure whether to advance or retreat.

'Carry on, Xinran's hardly an outsider. At her age she's seen it all! Keep talking!' This was from Wing, whose 'channel had been changed'.

It all sounded a bit peculiar, so I asked the girls, 'What are you talking about, all furtive and hangdog? Hiding something from me, are you?'

The girls giggled, but none of them spoke. Wing explained, laughing, 'We're discussing men!'

Discussing men? It seemed that China's age of earth-shaking changes had truly transformed its people, from inside out. When I was Wing's age, I would never have dared to talk about men in public. To do so would at the very least have been bad manners, at most downright 'hooliganism'. I warned myself, don't go showing your ignorance of the times! This is London, and you're with another generation, they can talk about whatever they like. But what are they saying about men? I was filled with curiosity.

'I . . . If I don't say anything at all, can I just sit here and listen in?' I implored.

In addition to Wing, the group also included an Italian, an American and a Swiss girl. The Italian said, 'Travel is a good way to find the right man, as it gives you opportunities to test his responsibility and general know-how.' The Swiss girl said, 'The man you meet in your normal life will be the most dependable, as everyday situations are the closest to home life.' The American said, 'It doesn't matter where you are when you run into him, as long as it feels good you can be with him; if it doesn't work out then you part company . . .'

All of a sudden Wing piped up with something that surprised us all: 'When I need a man I don't wait for the opportunity to travel or some special event, I head straight for a bar or a place that interests me, and take the initiative to get to know whoever takes my fancy. If we get along we can have a one-night stand, if we don't it's a couple of drinks and then bye-bye. Why use a formula to find men? The relations between men and women are all about feelings, why add all these humdrum formulas into the mix?'

'You Chinese girls seem so open, don't your family mind? Were you like this when you were in China? What about other Chinese girls? I thought the Chinese were meant to be very traditional?' several of the other girls blurted out eagerly.

'Me? When I was in China? I grew up in a desert, with no real human beings, so there's little by way of comparison. Sex is a universal human instinct, it can't be pigeon-holed as modern or traditional, nor is it something parents have the right to meddle in. Why should I care about other people's crass comments?' Wing said matter-of-factly.

I quietly clapped a hand over my mouth for fear I would cry out. Good heavens above, I thought to myself, is Beijing a desert, empty of human beings? Do her parents know about their perfect daughter's sexual habits?

Actually, Wing's attitude was far from unique, the 'novelty' of sex before marriage having begun a decade earlier with the first generation of China's only children. Prior to that, Chinese people would generally get married at between twenty-three and twenty-five years of age, and then have children. This was seen as fulfilling one's responsibilities to the family line. People who remained unmarried past this time were looked down on as pitiful creatures, while sex before marriage was a disgrace, too shameful to discuss. Nowadays everything has been turned upside down, and those who marry 'excessively early' have become the pitiful creatures. The first generation of only children pioneered China's marriage revolution. They began to view sex before marriage as a lifestyle choice, almost completely throwing off the family or political fetters that had been clapped on earlier generations. Instead, they chose their partners for love and romance, money, novelty value or even to relieve boredom. A quantum leap had taken place in the institution of Chinese marriage, throwing out old-fashioned ideas about a stable, dependable relationship where feelings might develop over time.

Back then I had never come across such pioneering opinions about men, especially from the lips of such a normally reserved girl as Wing. I was astonished and baffled by Wing's remarks. As a contemporary of her mother, just how much did we really understand about our children? The majority of us parents believe that our job is to prepare our children for the world as we see it. However, we often overlook that we have already changed the world that was left in our hands into something our forebears would think strange, ingenious and unbelievable.

I was desperate to understand their ideas and thought processes, not only because of the task Wing's mother had set me, but also as my son Panpan was just entering adolescence. I was often left not knowing whether to laugh or cry when faced with his 'pearls of wisdom', and yet I did not want to show any lack of understanding or disrespect, as young minds need encouragement like plants need the sun. Searching for some kind of common ground with my son gradually became an all-encompassing endeavour. But despite playing down my life experience and knowledge, and not pushing my own ideas on him, he still called me an 'unfeeling and unloving mother who did not understand him'. He would rather be the butt of his friends' jokes than believe his mother's heartfelt words.

One day, I invited Wing for a meal at New Fortune Cookie on Queensway in London. My excuse was that I wanted to ask her advice on the difficulties I was having with my son. As a mother, how was I supposed to understand a son going through puberty? How could I make him understand that the only unconditional gift in life is the love and care from one's family? That my attempts to correct his mistakes were done with an aching heart, not out of a desire to bend him to my will.

'Do you want to know what I really think, or would you rather some high-flown principles?' Wing asked me casually, sipping the French red wine I had ordered for her.

'What does that mean?' I said defensively. High-flown principles, I thought to myself, did she really think she knew more than me? I had a mind to . . .

But Wing had seen right through me. 'Do you think just because you presented a programme on women's issues for eight years that you know everything about life? Life changes, why can't principles?'

I was stunned. Was this young woman in front of me really Wing? She had truly 'changed the channel' this time. Her words were razor sharp!

Wing looked at me. 'What's the problem? You parents are always making a fuss about nothing.'

I was even more bewildered. Were age and experience no longer able to stand up to our children saying, 'You're making a fuss about nothing'?

Wing flashed me a wicked grin. 'You see, you can't handle the truth, can you?' Her smile brought me back from my reverie. Despite what she had said, it was still a very Wing smile, all embarrassment and anguish rolled into one.

'I can take it, I can take it, keep going. I promise I'll try my hardest to digest what you have to say.' I knew that her truth on the matter was precisely what I was looking for.

'I've never been a mum, I've only just kissed puberty goodbye,' Wing said, absorbed in the task of stripping off the packaging from her chopsticks. 'Don't worry about your son, he's a lot luckier than most of us only children! He's had heaps of opportunities and expe-riences, at home and in the outside world. Besides, boys are different from girls, they open their eyes to the world late and mature slowly. Your son is already doing pretty well. I went through some of the stuff he'd written when I was staying with you, and—'

'What? You've read my son's diary? Even I, his own mother, haven't gone through his things and read his diary.' I was rather put out, as I have always believed in respecting privacy, even between family members.

'Xinran, you've become too Westernised. All Chinese parents pry into their children's lives, peeling them open from skin to core. Chinese children are the property of their parents, and we single children in particular are the property of all the generations before us.' Wing drew a little circle on the dining table with a chopstick, then a series of bigger circles around it, building up the layers of generations.

I disagreed. 'I'm sorry, Wing, but not every Chinese parent thinks that way. I've always believed that in or out of the family, male or female, old or young, everyone should have their own space. Respect for others starts in the family. As a child, you formed your ideas about the outside world from family meals around the kitchen table.'

On hearing these words a flicker of doubt passed across Wing's face and her eyebrows twitched for a moment. 'In principle it's like that, but in real life things are a bit different. Where does the closeness between family members come from? It comes from a deep under-standing of each other. Aren't friends a bit like that too? You understand a lot more about the friends you share a dormitory with than the ones you see in class. This is because you know every last grubby detail of their lives! Take you, for example: if I hadn't stayed in your home and gone through all your clothes, I would never have discovered that you're no more a follower of fashion that I am. How else would I know that we have similar tastes in lingerie and accessories?'

'What? You went through my clothes?' I said, frowning with increasing discomfort.

Wing plainly found my reaction strange. 'When you invited me to your flat, didn't you say that I should treat your home as if it were my own? That meant I could go anywhere you hadn't locked, right?'

Wing's eloquent self-justification left me speechless! For a very long time after that, every time I opened my wardrobe I had visions of another pair of hands rifling through my underwear. Words could not describe how cringingly embarrassed I felt.

Wing seemed entirely unaware of my disquiet. She raised her wine glass and took a long gulp. 'You parents are always terrified about what might happen. Not everybody goes through hell during puberty. In my case? I don't know. Perhaps my childhood wasn't typical. Ever since I was little my life's been ruled by the second hand of a clock, revolving around the face of my parents, every second, every tick. I didn't lose a second in twenty years. The changes across the country, moving house, going up a grade at school, even biological shifts, to me were just different numbers on that clock. All I knew was that as long as I kept pace with that ticking second hand my parents would be happy, I wouldn't be scolded by my teachers or teased by my classmates.

'I never thought about what kind of person might want me when I grew up. Never knew my parents' hopes and dreams for me besides study and health. I didn't even know I had any rights and opportunities beyond studying, eating and sleeping. I never watched TV at home, as it was only for my parents to watch the news. My father said there was no point in me watching the news, as it was all made up and sensationalist. I never went outside during the holidays, as my parents thought the world was full of kidnappers and con-artists. At Chinese New Year and other festivals we would visit relatives, but as a girl I was expected to "sit like this and stand like that", tearing around any old how was definitely out and a sign of a poor upbringing. I didn't understand my classmates' games and couldn't join in their conversations. I could only secretly play by myself . . .'

'Secretly play by yourself? Can it really be possible that your parents didn't even let you play?' I felt waves of heart-wrenching pain crash against my body as she spoke. Disarmed by her words, I totally forgot my irritation of a few minutes earlier.

Wing smiled weakly again. 'Well, maybe they could have paid more attention. But if they had known they wouldn't have been happy any more.'

Once again I clapped a hand over my mouth, wishing I could cover my eyes that were welling up with tears. For the sake of her parents' pride and happiness, this young woman in front of me had sacrificed her childhood happiness, abandoned her dreams and even stifled her youthful impulses. I wondered whether her mother had the slightest idea about any of this.

Our food arrived, yet I could swallow nothing. I picked at the rice with my chopsticks, struggling with one grain at a time. I couldn't help wondering if my own son was suffering silently in corners I knew nothing about. I suddenly remembered a diary entry from a few years earlier.

6 May 2000

A busy Monday. Had to start work at 7.30 a.m. today. I said to my son as he woke up, 'Happy birthday, Panpan! Would you like to do something special today for your birthday present?' It is his first birthday in Britain.

He looked at me for a moment, not saying a word. Then in a tiny voice he said, 'Mum, I don't want anything for my birthday. I just want you to lie down with me for a few minutes. Is that OK?'

I froze. My heart ached and tears streamed down my face. I lay down next to him and put my arm around my boy. Neither of us said a word.

Lying there with my son, I was suddenly transported back twelve years. When I was pregnant with Panpan, I dreamed of bringing him up with my passion for music, even though I can't play anything myself. Of introducing him to art, even though I've never succeeded in painting anything. Of teaching him the poetry I've read, even though I've written my own since I was a teenager. I dreamed of playing with him and cooking his three meals a day. Taking him to see the world, from our local farmers' market to far-off climes. Picking up fallen tree leaves, trying different foods, strolling through different cultures. My boy has to live on the world stage, not just in one corner of it. I dreamed, dreamed every single day. I bought four Chinese dictionaries and one English one to trawl for children's names. The first name I chose was Yibo (翌博) – *yi* means 'feather wings ready for flying'; *bo* means 'to gain rich and deep life knowledge' – wings feathered, he can fly with a rich and deep life knowledge. Then I also wanted to give him an English name, since my family has so many ties overseas. Chinese is such a rich language, with over 18,000 surviving characters, and English has all the combinations of the twenty-six letters. I wanted my son's name to have strong energy and imagery in both languages. Panpan is very meaningful in Chinese characters, symbolising hope, observation, expectation and wishes. In English, as I discovered from the dictionary, it means half human, half god. That is how I feel when I see my son.

When I heard Panpan's first cry at 2.16 a.m. on 6 May 1988, I promised my boy I would devote myself to giving him a happy life.

I'm working day and night, as any other Chinese mother would. I'm trying as hard as I can to build a better future for him. However, it never occurred to me that what he really needs as he grows up is for me to be a mother to him. A mother who can spend time with him. He craves this as much as he craved milk and sleep as a baby.

Lying there with Panpan on his first birthday in Britain, I realised that I had already missed so much of my son's childhood. Was this any different from how my own mother missed so much of mine?

As a child, I used to believe I was an orphan, because my mother gave me a life but had no time to love me, or maybe she never thought that she should be with me. From the 1950s to 1970s, my mother, like most Chinese women then, followed the Communist Party's call. Everyone was expected to 'put their lives in order', meaning put the party first, the motherland second, and helping others third. Anyone showing care for their family and children was deemed a capitalist and could be punished. At the very least you would be looked down upon by everyone, including your own family. When I was a month old, I was sent away to live with my grandmothers in Nanjing and Beijing. Like millions of other Chinese children, I grew up without my mother throughout that whole Red period. Their busy careers as liberated women and victimisation in the Cultural Revolution kept them away from their children. Later on, for a number of reasons, we lived in different cities, countries and time zones.

I still miss my mum during the day when chatting to my family, writing or on book tours around the world. At night, I often dream of being a little girl again, one hand holding the doll that was taken by a female Red Guard the first day the Cultural Revolution came to my town, the other clasping my mother's two fingers. In my dreams she wears the purple silk dress she wore when, aged five, I first saw her. My grandmother took me to the train station to meet her while she was on a business trip. 'This is your mother. You should call her Mama not Auntie,' my grandmother corrected me, deeply embarrassed. Wide-eyed and silent, I stared at the woman in the purple dress. Her eyes filled with tears, but she forced her face into a sad, tired smile. My grandmother did not prompt me again, as the two women stood frozen in front of each other.

This particular memory has haunted me throughout the years. I felt the pain of it most keenly after becoming a mother myself, and experienced that atavistic, inescapable bond of mother and child.

What could my mother have said, faced with her daughter calling her Auntie?

Why have two generations of Chinese mothers, across different political and social times, made the same mistakes? Why was I unable to be the mother that my son Panpan wanted and needed? They are the same wants and needs that I had for my own mother.

I spent the rest of that day with Panpan, and as many as I could afterwards. I cut my busy work schedule to spend time, travel and play with him. But before long he became a Westernised teenager, with his own ideas and independence from his mum. Now he's grown up, and is both Chinese and English. He can cook Chinese food for me as a Chinese man, and help me with my English and computers as a Westerner. We talk about life and international politics as friends, but I still miss my baby boy. I wonder whether he too misses the days when his tiny hand clasped my fingers.

I once asked my mother how long she thought it had taken Panpan to realise that he just wanted to be with his mother on his birthday.

'Twelve years you think? Xinran, he has been asking you that since the day he was born,' she said quietly.

My heart nearly stopped.

'Go on, eat, what are you gawping at?' Wing called me back from the depths of my painful memories. 'Don't waste your tears on the state of the world for my sake. I actually have a pretty good life. After uni I carried on studying computers, and spent every day on the internet for three years! I've had my fill of fun from the news and on-line gaming. I won't lie to you, I saw loads of juicy things from all over the world on the internet, including how men and women pleasure each other, I just didn't want to deal with real people. Ha ha, go on, eat!' Wing teasingly encouraged me.

'Do you hate your parents?' I couldn't stop myself from asking her this question.

'Why should I hate them? They gave me life, spent twenty years raising me, and they're still paying for my overseas studies. What reason would I have to hate them?' Wing stared blankly at her chopsticks as she spoke.

'So do you call or write to them often?' I asked cautiously.

'I think you know perfectly well the answer to that question, so why ask? Has my mum been on to you?' Wing continued eating and drinking her wine, apparently indifferent to whatever her mother had told me. However, less than a minute later, she suddenly became very emotional. 'Think about it, Xinran, I've lived by their clock without feeling or desire, dotting every i and crossing every t, for twenty-two years. As a child I didn't know any better, then I learned to endure it, later on it became a prison. I never complained about anything to them, all so that they would be happy; this was my way of repaying the debt of gratitude I owed them for raising me. I wonder if it ever occurred to them that out of their machine-like life I would grow into a real flesh and blood person with joys and sorrows of my own? They never even seemed to worry that I might be physically or mentally abnormal. I've often wondered about this, because I seem to be scared of everything, afraid to see people, afraid to do things, afraid of anything new.

'After I left China I decided to set myself challenges. I forced myself to learn by trying the bitter, difficult things in life. I went to the country I was most afraid of, Nepal, because pictures of the poverty there had once given me nightmares. After I arrived in England, I spent a week going around London on foot, because I was afraid people would laugh at me for not knowing about the city where I lived. I would force myself to buy food I'd never tried; twice I ended up eating tinned cat food by mistake! I was afraid Westerners would laugh at my ignorance of food. I went to bars three times a week, to forced myself to face my fear of men. I used to think that if men were nice to me they were probably up to no good. I didn't want to end up on the shelf like some kind of "reduced to clear" product, but even less did I want people to think that I lacked the "seven emotions and six desires".* I wasn't rebelling, I was fleeing! Escaping from an only child's prison. But did I dare tell my parents about these experiences? Wouldn't that be the death of them? If I asked their permission and reported everything back to them, would they still be able to carry on with their lives? I don't mind them thinking I'm heartless, I'd rather that than they live in fear. No one should have to live in fear . . .' Wing unconsciously picked at the remains of her food with her chopsticks; she was breathing hard.

I looked at Wing intently. What could I say? I was lost for words, as they piled up in their thousands like a traffic jam in my throat. What a hopelessly struggling, despairing, yet kind and self-improving girl! Wing and I formed a bond that day, over those four dishes and bottle of wine. I no longer felt I was waving silently to her from the opposite bank of a river. I hoped I would be able to teach Wing that families need to communicate, that her ageing parents longed for the comfort of their daughter's presence and trust in their remaining years. I hoped she would realise that the same strength coursing through her veins, allowing her to face and conquer her fears, also flowed through her parents'.

In the spring of Wing's second year volunteering for MBL, we sent her to southern England to help a group of parents who had all adopted girls from China. A week later, we listened closely to her debrief in the office. When Wing and I were finally alone, she suddenly looked at me, her face brimming with emotion. 'Xinran, I finally understand what made you set up Mothers' Bridge of Love. While I was with those families I could feel their helplessness. They

---

* The 'seven emotions and six desires' *qiqingliuyu* 七情六欲 represent the inescapable feelings of the human condition: happiness, anger, sorrow, fear, love, hate and longing, as well as desires of the flesh.

were so kind to their new Chinese daughters, talking over their days with them at mealtimes, reading them bedtime stories. They seemed so cultured, with their own successful careers, yet they have so little understanding of their adopted children's country. They don't know how to answer their questions. I've never experienced anything like it. China is so poorly understood in the world, there are so many Chinese girls who can't even speak Chinese! The parents kept asking me, "Why didn't their Chinese mothers want them?" I looked into their longing eyes, really wanting to give them an answer. I'm Chinese, but I truly couldn't say why their mothers didn't want them. I hope we'll be able to spend more time helping them search for these answers. The girls miss their real mothers so much, and spend all their time trying to imagine them. How much more must their mothers be thinking of them. Do you think there is some special connection between mothers and daughters that transcends space, time and culture?'

Wing burst into tears. It was the first time I had seen her make no attempt to conceal her emotions.

I hugged her. 'Yes, of all the things in the world, a mother's love is the only one that is universal. Strength and support have their limits, but we are all doing our best, a little at a time, like the Foolish Old Man Who Moved the Mountains.* One day, sooner or later, more people will think and feel the way we do. When that day comes, we little drops of water will come together into streams, rivers, lakes and oceans. People will begin to take notice and want to help those Chinese girls. Thank you, Wing!'

---

* The Foolish Old Man Who Moved the Mountains is a story by the philosopher *Liezi* 列子, about an old man who did not fear being mocked as a fool by the wise. He was not afraid of hardship, and persisted in his struggle to remove two mountains in front of his house. He made his family dig ceaselessly into the mountains, until the Lord of Heaven was moved, and sent two heavenly generals to move them.

Wing worked in the UK for two years after completing her studies, then emigrated to Australia in 2010, where she found a job researching South-east Asian Chinese culture. In 2011 I was pleasantly surprised to receive an email from her mother. She wished me a happy Chinese New Year, and informed me that the whole family was moving to Australia to be with Wing. Their daughter was still the only sun in their solar system. They were following the fuse that brought light to their home. Maybe such a thing could only happen in a Chinese only-child family.

Her email came with an attachment:

My child, please read these words.

One day, as you see me getting older, when I become clumsy, when my health begins to fail, please be patient, try to understand me and sympathise . . .

When I dribble food around my mouth, or when I can no longer dress myself, please don't laugh at me, have a little patience and think of how much blood, sweat and tears your mother spent teaching you these very same things . . .

When you and I are talking, and I suddenly forget what I was going to say, please give me a little time. If I really am hopeless, don't fret, because for your old mother the important thing is not talking but being with her daughter.

When I go out and forget my way home, please don't be angry, but slowly lead me back home. Remember that when you were small, Mummy waited anxiously for you at the school gates every day . . .

When my legs start to fail me, please lend me an arm in support. Just as I supported you as you took your first steps in life . . .

When one day I tell you I don't want to carry on living, please don't be angry. One day you will know that days spent with one foot in the grave are painful and hard to endure . . .

My darling child, in the course of your growing up I always did the best I could and gave you the best of everything. It was all new to me, and the mother of an only child gets no second chances. I know I have done many things wrong, but please don't get angry or blame me too much. No one is born a mother, we all learn as we stumble our way through life. Please stay beside me and tell me of your loss and disappointment calmly and with an even temper, like in the early days when I was helping you to explore your life . . .

My child, give your old mother a helping hand, and with your love and patience walk with me on my life's road till it comes to an end. I will repay you with eternal smiles and a love that has never changed over all the days and nights of your life.

I love you, my only child! One day we will look back on all the things that we did not manage to do for each other, and they will beat like heavy hammer blows on our hearts and memories. Living is a gift, a heaven-sent chance to love each other tenderly.

When you were wailing in swaddling clothes, my love was a warm embrace. When you were babbling your first words, my love patiently taught and guided you. When you were travelling far from home and when you overcame obstacles to succeed, my love was the tears pouring down my face. When you were ill in bed, my love was a pair of tired, bloodshot eyes. When you succumbed to bad habits, my love was warm with heartfelt warnings and advice. When you refused to heed my words, my love was the healing salt sprinkled on your wounds and the pain in your heart . . .

I asked Wing's mother if she hoped I would forward her attachment to Wing.

She wrote back saying that Wing had copied it from the internet, edited it and sent it to her. Perhaps she wanted to use this as a key to open the door between her and her parents?

I thought back to her words: 'I wasn't rebelling, I was fleeing!

Escaping from an only child's prison.' Was Panpan fleeing too? I dared not pursue this thought any further.

———————

How do you view the Yao Jiaxin incident? Why is Chinese society debating him (a post-80s man) so fiercely?

Recent, more in-depth media surveys have demonstrated how the victim has to some extent been hijacked by the extremes of popular opinion. However, many aspects of the incident are not actually that bad. The long-term lack of fairness in Chinese society has created a tendency to overcompensate when judging wrongs, and this is reflected in the justice system. If you trace the incident back to its root, it reflects a general lack of moral integrity in society. I don't see that Yao Jiaxin being an only child affects the incident in any fundamental way.

LILY | 4

M ANY CHINESE families feel they have lost their way amid the country's breakneck struggle to transform and modernise, and an increasing number are turning to miracle 'cures' from the West or returning to the teachings of their ancestors. In 2009 a big debate broke out over the *Dizigui*, one of the great Chinese educational classics. It represents thousands of years of civilisation, and has survived under the dust and rubble of a hundred years of chaos and war. If Confucius is the basis of Han Chinese culture, then the *Dizigui* is the 'Ten Commandments' of education.* It was compiled from Confucius's writings by Li Yuxiu in the reign of the Kangxi emperor towards the end of the seventeenth and early eighteenth centuries, and consists of a list of educational aphorisms. In prime place is filial piety towards parents and love of siblings, followed by self-control and keeping one's word, then fairness, altruism, family unity and choosing virtuous friends. It emphasises studying the six traditional arts of ritual, music, archery, horsemanship, calligraphy and logic, and states that one can only be considered educated through an exhaustive study of the Chinese classics. The debate in society centred around the relevance of the traditional *Dizigui* in a modern globalised age. Can and should it be taught to children nowadays? Should it be preserved as part of the world's cultural heritage?

Those in favour included Professor Qian Wenzhong of Shanghai's Fudan University. He maintained that while many people nowadays

* See Appendix II: The *Dizigui*.

consider it old-fashioned and harking back to feudal times, it is impossible to overestimate its real value. Although old, it deals with very current problems like happiness, children's education and how to be a good citizen. It could again become the foundation stone for the nation and bring a civilising influence to family and society. We should treat traditional culture with the gratitude and respect it deserves, and make use of its teachings on filial piety and morality to create a happier society. This happiness should come from an acknowledgement of our current level of civilisation, and from giving our children a first-rate education.

Those opposed to the *Dizigui* maintained that traditional culture is secretive, morbid and dark, while modern culture is open, healthy and bright. Many Chinese people have been influenced by Western materialist ideas like 'matter determines spirit', 'existence determines awareness' and 'economics are the foundations for growth'. They believe that happiness is solely linked to increasing GDP and material wealth.

I personally support those in favour of the *Dizigui*, because no matter what happens in the future or how our environment changes, if we continue to live in an age without virtue and a society that has forgotten its cultural roots, the people will lose their culture and regional diversity will disappear. They will become like flowers in a display, living a kind of cut-off life temporarily supported by nutrients, but unable to live long in their own soil.

But for those only children whose families believed in the *Dizigui*, has it acted as a charm to ward off evil? The experiences of Lily and her classmate may provide an answer.

My husband Toby, a literary agent, has spent many years exploring the translation and publication of books into different languages. His work has taken him to many non-English-speaking countries, and put him in touch with many authors and literature professors. Most years he attends two Chinese publishing events, the spring sowing and the autumn harvest, and over the years has acted as agent to many Chinese writers. One summer in the late 1990s he was invited to Shanghai, and while snatching a moment of peace in the newly built Shanghai Museum, asked one of the young staff where he could see traditional life and religion in Shanghai and Beijing. To his surprise, the young university student took the time to show him the city's old courtyard houses still surviving down narrow alleys between skyscrapers. She also left him some information on religious sites in Beijing, including the Yonghegong Tibetan Buddhist temple, Shishahai Han Buddhist lake and the Eight Great Buildings from the Ming and Qing dynasties.

When Toby told me about this young woman, I found it hard to believe that amid the craze for computer games (on-line gaming was yet to take off) and fast-food culture, which was spreading like wildfire through society, there was still a young person who cared about history and traditional culture. Especially as it was all being swept away in the enthusiasm for modernisation.

I wanted to meet this exceptional young woman, and very soon my wish was granted. Lily was an architecture student specialising in urban art at a university in Shanghai. She spent her holidays working as a part-time interpreter at the Shanghai Museum, which she had fallen in love with when she was a little girl. Because of our common interests, Lily and I soon became good friends. Later on we discovered a connection between our families, and restored a link that had been severed since the Cultural Revolution.

Lily was an unusual young woman, with a fine physique, an appreciation for art and an impressive educational background. However, she later told me that she only studied architecture because she was not accepted into the military. Lily seemed to regret this, as it was clear that she had modelled herself on the army for many years. She exhibited great self-control and was instinctively respectful of others. She dressed with military simplicity and elegance, and had very precise body language. She hardly ever made exaggerated gestures, even during extremes of emotion. I guessed that her general style came from her family, who were part of the military aristocracy, having held high military posts for several generations.

There is a particular class within Chinese society known as 'inside the residential compound'. The residential compound is the army. Chinese military academies were the only places that maintained normal education and discipline during the Cultural Revolution. The military is one of the master controls of the nation, and to this day enjoys preferential treatment. Children growing up in those guarded compounds never lacked for food or clothing when times were hard. There were never any worries over choosing the right school. Housing, life, clothes, even festivals were all set out according to the military calendar. However, there was also little opportunity for individual expression. The vast majority of young people from these compounds received a first-rate education and were comparatively public-spirited. They tend to be very determined, not afraid of hardship and have a strong sense of responsibility, although the big residential compounds also produce their fair share of tearaways. At first, I thought that Lily's innate self-control came from her 'compound' upbringing. However, as soon as I met her mother, I realised the true source of her strength.

Her mother told me, 'My husband and I come from a long line of scholars. Although our families have been completely absorbed in military affairs and the construction of academies for the past two generations, our parents gave us a traditional education. Even during the height of the Cultural Revolution, my father would have me and my sisters recite the *Three-Character Classic* * and the *Dizigui*. My father, who was a maths professor in a military academy, used to tell me that the three Chinese educational classics, the *I Ching*, the *Three-Character*

---

* The *Three-Character Classic, sanzijing* 三字經, believed to have been written in the thirteenth century, is an educational primer to teach children the basics of Confucian thought.

Classic and the *Dizigui*, are China's 'maths, physics and chemistry'. Once you know them, you can face any situation in the world without fear. Soon after, we were sent down to a poverty-stricken mountainous area in Jiangxi province. Many similar families were sent there with us, and spent almost the whole ten years bemoaning their fate. But my parents made us memorise the classics and read books, hunt for different types of grass and insects, and pick wild vegetables. I don't think I had one boring day in all those ten years!

'Conditions improved after we moved back to the city and civilisation. We were paupers compared to other families, but we had the benefit of ancient philosophy. We never complained or got upset at "not having". Later when I was looking for a husband, the clincher was whether he knew the *Three-Character Classic* and the *Dizigui*. It might sound strange now, but in 1980s China there were only two sorts of people: those chasing after political power and those chasing after money. When I said I wanted to marry a man who knew the classics, everyone thought there was something wrong with my head! Fortunately, my husband's family were cultural diehards too, so we hit it off very quickly.

'After our daughter was born we took turns to read her the *Three-Character Classic* and the *Dizigui*. My husband thought the *I Ching* was too difficult to read to her immediately, and something that should be learned slowly over a lifetime. When Lily was just three years old, she started memorising the *Dizigui*, one character at a time. I remember one day, not long after she started at primary school, she came home and said with a pout that none of her classmates had heard of the *Dizigui*, and her teacher had said it was old and of no use to anyone. She asked us why she had to memorise a text that nobody knew or cared about. I didn't know how to answer her, but my husband quickly replied that the *Dizigui* is useful for getting into the best universities. Years later, Lily really did get into one of China's top universities.'

When Lily's mother told me this story, Lily was about to finish her course. Her mother and I came to an agreement that some time after her graduation Lily would live with us in London for two months. The aim was to broaden her horizons, give her a feel for European civilisation, and teach her about the world outside the *Dizigui* and China's politicised classrooms.

Lily graduated from university in 2003, and soon found her *Dizigui*-centred academic life crashing headlong into the hustle and bustle of Chinese city life. But this meeting of worlds left her scarred and bruised. She could not understand it. China's ever hungry capitalist beast was swallowing up the city's traditional architecture totally unimpeded. Nobody was talking about it, development policy was in a shambles, and officials seemed locked in petty power struggles. Her family and university education had led her to believe that her knowledge would be respected and her ideas welcome, especially as the country went through major reforms. However, as soon as she started work she discovered the harsh reality. Either she could be a spare part in an outdated production line, where those who went with the flow flourished, while those who went against it floundered. Or she could be just one more obsolete tool in the barbarism of modernity, to whom no one would give a thought. Either way she would have to bide her time for an opportunity in a bloated hierarchical system where promotion was based on seniority. Three years passed, and the crisp blueprints that she clutched to her chest were slowly trampled under the feet of reality until faded and yellow.

In autumn 2006 Lily brought her injured heart to London. I took her to see many buildings, including the mix of modern and Gothic that jostled like neighbours along the banks of the Thames. Lily was beside herself with excitement at the Royal Albert Hall, Queen Elizabeth Hall, the National Theatre and London Television Centre, at all those geometric lines and higgledy-piggledy rooflines.

However, she was puzzled by groups of buildings that seemed neither fish nor fowl in terms of historical continuity. 'How has nobody noticed that the design of this group damages the artistic landscape of accumulated centuries on both sides of the Thames?' she would ask incredulously.

In the three months Lily spent exploring Britain and Europe, over half my time was spent listening to her rigidly held opinions. 'Shining such a strong light on the exhibit will spoil people's appreciation of it, and damage the precious artefact. It's wrong. Why hasn't anyone corrected it? That refit has damaged the original style of the building, why have so many generations overlooked this? Art is like the four seasons, with design elements as living things. Just like the tiger is found in Asia, or the lion in Africa, how can they just change things with no awareness of the environment? That's not art, that's messing around with technique!' On and on she went . . .

Lily's concept of good and bad was as rigid as reinforced concrete. Many people think this Chinese black and white mindset comes from the last one hundred years of turmoil. During those years, everything had to be either good or bad, black or white, with none of the shades of light and dark grey found in ancient Chinese paintings. But I think this is only part of the picture. It also has to do with how people perceive culture and civilisation, and how in modern society the boundary between these two words has become increasingly murky. In fact, culture is not the same as civilisation. Every clod of earth develops its own culture, but civilisation only arises when we have learned to understand, respect and make use of culture. However, in twenty-first-century China, destroying traditional civilisation through new educational models is a trend we have become accustomed to and no longer see as strange.

In order to test something I had heard in China, I invited Lily and two other Chinese students to afternoon tea. One was from Peking University and the other from Shanghai's Fudan University.

I told them about a Beijing Union University survey in 2002 that had greatly surprised me. A group of second-year female students had no idea from which part of the body babies were born. Some said they came out of the armpit, some from the belly button, there were even girls who said that babies were born out of the head! The students were asked where they got their ideas from. One said, 'Well, don't women who've just had children bind their heads up?' True enough, I thought, country women do believe that they should wrap up warm and avoid wind and water after giving birth, so as to avoid arthritis and headaches in later life. A second said, 'Haven't you heard of the belly button? Children are born through the belly button, and then the umbilical cord is cut.' Another said, 'I've heard people say babies come from that place where women have hair, right?'

I asked the three girls in front of me whether they believed these findings.

The girl from Peking University replied, 'What's so unusual about that? When we were at university, we got everything we knew about sex from classmates from the countryside who in turn learned about it from watching farm animals! City families tended to be more prudish, and never discussed sex at home. Students from small towns pretended to understand but didn't really. But they did have more freedom to talk about it, and had covered a bit more ground than us big-city girls. It was different in those days. Now you can watch it all secretly on the internet, but back then we had to wait till lights out to discuss men and women.'

The girl from Fudan University said, 'We were all in the same boat. At home we had no sisters to "pass on the jewels of experience". Away from home we were indoctrinated by other family members and teachers, ten of them to every one of us. Aside from homework, all we had was our daydreams and mad fancies at night. Still, I think that talking about these things is foolish. If you want to know about men and having babies you should go and experience it for yourself!'

'Experience? Is it really the sort of thing you can experience?' Lily asked, her eyes huge. 'Xinran, have you experienced it? How do you go about it?'

'Me? Oh, I used to be appallingly ignorant, I was a very late bloomer,' I told them. 'In my day, if you even discussed sex you'd end up in jail. I once read a book called *Beacons on the Grassland*, which contained a passage about love. "They sat shoulder-to-shoulder under the moonlight, holding hands . . . The following year they had a fat baby boy." When I was twenty-two, our political instructor wanted to hold hands beside the campfire. I got very scared and angry, and turned him down outright. I thought he was sexually harassing me, wanting to get me pregnant out of wedlock! I'm part of the older generation, and still find it hard to accept your ideas of "experience". Even after I was married, I still often did not know what to do. We all grew up in a sexual desert.'

The girl from Fudan University was from Shanghai, China's most modern city, and it showed in her forthright attitude. 'Experience is getting to know men, coming into contact with them. It's nothing to worry about, you're not going to get pregnant from touching and stroking.'

The Beijing student was equally as direct. 'Modern families don't necessarily need a man and a woman to have a child. All you need to do is find a good-looking guy, have a child and live by yourself. Isn't that a better way of doing it?'

I suddenly noticed that Lily's expression had changed. She was looking down and seemed unusually reserved. Her eyes were fixed on her two hands, which she was rubbing together nervously. I wanted to put it all in some kind of historical context she would understand, so I said, 'When society was mainly agrarian, Chinese rules on sex were very cruel. From princesses and nobles to peasants, if a girl was touched by a man out of marriage it would signify the end of her life as she knew it, and she would be labelled "dirty goods". The pleasures of sex were for men only. For the emperor, kings, generals and ministers. Many women never experienced a moment's pleasure from sex in their whole lives, and regarded themselves as sacrificial cattle . . .'

All of a sudden, Lily surged to her feet and stormed into the bedroom, gasping with rage. The rest of us were stunned, not knowing what had just happened. We followed her to the bedroom only to find her in tears. When she saw me she said, face scarlet and streaming tears, 'Xinran! It was only because my mother trusted you so much, and we thought you were a moral person, that I came to visit you in the UK in the first place. Now here you are talking to me about these filthy, horrid, indecent things!'

'I . . .' For a moment I could not find the words to reply to her indignation.

I had been away from China for almost ten years. Each time I returned during that period I would seek out the old familiar feelings of home in those utterly transformed streets and thronging crowds, but they always seemed to have been lost among the changes of Reform and Opening-up policies. Time and again I felt abandoned on a branch line of history by my madly sprinting motherland. But I never thought that I would have such a young fellow branch-line traveller. That at twenty-five Lily could still possess such childlike innocence!

Seeing my bewilderment, the girl from Beijing commented, 'Students from China's top universities are all this naïve, and that's not to mention those from smaller universities.'

The girl from Shanghai said, 'Xinran, the facts of the matter are right here in front of you. Is there anything else you'd like us to confirm?'

After seeing out the two girls, I asked Lily, 'Have you really never had a boyfriend since leaving university?'

Lily was still angry. 'I'm not the kind of person you think I am!'

'What kind of person do you think I think you are?' I genuinely did not understand.

'I've never carried on with a man like that!' Lily said in a definite tone.

'Have you ever had any male friends before? Have you ever gone for meals or just chatted with them?' As I asked this question, countless girls like Lily flashed before my eyes. Caught up in the conflict between Chinese traditions and Western openness, they defended their chastity and morals with a painful uncertainty.

'No, I haven't. In the day I go to work, and have an office to myself. When work finishes at six, I go back home to my mother, who has a meal waiting for me,' Lily said blandly.

'Are you still living with your parents?'

'Of course, I'm not married yet. How could I live with anyone else?'

'Nowadays lots of young people rent a flat with friends or colleagues. Why couldn't you live with other people?'

'If I did that then how would I be able to prove my purity?'

'Why would you want to be able to prove your purity?'

'If I can't clearly prove my purity, won't my parents lose face? Won't I have gone to university for nothing? Xinran, I'm living my life according to the *Dizigui*!'

Listening to Lily's traditional ideas on chastity made me realise how disconnected she was from modern China. I once again felt the strength of tradition and culture in the development of human civilisation. It was a force that not even Chinese politics or modernisation programmes could stand up to, let alone one-child families cherishing their little 'one-and-onlies'. In this way the ancient Chinese were much like many other peoples. They believed that love and courtship were only a small part of reproduction, to be respected, but certainly not required. Giving in to human desires was a sin, and locking up young people's sexuality a parent's duty. However, does this rigid view of chastity and morality, pure as crystal though it is, lower people's immunity to living in a diverse society? Does it in fact leave them unable to defend themselves? Chinese academics are very concerned about how these traditional ideas could damage or even split up families if, in the fast-changing modern world, young people reject these ideas, and their parents who taught them.

I told Lily my personal belief that a woman may have as many as three men over the course of her life. One is like a huge tree in which you can build a nest and raise children. One is like light itself, having little influence on your daily life, but appearing when you are in the depths of despair, moving mountains and crossing oceans for you. The third is a combination of the two. This is the man of your dreams. Perhaps you will never encounter him, but he plants in your life the hope for a good man and the things you want of him.

'Lily, be brave for a moment and try to imagine the man of your dreams. Make a few male friends, you don't have to have any physical contact that your family might worry about. Learn to experience the feeling of men and women being drawn to each other. There is nothing low about this kind of awareness, nor is it improper. It is the gift of culture and the delight of civilisation.' With these words of encouragement I drove Lily to the airport for her return to China.

I caught up with Lily again on my next visit to China. 'Xinran, I've been very brave, and not just in my thoughts, I've had some new experiences too!' she blurted out as soon as we met. Her body language was as controlled as ever, but her eyes were brimming with excitement. She had softened her stark, military-style clothes with a brightly coloured silk scarf, displaying the style of a woman of the arts.

'Brave? Why do you say brave, is there something dangerous

about men?' I asked, puzzled. I had forgotten about Lily's distinctive way of talking.

'Of course there is! Otherwise, why would so many people lay down their lives or break up their families for love? The art of human life is on another level of complexity altogether compared to city design. It's just about the only art that people are powerless to alter. Don't you think, Xinran?' Lily looked at me, apparently surprised at my shallowness. Evidently new discoveries were coming thick and fast for her. 'Do you know? In the past I never thought there could be such passion between men and women, aside from what you do to make babies. Somebody can be several metres away, but a single glance can whisk you off to a fantasy land that is totally out of your control, it can even send you out of your mind. It's fascinating. If you've never experienced it you wouldn't believe it possible, but once you do, boy, do you get a shock! Those traditional love stories really weren't made up, they're a record of actual love, to be passed down through the ages. Could my parents' and grandparents' generation really have condemned these powerful emotions as hooliganism? I know it happens, but I still don't understand it. People know full well that disaster may be looming over them, but they still charge blindly into enemy lines. The power of love is irresistible. How can you say that's not brave?'

I later discovered that Lily was not as brave in real life as she believed. In the subsequent two years I did not hear any news of her 'material progress'. However, her clothes and make-up suggested a blossoming of her emotions. Her style was inching towards a feminine warmth, with colours changing daily to match her dress and accessories. Occasionally I would even see jewellery peeping shyly from her new hairdo. I would often tease her, 'Next time you visit us, it'll be as a couple.' To which she would reply bashfully, 'Before introducing any boyfriend to my family he'll need to pass the test of time. I wouldn't want him scaring them to death over something!'

Toby never really understood where she was coming from. 'Men and women finding happiness together is their own business. Why does Lily care so much about what her family thinks?'

I tried to explain: 'In traditional Chinese culture, filial piety comes first, then duty to the whole family, then children's education. For a girl, there's also the added duty of bearing a son. If you don't give the family a son you're spurned by society. You have to understand that Lily grew up with the *Dizigui*, the equivalent of Moses' Ten Commandments for children. It's very hard for these beliefs just to be washed away by new trends or politics. But Lily is also an exception, as hardly any families teach their children the *Dizigui* these days.'

However, despite Lily's upbringing, at twenty-seven she was already past normal marrying age. Could she really stand by unaffected while her contemporaries were all roosting in their own little nests? What was it that made her so cautious? Why did she think romance was like skating on thin ice? Was it fear of her parents? Did she lack confidence? Or had she fallen in love with a man who did not belong to her? I had no way of answering her mother's probing questions. Sometimes she even suspected us of colluding together to deceive her, of 'crossing the sea under cover of darkness'.

Lily finally told me that Chinese people think men can do no wrong, that they cannot marry the wrong woman. She wanted to look around and play the field for a while, to test her own judgement of men through experience, and make sure she was prepared for marriage. She was wary of destroying her parents' hopes and dreams for her in some moment of passion that she would later live to regret. She wanted to be certain that the man she chose would walk the road of life with her till the very end. She required more than promises, more than romance, she was seeking the wisdom to plan ahead for the rest of her life.

When I heard her words I could not suppress a deep sigh of

emotion. In today's China, where great and ancient things are collapsing and we are being whittled down to a fast-food society that only knows how to snatch and compete, who would have thought that a young woman like Lily could still exist. A young woman who, without fuss or hurry, looks around with a cool gaze. I wondered whether her logical and reasonable outlook was based on great wisdom or great fear? I often feel that higher education grants both of these things. The wisdom to be aware of risks that others are blind to, but also the fear that comes with awareness, and the opportunity for greater wisdom through facing this fear. I have seen this pattern played out many times over the years, particularly in only-child families, and particularly when Chinese and Western education systems are flung together without a thought.

Perhaps it was in order to explain the dangers of haste that Lily introduced me to Lotus, a friend of hers famous for her good looks at university. Lotus had a striking face and an elegant, refined manner. An artist through and through who, in Lily's words, was 'a public work of art' wherever she went. She was a pedestal to which boys would gravitate to put themselves on display. They would flock around her, but almost none had the nerve to possess her. A single date with her was worth several weeks' boasting. The other girls were jealous of the competition, and there was much gossip over which prince would have the good fortune to marry this paragon of beauty.

After graduating from university, Lotus met an art critic from Germany called Karl at an international art event. Karl had come to Beijing to research the roots of Chinese performance art. What intrigued Karl the most was how there could be so much transcendental awareness in Chinese art. The country had been cut off by war and chaos for almost a hundred years, but was still able to produce pieces that wowed the world, even against the backdrop of modern art so popular since the 1960s. Lotus was Karl's assistant and translator in China, and their investigations led them to a very unusual artistic community.

The community was a research group on the ancient Chinese 'Art of the Bedchamber' (*Fang zhong shu*), an ancient text on Daoist sexual practices. Each group consisted of one male director-trainer and three women. They not only lived under the same roof, but would also sleep in the same antique four-poster bed. According to the 'requirements of the research', the three women had to come from different cultural and educational backgrounds, in order to obtain evidence of the relationship between sexual culture and background. The highest educated woman was granted the title of Elegant Lady of Talent. Her role was to make love in the ancient, warm and soft ways, and to explore Chinese sexual behaviour. The most beautiful or culturally unusual woman was called Beautiful Concubine or International Beautiful Concubine. Her role was to explore the senses in modern frenzied lovemaking. The third woman was the Uneducated Peasant, whose role was to allow the male artist full scope in sexual violence, based on the idea that men are superior to women.

As I got to know Lotus better, she introduced me to more of the research, in the hope that I would support their artistic freedom. She said that the government refused to accept that it was performance art, and that Chinese artists had no freedom of expression. Lotus told me that there was a fair amount of evidence to support her view, as over the last thousand years art had belonged to one of the 'low nine groups', and been banned for a long time. 'But do you really think this is what the men in the group are researching? Or are they just . . .' I asked Lotus, unconvinced.

'Xinran, I know what you're thinking. When Karl and I first heard about it we were left open-mouthed too. Several of the male sex director-trainers explained to us that they were "excavating and researching" China's ancient arts of the bedchamber, which are at the heart of Chinese culture. They said that if it is to be understood and passed on people need to rush headlong into the experience. Ancient Chinese is being polluted by Western junk. It's in danger of being supplanted by American fast-food culture. Any Chinese person who can should stand up and do something about it, and safeguard the continuation of a thousand years of civilisation. When I heard the passion in their voices, a feeling of great responsibility arose in my heart. I realised that I had a responsibility to help these artists perfect their knowledge of ancient culture, including the arts of the bedchamber.'

'Then . . . you joined in?' I asked Lotus. At that moment my body felt as if it had fallen into two different worlds, freezing and burning up all at once. Shameless? Degenerate? Ridiculous? Foolish? Hooligan? Out of all the 18,000 Chinese characters that have survived 5,000 years of Chinese civilisation, I could not find one word or phrase adequate to describe this kind of cultural confidence trick!

'I haven't signed a contract with them yet, as I have to help Karl finish his project. My first agreement was with him, so I can't break that,' she said.

What a responsible girl, I thought! All my instincts warned me that this was some kind of cultural trap. After the event, I did some research among China's artistic elite and discovered that research into the ancient arts of the bedchamber really did exist. I had naïvely hoped that what Lotus had described was one of a kind. As it turned out, the facts were shocking. There is indeed a hidden movement in Chinese society, set up by male artists to pursue 'the art of human nature', 'primitive cultural moulding' and 'art through international sexual blending'. These are essentially groups of conmen dressed up in the golden robes of artists, trampling traditional morals underfoot, and violating young girls' yearnings for art and natural human feelings.

A female migrant worker who had been duped into taking part in this 'sexual culture research' told me: 'A job centre official said there was a bloke who wanted a few of us to help him with some kind of cultural work. Those cultured city guys are strange though. They say and do things that country people wouldn't even dare to think. I don't understand how city women can live with them. If I hadn't wanted to build up a nest egg, so I couldn't be pushed around when married, I would never have kept my family in the dark and done this sort of "sexual education", that's for sure. If all city education is like this, I'd be better off going back to the countryside and marrying a totally uneducated man. At least then I'd be living a proper life.'

This was the last time I saw Lotus, but my brief contact with her left me with many unanswered questions. I wondered what became of her after that.

In spring 2009 Lily sent me two pieces of news, one happy, one tragic.

The happy news was a natural reflection of her increasing emotional maturity. The currents of common interest and personality had brought a man into her life. After flying together for a year and a half they had decided to build a nest and have a child. It was just as Lily's mother said: 'As a mother, I can finally see my life's work completed. In a one-child family such as ours, this is such a one-off opportunity, such a one-off labour. I've waited nearly thirty years with my heart in my mouth!'

The tragic news was related to Lotus and her pursuit of the arts. Her involvement with the Art of the Bedchamber research group had left her physically and mentally scarred. The realities of sex research finally made her come to her senses and realise that she had become a sex slave. Her elegant and refined heart had been broken. After all the education she had received to the contrary, she was unable to face up to her own family and beliefs. But what made the memories of that time most unbearable was that her elderly father had to come and rescue his child, once his pride and joy. He faced down the artistic director who, realising that he was losing Lotus, had begun to behave appallingly towards her. However, after returning home, her father collapsed, never to rise again. Lotus remained at home thereafter, full of sadness, refusing to see anyone.

In summer 2010 I received an email from Germany with news about Lotus. She said that when Karl, who had always admired her from afar, heard she had given up the sexual culture research, he hurried back to China to ask her to marry him. He had enveloped her injured heart with all his love, and they had moved to Germany together. Apparently she felt that she suited German seriousness and their precise way of working, and that her Chinese art was going down well in northern Europe. However, from time to time her hidden pain and shame would still surface and overwhelm her.

Lotus asked me in the email: 'Lily and I grew up together, but one of us is sipping sweet nectar in peaceful tranquillity, while the other is chewing on bitter memories. Why is this? Has all the beauty in my life been corrupted by the dirty mud and foul waters of my past?'

I replied: 'Why don't you do what Lily does, read ancient Chinese philosophy and that will help you attain peace. Remember that your name is Lotus, a flower that emerges from the mud with no stain on her!'

In 2012 Lily, now a mother, was still researching the urban art history she so loved. She had already started to read the *Dizigui* to her child, who was not even old enough to talk. She said to me, 'In the past, the *Dizigui* only existed in black and white in an old book, but now it is guiding me towards happiness and ease in my daily life. After getting lost for a while when I was growing up, when I reread the *Dizigui*, it helps me re-evaluate life's losses and gains. The journey through life is like driving a car or sailing a boat, many people lose their way through ignorance or curiosity. However, the subsequent panic and moaning causes so many people to give up before they're halfway through, or even give up and live the rest of their lives in despair. To me, the *Dizigui* is the compass on my journey through life, or a set of rules for the art of living.'

Lily once asked me, 'Why would something like this happen to Lotus? What has life revealed and taught to generations of people like her? Why do so many young people courageously sacrifice themselves to ignorance this way? To destroy their parents' hearts and lives with this ignorance and fearlessness? Can they ever know peace again?'

I was unable to answer Lily's questions. I do not know how many hothoused 'emotional infants' modern China has created, who go charging blindly into the tumultuous winds and rains of sexual relationships. Nobody has yet produced a practical and effective way of educating a society of only children, whether in China or abroad, in ancient times or today. China has still to develop a 'social vaccine' to solve the problems faced by this first generation of only children.

How do you view the Yao Jiaxin incident? Why is Chinese society debating him (a post-80s man) so fiercely?

I do not understand the whole story, but from Google searches after the event I came across a few things. From the first to second sentencing, there was a general dissatisfaction with the special rights enjoyed by second-generation nouveaux riches and officials. The focus of the incident has become whether or not everyone is truly equal in a society under the rule of law. I once asked a lawyer what he had learned from studying law. He said, smiling, that the first chapter of the first lesson in law school is that everybody is equal before the law. These words left a particularly deep impression on me. I personally believe that adults have to be responsible for their actions, without exception, even if they are 'only children'.

5 | MOON

J UST AS I finished editing the second draft of this book, I received a call from the BBC's international news office asking me to comment on the following story.

A young Chinese couple had sold three of their own flesh and blood to pay for three years of internet connection.

While in prison awaiting trial in Jiangyong county in southern China's Hunan province, the pair of post-90s lovers were not in the least distressed when questioned by the police. In fact they asked, smiling, 'When do we get to go home?' In the space of three years they had sold three of their own children, saying, 'We didn't want to raise them, so we sold them off in order to earn money to go on the internet.'

The man's father had died when he was a year and a half old. At thirteen he went with his mother to Guangdong province to find work, and in doing so lost his right to state education, as he moved from the place where he was registered. As a result, he lacked even the most basic knowledge of human life. His partner was in her second year of middle school when they met, and they 'tasted the forbidden fruit' on their first date.

The Chinese have a saying that 'our children are either the flesh of our palms or the back of our hands, to part with either is agony'. But this couple appeared to have turned traditional values on their head, selling their own children without a second thought. Many Chinese sociologists believed that while their biological and psychological needs were perfectly natural, their attitude to the results of sex was very unusual. It was more than just a lack of sex education, they had barely received any education on human nature. Their extreme indifference towards their own flesh and blood suggested an exceptional lack of education on even the most basic human nature.

I was shocked by this story, but I also very much wanted to know how this total lack of awareness of their own human nature came about.

China's first generation of only children, who I have been following for ten years, began to reach normal marrying and childbearing age in 2002. By now more than 10 million families from this generation are raising their own only children. This has given rise to an 'age of only-child parents' that is unprecedented in Chinese history. According to some statistics, over 75 per cent of only-child parents are financially independent. They are relatively adaptable in society, but lukewarm about having children, terrified that their own child will usurp their position as overlord in the family. Many only children lack a sense of responsibility after they become parents, and the phenomenon of parents who are unwilling to raise their children has become widespread; some even resent their child for the time and space they take up. If romantic love and motherly love, the two greatest loves in life, can be knocked down like straw men in many only-child families, then what remains sacrosanct in human nature? However, at the same time as judging and blaming them for their lack of humanity, how many people actually understand the price that these parents, only children themselves, have paid?

The writer Lu Xun* wrote that it is not the dead who suffer the pain of death, but the living who are left behind. At a time when

---

* Lu Xun was the pen name of Zhao Shuren (1881–1936), the most famous Chinese writer of the twentieth century. Born in Shaoxing city in Zhejiang province, he was the leader of the New Culture Movement and a keen supporter of the left-wing movement.

romantic and motherly love are perishing amid the indifference and warped views on human nature of some only children, will it not be us and our descendants who feel the pain? We are left grieved and indignant at the news of children sold to pay for internet access, distressed that so many only-child parents cannot rejoice in romantic and motherly love, and our hearts ache for the only children left scarred by their lonely struggles between good and bad.

Out of all the heroes and heroines of this book, the one I discussed these issues the most with was Moon.

I first met Moon in 1989, when she was only nine years old. Her father was a colleague of mine at Radio China. After I left China, Moon's father was transferred to a government post in Guangzhou, supervising news broadcasting. Not long after he took up the job, he phoned me asking for help. He said that a TV station under his jurisdiction was trying to make a foreign history documentary by 'cooking a meal without rice'. At the time, there was barely enough content for one broadcast every day. Apart from experimental channels and some natural history films from the National Geographic Society, China had almost no foreign history programmes. He hoped that my husband Toby and I could pull some strings and help him build bridges with Western broadcasters. We in turn very naïvely thought that after nearly thirty years of Reform and Opening-up, it might now be possible for the Chinese media to work with foreign companies. When we visited in 2003, Toby brought Moon's father several documentaries on European history as a taster and an experiment.

China has always been very stringent on foreign publications; even Second World War history programmes had to go through three levels of 'political reliability' checks. Moon's father set up a meeting to review Toby's documentaries.

In the meeting, several Chinese news officials did not understand either the timing or the contents of the documentaries. Why were we planning on broadcasting them at peak time after the news, a slot that they saw as an opportunity to make money from entertainment programmes? If the TV station did not earn money how was it to expand? Moreover, they didn't understand how there could be no documentaries about China on the international stage. 'We are an ancient nation, one of the Four Great Civilisations, a giant in the world, how do we not have an important place in Western media?' they said. Toby told them frankly that there was virtually no news about China in mainstream global media, and almost no mention of China's 5,000 years of civilisation. Several news officials frowned at Toby's remarks. 'That's impossible,' they said. 'It can't be true, can it? Chinese newspapers have almost more international news than domestic! We sometimes think that everybody in the world must wake up wondering about what is going on in China today.'

Afterwards, over dinner, Moon's father said to us quietly, 'Don't worry about those officials not believing the world's apathy about what is going on in China. Although to tell you the truth, I've also got my doubts. My daughter Moon has been studying in the UK for a year and a half already, and she's never mentioned anything about the world not understanding China.'

Toby replied jokingly, 'If that's so, I'd like to meet your daughter. Perhaps the world she sees is different to the one we live in.'

Later on this joke became a reality, as it prompted Moon to come and stay with us after completing her Master's in Britain. By this time, the callow little girl from my memory had been transformed into a bright, lively and beautiful young lady, with classic Chinese good looks. A melon-seed-shaped face, sloping shoulders, narrow waist, petite stature, and very gentle and quiet.

One day after supper we sat around the table discussing China's distance from the world. Toby said that if China itself does not open the door, it will be very difficult for outsiders to get in. However, it is also not fair for Western media to make frivolous comments about China based on distant sounds heard through the keyhole. Moon replied that it was more that the outside world did not want to know about China, rather than China not wanting to open up. The two of them debated this issue at some length. Toby, who normally goes to bed at half past nine, eventually got up to go to bed. To our great surprise, Moon leapt to her feet and grabbed hold of Toby's lapels saying, 'You can't go, we're not done yet!' Toby, who is 1.9 metres tall, lowered his head and looked down at this slight, gentle Chinese girl hanging on to him for dear life. For a moment he seemed genuinely at a loss as to how to react. I suspected this was the first time in his life that someone had grabbed his lapels during a discussion. Moon however was unwilling to give an inch, vehement about what she considered to be 'the truth'. Her English had the fast rhythm of people from the Yangtze delta, and reminded me of what my grandmother used to call 'Shanghai Yangjingbin'.*

Toby said helplessly, 'I really am very tired, I have to sleep, we'll talk again tomorrow, all right?'

I could see that Moon was about to say that this was not all right, so I gestured to her to let Toby off the hook.

From then on, every time I got into an argument with Toby, and my English was not up to the task, I would find myself wishing I could be more like Moon, and grab him by the lapels, but I never quite did!

Compared with other parents of only children, Moon's parents were not that worried about their daughter, and hardly ever telephoned me to prise out information on their daughter's life. Her mother once said to me: 'Children only go to their parents when they need

---

* Yangjingbin 洋泾浜 was a district outside Shanghai's pre-1949 foreign concessions, where Chinese and foreigners lived side by side. Their languages mixed together, with some Chinese using English vocabulary with Chinese sentence structure when talking to British and Americans. This English was satirically known as 'Yangjingbin' English. The term was also more generally used to indicate non-standard foreign languages.

something, when nothing's wrong they don't even think about family. It's only when they've grown up in body and mind that family will be in their thoughts daily. If they manage to learn about right and wrong before marriage and a career, that's just good luck for the parents, as some people reach old age without ever having grown up.' Her wise words have proved true over the years of watching many children grow up around me, including her daughter Moon.

Over the year that Moon spent in Britain for her Master's course, she only came to me for help three times. First when she felt lonely, next when she was torn between her studies in the West and in China, and lastly when she was faced with the choice of either being with her parents in China or developing her future overseas.

Moon always came and went in a hurry, and would always fly off before I had a chance to digest her questions, so I was usually only able to give her a few brief suggestions. For her feelings of loneliness and helplessness in another country far from home, especially when she had fallen in love with someone she thought inappropriate, I could only console her by saying that finding pleasure while abroad is one of the tests of life. Only those who are truly able to embrace the art of living will find points of sympathy when surrounded by a different culture. As for sex, emotions and love, these are three separate things, with different degrees. One can be pleased to see someone and sad when he is not there, and then there is being willing to change yourself for someone else; only the latter can be called true love. Love is eternal, but it has to have a moral bottom line. As for feeling torn between China and the West, I told her this was something that required some traffic-light thinking, to guide behaviour and prevent clashes between people from different cultures. With regard to not wanting to let her parents down by staying abroad, I told her it was not a question of location, as her happiness and success would always be her parents' greatest wish for her.

However, it was not until Moon's studies were over and she came to stay with us for a while that I realised her questions were not as simple as I had thought. Rather they represented a bottleneck of the many problems faced by all only children studying overseas.

Moon told me that during her time as an overseas student she always seemed to be the one most affected by the clash between East and West. She felt beset on all sides by English explanations, Europeanisms and Americanisms, Western ways of thinking; from three meals a day to her classes, there was nowhere for a Chinese student to hide!

The thing she found hardest to accept in her studies was why Westerners looked down upon China's riches and abrupt rise to prosperity. And why did they not believe that Chinese only children could be self-reliant too? Isn't the point of studying to learn from intelligence? Why did they have to ask so many challenging questions? In China, challenging scholars is considered wild arrogance and gross disrespect! Why do lecturers praise students, then not let them pass exams? Isn't that hypocrisy? In China, lecturers never praise students, but they always reap the rewards come exams. As the saying goes, 'strict teachers produce top students'. In this international age, why is only the British-American education system used, instead of one more compatible with China, India or Arabic-speaking countries? After all, our combined populations and landmass far exceed those of the English-speaking world!

Once, Moon talked to me about the subject she was studying, multi-media. 'When I began it was a trail-blazing subject globally, but my British supervisor thought I shouldn't add in so many Chinese elements. He was worried that Westerners in the industry would be afraid of the sections they did not understand, and reject my work as a result. One supervisor hinted to me, "Chinese culture is not the sun in the sky, you know." I came this close to asking him, "So what is, British? American?"'

Moon's graduation piece was a thought-provoking digital advert. She arranged various news snippets from around the world on a screen, including ancient legends, different languages, lectures from experts and whispering voices, which gradually morphed into the smiling face of American President George W. Bush. The text then coalesced into three topics: democracy, freedom and human rights. When clicked on, the words opened a series of short films. Democracy led to a war film, freedom turned into a scene of street violence and drunkenness, while human rights led to a clip of weeping mothers and crying babies. When Bush's face was clicked on, the image shattered and sent shards flying into democracy, freedom and human rights, which then exploded. As the flurry on the screen subsided, an oil company logo gradually appeared to the lingering sound of Chinese drums and gongs.

This three-minute piece left a deep impression on me. Not just because of its multiculturalism and the way it used modern scientific method to attack the hypocrisy of political power and the voraciousness of material desires throughout history, but also because it bolstered my hopes for Chinese only children. They are currently watching from the wings, but will one day be responsible for our future.

Her project was so successful that the university chose her to take part in an international academic conference, the first Chinese student ever invited. We were all excited and proud of her, yet Moon went around with a long face. I asked her why she was not more pleased with herself, and she replied that she had already spent two weeks trying to learn six pages of English by heart, but just could not take it all in.

'Why do you have to learn it by heart?' I asked, puzzled.

'If I don't know it by heart, how can I make the speech?' Moon replied, equally puzzled at my question.

I did not know whether to laugh or cry. 'Think for a moment,

Moon. You're presenting an interactive piece, so your speech shouldn't be fixed in stone. You need to be able to improvise on the spur of the moment, as the audience might ask you to click on different pictures. They might interrupt your speech and ask you to go into specifics. If all you can do is recite a speech from memory, you won't be able to answer their questions. Is that really interactive communication? Besides, this is your own concept, your own work that you've produced after long consideration, why would you want to present it to them in the form of a fixed model or dogma even?'

'OK . . . that's a good point,' Moon said, deep in thought. However, a glimmer of fear still shone in her eyes. 'But . . . my mother and father always say that as their only child I'm their face in the world. I can't lose face for them no matter what!'

When I heard these words, I wished I could yell at the whole of China, 'Don't pile more of these antiquated pressures onto our children. How can face be more important than our children ending up with fearful and empty hearts?'

I could not bring myself to say this to Moon directly, so said, 'As soon as you step onto the platform they'll know from your Chinese face and the colour of your skin that your English is unlikely to be as good as theirs. You needn't worry about your language. They'll also make allowances for how young you are, right? Remember, for all the flashy power of the Western world, not one of them can speak Chinese. So they won't expect a young woman like you to be perfect in every way. They're all coming to hear you talk, to listen to your wisdom, and hear what Chinese people think about these issues. They're not coming to test your English, or judge you by your appearance or way of speaking.'

After our conversation, Moon spent almost four days practising her speech in front of a mirror. I invited several friends with an interest in advertising and computers for afternoon tea, and asked them to listen and ask questions. I even invited two media friends over for a meal, and got them to ask questions about Moon's presentation. After this repeated 'education by the masses', Moon's evident talent and intelligence no longer seemed locked away in the deep recesses of her heart, and no longer confined to her computer. Even her psychological block about speaking English was no longer the tiger barring the way that it once was.

Upon her return from the conference she told me that she was a little nervous walking onto the stage, but repeated my words over and over to herself: *Hardly anyone in the West can speak Chinese, so why should I be perfect in every way?* After this she soon started to enjoy the feeling of standing on stage answering questions. She felt like a beautiful swan beating its powerful wings. She was no longer a nervous, frightened ugly duckling!

Moon's father was a senior government official in broadcasting, while her mother was one of the first dealers in Western art after China's economic reforms. However, their personal success and the rigorous education they put Moon through often left her feeling caught between two competing ideals, desperately trying to find herself. She frequently racked her brains over how to make her parents proud and happy, and how to manifest the family intelligence in her life. As their precious one-and-only, she felt she should have both her father's ability in the public sphere as well as her mother's artistic talent. However, she grew up in the rarefied atmosphere of a one-child family, with no exposure to 'the masses'. She followed the trends of the Chinese job market into the artistic desert of the high-tech age, and felt that she had no opportunity to show the intelligence passed down to her from her parents. At the same time, she herself yearned for the rustic, idealised life described in literature, where men till the fields and women weave cloth. It was not hard to see the twists and turns of Moon's life that led her to her choice of profession.

I remember one time seeing Moon sitting at her desk staring into space. I asked her, 'Just what is it about choosing a career that makes you so afraid?'

She replied with eyes reddened from unshed tears, 'My worst fear is that my mother will be left bed-ridden by some disease, never to rise again, and I won't be able to get there in time. I won't be able to stroke her hand, and tell her that I'll be there to protect her.'

I suspected that Moon's ideal job (creating a digital platform for cultural exchange) was very far removed from that envisaged by her father and mother for her, otherwise she would not be feeling so sad. I asked her, 'If your mother knew that you had given up your ambitions and happiness for her sake, do you think this would be a comfort to her? You should think about the fact that you are all they have, their one child.'

In the end, Moon chose to go back to China to be by her parents' side. She told me that she would never let her parents know her true dream, because the first duty of a Chinese child is to pay back the debt of gratitude to one's parents. Her words moved me deeply. In today's only-child society, where everyone is frantically chasing self-fulfilment, how many daughters would approach their role with such unselfishness as Moon?

The day before Moon's return to China, we were cooking supper together when she suddenly asked me, 'Xinran, tell me truthfully, what should a good daughter be like? It's plain that you see things very differently from a lot of Chinese mothers.'

'Really?' I said. 'I think all women and mothers have basically the same feelings. The heavy burden carried by Chinese women is one that we all bear, in spite of being blamed for all the problems with today's youth. Do I think differently? I think it's just because I've had different experiences, nothing more than that. In reality, most people from the same generation are all marked by the same brush of their time.' I replied in an off-hand manner as I cut up the vegetables.

'You're wrong about that,' Moon said lightly but very definitively.

'So many Chinese mothers live in a cage, and then later on stuff their own child into it too!'

I was startled by her comment, almost bringing the chopper down on my fingertip. 'What makes you think that?' I said.

Moon said coolly, but far from calmly, 'Originally I was going to ask you for help, but you ended up helping me anyway by teaching me how to make my life take flight. After that, I started to have self-belief and courage. I began to unload the heaviness in my heart, and truly live in freedom. Even if my parents never forgive me, I'll have no regrets. As you said, honesty and straightforwardness are the skies in which freedom flies. It's just that I have this friend (Ping) who is shut up in her mother's cage. She sighs as she looks out at my sky, and sends me emails from time to time, asking me how she can escape her parents' cage.'

I asked her, 'Just what has happened to give this friend of yours such a terrible burden, to think that she's been imprisoned by her own family? Perhaps she's at a crossroads in her life, or struggling between her parents' choices for her and her own longings?' My brain was whirring at a rate of knots, as I self-righteously sifted through all the possible causes of such anguish in a young person.

Moon levelled me with a frank gaze, both pain and helplessness shining from her bright, expressive eyes. 'How about I show you her email right now? It's already late at night in China, but she'll still be up waiting for my reply. I really want to help her unravel the knot in her heart, or at least let her know that she is not a wicked girl. I've tried several times, but never managed to talk her round. Do you think you could help?'

I could tell from Moon's expectant glance that tonight's first dish was going to be emailing her friend.

The email had a pink background, on which floated line after line of elegant Chinese characters. Chinese girls often personalise their emails in this way, filling them with longings beyond the realm of their parents and studies. But many of the words they tap out on their keyboards are soaked through with tears, just like the letter I read on Moon's computer.

Hi Moon,

To me, life sometimes just feels too dangerous. I used to think that as long as I studied hard, I would be able to be on my guard against it, but I never realised how cruel loneliness can be. Do you remember that I once came to you in London for help with feeling lonely? Well, last term I made friends with another Chinese student at university. He was in his forties, studying on his own in the UK, and never mentioned anything about having a family. The first time we met he told me that the life I was leading was too solitary, that there was no spice to it. I was really lonely, and felt like I didn't have friends, family or good enough language. All I wanted was to study well so that I could be worthy of my parents paying all this money for me to be here. Every morning as soon as I opened my eyes, it was like I was waking up in a cage. He was always giving me and a few other Chinese girls advice, saying that being too lonely is bad for women's physical and mental health. He told us about how Western women live and what they want out of life. 'Don't be afraid of the opposite sex,' he said, 'you should enjoy your physicality, it's one of the best feelings. As long as you don't let yourself or anyone else down you shouldn't worry about it.' To tell you the truth, nothing he said was actually bad. We're meant to be a new generation of women now, aren't we? I know we're not as open as Western society, but we're way different from the generations above us. We all know that sex isn't bad and that what men and women do together is perfectly natural, but most of our parents' generation are still steaming along under the momentum of their traditions. More to the point, they place these restrictions and expectations on our shoulders. They still believe that it's somehow honourable to be a virgin, and that to lose your virginity is shameful.

Apart from at parties with classmates, I'd never actually been alone with a man, and didn't know anything about how dangerous it can be not to have any experience at all! One time after this weekend party with some classmates, a few of us walked back to the dorm under the full moon. In the end there was only me and this guy left. When we were saying goodnight he took me in his arms and kissed my forehead saying, 'Let me make you happy, let me teach you about the pleasures of being a woman!' Can you believe it?! I won't lie to you, at that moment my body seemed to fly apart. I'd never felt anything like it. It was like I was under a spell, unable to resist his caresses. That night I became a real woman!

That guy really knew how to make love! It was like I was crazy drunk or something, I could barely keep away from him for a day. He replaced everything in my life, even my family. But when our course was over, he told me that he had a family back in China. That he loved his wife and daughter very much, so he had to go back to be with them, and he hoped I wouldn't bother him any more. The day he left he said to me, 'I made you a woman, gave you a great time and satisfied you like you'd never been satisfied in your whole life.' And then he left! Just like that he sent me packing, thrusting me back into my desert of loneliness! Back in that loneliness, all my parents' teachings and expectations suddenly flooded back into my life. It was only then that I realised that in their eyes I was the guilty one. I was no longer their cherished little girl. I was unworthy of them. However much they loved me, they would never forgive me for having sex before marriage, and with a married man no less, oh my god!

Moon, tell me the truth, am I really bad? My parents are so going to be big-time disappointed, aren't they? What if my future husband will hate me for this? What if I've destroyed all my self-respect and right to have a voice just because of a few months of passion and romance? If you were me, would you still be flying high? Would there even be skies left for you to fly in? Would you still be able to look your parents in the eye? Our generation is tied down by chains that are both ancient and modern, Chinese and foreign, some dragging us forward, some binding our hands and feet, and some flogging us on in a particular direction . . .

Moon, who all the while had been looking straight at me, took a deep breath then slowly let it out. 'She says she doesn't dare imagine how her mother will react, let alone how much her father will hang his head in shame. I've tried to tell her to trust her parents, to tell them the truth. She won't be able to bring herself to hurt them by lying to them. Besides, you can't be free while surrounded by your own lies.'

I interrupted her, 'But in this day and age? Her parents work in China's most cosmopolitan city. How can they reproach her with all those outdated notions of chastity?' I was very surprised to hear how this Chinese girl, who had been though a modern scientific education, could be so conservative. I suspected that her own psychological make-up was the real cause of her grief.

Moon did not understand my surprise at all. 'Oh, but they would reproach her. Actually, parents of only children in cities are a lot more conservative than countryside parents. As far as my parents are concerned, if I'm ever to be worthy of their goodness in raising me, I must not only be an unblemished piece of jade, but also their face in society, which cannot be tainted by a single speck of dust. They would never approve of this kind of face-shaming behaviour.'

What Moon said was the reality of the situation, but this reality was also like a sandcastle, vulnerable to being spoiled or even swept away by the huge tide of China's opening up. Moon's generation was living in an age where heavy breakers were crashing through the sands. Standards of behaviour were like sand and stones on a beach, some swept to the bottom of the sea, while others were washed up on the beach.

We did not enjoy the feast we had planned for supper that day.

Even after Moon had replied, she and I remained preoccupied by the heaviness in her friend's heart, tasting the bitterness in her life.

'Why does your friend think she has lost face?' I asked Moon. 'Every culture and age has different definitions and standards for sexual experience. How does she know that when her parents got married they were as pure as the driven snow? You say her mother works in the arts, but are not artists more able than most to understand the pleasures of men and women in modern society? Maybe your friend is just projecting her own worries onto her parents? If that's the case, then it's unfair. We shouldn't live with the anxieties of the past, nor should we go rushing out to meet trouble halfway.'

'That's easy to say, but difficult to do.' Moon's usual happiness and brightness seemed dimmed by clouds of worry in her eyes.

Moon became a university teacher after returning to Guangzhou. We hardly had any chance to meet, but spoke often on the phone. I went to Guangzhou in 2009 for a meeting, and finally managed to have a meal with her and her parents. Moon brought along her friend Ping and Ping's fiancé, who, according to Moon, had been selected by her mother. During the meal we discussed the decline in Chinese morality. Moon's mother said, 'Many Chinese men are absolutely shameless these days, polluting girls who have no immunity against them with their selfish desires, even proclaiming that they're giving them happiness! I pity those poor girls, who become sacrificial objects to those rakes without even knowing it. They often even remain sentimentally attached to all that filthy biological behaviour!' Her elegant, refined art dealer eyes burned with disgust and hate. I instinctively glanced at Moon's friend. She was picking up morsels of food with her chopsticks, head lowered. I noticed that her cheeks were already bulging, but she continued stuffing more food in . . .

From a series of phone calls with Moon, I learned that her friend had got married, become pregnant and given birth to a daughter, who before long was toddling around. She said to me, 'But her friends have never heard her say anything about the joys of setting up home, about being a proud mother or a happy wife.'

Could it be that this swan had finally taken wing, only to be turned into a sacrificial object for chastity? I dared not think about it any further.

I had been discussing with Moon the joys and sorrows of only-child parents since starting the outline for this book. Moon told me that among the group of white-collar only-child parents around her, the majority were mother and father in name only, and felt none of the responsibilities or emotions of being parents. Many women thought that getting pregnant marked the end of their womanly charms, and that parenthood was a 'life sentence'. Some only-child parents dumped their child in the care of their own parents straight after birth, like pushing away their chopsticks and bowls at the end of a meal, and then went home to surf the net. Some projected resentment at their loss of position as the focus of their family's attention, and believed that they had been usurped by this new 'precious treasure'. It was common for only-child parents regularly to beat or viciously tell off their children. As for the government allowing only-child parents to have two children, many young mothers and fathers cried out at this. 'One has nearly driven us crazy with exhaustion, another would kill us!' Many thought of their own child as a force robbing them of happiness, even as an enemy.

Moon's words reminded me of similar scenes I had witnessed at airports all across America. Crowds of Chinese grandmothers and grandfathers carrying in their arms a child barely a month old. Some were Chinese nannies specially hired to courier babies under one hundred days old. Time and again I asked the airport staff for confirmation: 'This is just a seasonal thing, isn't it? At holiday time?' But no, no matter who I asked the answer was the same: 'In the last few years we see at least ten babies sent back to China every day.'

I asked Moon, 'Is it that the older generation are helping the baby's parents roam the world and fight for their freedom? Is this why they send their children back to China to be brought up?'

'No, those only-child parents are just fleeing parenthood. Many believe that while parting from their child will be painful, raising it will be more painful still!' Moon said decisively. 'In September last year [2010] the *Jinghua Times* published an article on an only child couple who were divorcing, and neither wanted custody of their six-year-old child.'

Moon also told me about what the experts had to say on the matter. 'Marriages between only children tend to have high levels of interference from the family, mainly because of the exceptional influence that family and society have already had on the couple's personalities. Marriages between this first generation of only children are already showing a trend of "marry in haste, divorce in haste". Some marriages only last a year or two, some even less. Many young people believe that intense emotions are synonymous with love, and once passion disappears the marriage is at an end.'

Moon also said that research from the Tianjin Family Education Research Association showed that 32 per cent of only children quarrel frequently after marriage, and that they are relatively ill-equipped to deal with family relationships. Restraints and pressures on China's first generation of only children have declined, along with parental interference in marriage, and more matches are chosen freely by the young people themselves. However, very many only children, after years of pampering from doting parents, have become accustomed to a life where they can reach out a hand and find clothes, and open their mouths and be fed. They have become stubborn, afraid of hard work, and are constantly comparing themselves to others. These and other psychological problems are all relatively pronounced in only-child parents, who find it harder than the previous generation to cope with life. When they bring their reliance on their parents and money into the marriage, any minor conflict results in an emotional crisis. Their ability when married to deal with problems and resolve conflicts is also weak, with clashes often escalating into divorce.

Moon passed on a lot of information to me over the phone, often including her wise and ingenious opinions, but she seldom mentioned her personal life. Did she really plan to spend the rest of her life with her mother, being no more than a filial daughter?

'Tell me something, Moon, has anyone claimed you for their own yet?' I asked her once before I could stop myself. As soon as the words were out of my mouth I regretted them. I was afraid that I would not like the reply.

Finally, one day, a trill of cheerful laughter came down the line. 'I've got a boyfriend, Xinran. We're still getting to know each other, which is no easy thing with men, especially because of the generation gap. It's quite impossible to find common ground with men from the older generation!'

They married a year later, and from then on most of her phone time with me was taken over by her little family. When we did catch up a few months later she could speak, but was obviously exhausted; she had become a mother! Feeding the baby by night and working by day left her with no energy to get worked up over society or other people. It was not until her son was a year old that Moon's conversations gradually returned to life in China, which was when I asked her: 'Are you happy being a mother? I'd like to know if only-child mothers enjoy the simple pleasures and take pride in being mothers more than we did?'

There was a long silence on the end of the telephone. I wondered if Moon was searching for her answer. How long would I have to wait? Several years? Until her baby could sleep through the night? When her little son went off happily to school? Until her child had grown up enough to think of rubbing her back and massaging her shoulders? When he was bathing happily in the river of love? Or when she grew bored of waiting, and realised that it was already too late? I prayed for Moon: 'Whatever you do, don't do that, for that was the fate of several generations of Chinese women before us.'

Moon never replied to my question, and we continued to discuss other people.

'Actually, my generation is a bit different from the post-80s and -90s,' Moon said to me. 'Our parents did not have enough time or experience to adapt to the one-child society. My generation were the guinea pigs for the whole country. By the time we reached puberty, we were overlooked in the clash of tradition and modernity, East and West. When the time came for us to marry, we were unable to let go, relax from work and enjoy family life because so many things had been lacking in our own families. But there's another important factor that can't be overlooked. Compared to parents of later generations, ours experienced much more political terror and disasters. The train that brought fear and change had already applied the brakes and come to a stop, but our parents still felt carried along by its momentum. We grew up affected by that momentum. Xinran, tell me, is it still affecting us? Or have we finally come to rest?'

Moon had asked a good question. And, by extension, was the momentum of thirty years of China's Reform and Opening-up still moving or had it stopped? Could the past be replaced? Can the future take us where we want to go? Will our only children have the chance to experience the normal pleasures of life, having normal relationships with their parents, and healthy ones with their own children?

———

How do you view the Yao Jiaxin incident? Why is Chinese society debating him (a post-80s man) so fiercely?

To tell you the truth, when I first heard about the Yao Jiaxin incident, my hair stood on end with fright. I just couldn't understand it. It was very hard for me to imagine that this was the behaviour of a normal person. The first reaction a normal person should have when they've caused harm is to think about how to make amends and make up for the pain they have caused. But this guy was actually capable of stabbing someone to death with eight blows from a fruit knife! Did the victim trying to note down Yao's number plate make him feel under threat, even violated, so that the idea of killing her took root in his mind? This seems like a very forced kind of logic to me. What is still more frightening is that he was a music student at university, grade 10 piano as well, and all this happened while he was on the way to pick up his girlfriend! This was a person who had love, learning and art, so why was his heart so cruel, unfeeling and bloodthirsty? His actions were more like those of a twisted homicidal maniac. Was it a deficiency in human nature, or a lack of morality? What caused all this to happen? Or was it just a random incident?

However, if you delve into all the extraordinary things that go on in our society, you soon find out that incidents such as this are not unique at all, it's just the degree of ghastliness that varies. Recently there's been a sickening rabbit cruelty video from a Chengdu University student doing the rounds on the internet. A young girl presses down a sheet of glass onto a little white rabbit, then sits on it, crushing the rabbit alive. Incredibly, two other girls are looking on as if nothing is the matter.

Next there's those 'bumping into porcelain' incidents. My parents have experienced these first hand. A pregnant woman will deliberately squat down behind your car and wait. As soon as you start the car she pretends she's been hit and collapses on the ground. Afterwards she demands money for not going to the police and through the courts. Can you imagine? There are actually mothers like that in this world who are willing to use that pure, sacred unborn life just to get hold of money?

I believe that rats do not start to steal as soon as they are born, but if they are immersed in it and their eyes and ears are full of it of course they will learn it. The Yao Jiaxin incident is most certainly not a one-off, it is a creation of our modern society. Of course it is an extreme manifestation, but it is one that should sound a warning bell for us all.

6 | SHINY

T HERE ARE Four Great Works in Chinese literary history, *The Three Kingdoms*, *Journey to the West*,* *The Water Margin* and *The Dream of the Red Chamber*. These four ancient tales are the classics of Chinese literature, like the works of Homer, the *Divine Comedy*, *Hamlet* and *Faust* in Europe. These stories, their characters and even the customs and objects that appear, all form part of Chinese cultural education, and have profoundly influenced the people's attitudes and values. It is a pity that although they have been translated many times into English, French and other languages, they have never entered mainstream Western education. When the worldwide craze for Harry Potter was at its height, many Chinese parents rebuked their children for being in such a mad rush to buy the books. 'We've had *Journey to the West* for the past 400 years, and everything described in that book, the dreams, illusions, ghosts, spirits and magic, all of it is just as exciting and magical as Harry Potter, maybe even more so!'

The plot of *Journey to the West* (or *Monkey King*) comes from the legend of the monk Xuanzang (pronounced *shwhen dzang*) who went in search of the Buddhist scriptures. It begins with the story of a magical monkey who raises havoc in heaven. He follows

---

* *Journey to the West* (*Monkey King*) was written by Ming dynasty author Wu Cheng'en in 1592. It is a classic novel of magical literature. Over the past few centuries it has been turned into countless local operas, comic books, animations, films and television series. Its influence can be seen outside China in a number of books from Japan and other Asian countries that feature Sun Wukong and the Red Child as their main characters.

Xuanzang west on his journey to collect the scriptures, using his unique talents and some help from the heavenly powers to drive out demons and defeat monsters along the way. He helps Xuanzang collect the scriptures and bring them back to the great Emperor of the Tang dynasty, attaining Buddhahood and immortality along the way through various trials and self-cultivation. The main characters in the book are Xuanzang, Sun Wukong (the monkey's Buddhist name), Pigsy and Sandy. They are all depicted in a lively fashion, and the well-structured plot is on a grand scale. It is one of the most romantic of all classical Chinese novels.

Journey to the West is not only loved by adult readers, its stories have also been told to countless children down the generations in Chinese homes. Even in far-off and desolate regions, everyone uses characters and scenes from the story as figures of speech to describe the people, events and objects in their daily life. For example, people who are gluttonous and lustful are often called Pigsy, while thoroughly decent but gullible people get called Xuanzang. People who work hard and get on with things quietly are called Sandy, while powerful people in positions of responsibility are called Sun Wukong. Lucky people are also called Sun the Monkey. Bewitching and malign women are called White-Bone Demons, while overbearing men are called Ox Demon Kings. People who like causing trouble in gangs are called shrimp soldiers and crab generals, while those good with their hands are praised as having an 'endless casket of treasures'.

After the only-child society came into being, many Chinese people said, 'We now not only have suns, emperors and princesses beyond measure, but we have also created countless Sun Wukong parents and Xuanzang sons and daughters, who spend their days and nights in search of the Buddhist scriptures from the stories. Parents are busy bringing all their skills into play, searching for the magic of life, battling with the demons of society, and defending their only children, their Xuanzangs. These parents will never attain enlightenment and immortality until they have found the scriptures – meaning that their child has a family of his or her own and is set up in a profession. Our deepest fear is that the powerful, vigilant Sun Wukong will leave Xuanzang's side for a moment. Xuanzang, left on his own to face ghosts and monsters, will be carried off to a boiling, seething cooking pot, and devoured by the White Bone Demon!'

Is it possible that these parents do not want their children to grow up into powerful Sun Wukongs? How could they not wish for it? Surely this is what every parent wants for their child? However, we often cannot bring ourselves to put our children through the trials Monkey has to face in order to become Sun Wukong. How many years of painful hardship must they endure? Should we allow our children to do wrong and create havoc in heaven, following Xuanzang on arduous journeys, scaling mountains and fording rivers, going through a hundred misadventures? No, no, impossible!

I am no different, as I often find myself in a state of anxiety over my only son, Panpan. I understand completely that the life experience he demands is a necessary part of his growing up, and that this is a common view among his contemporaries, but I seem unable to free myself from the fear of him being my 'one-and-only'. In order to teach him how to deal independently with the world he must face, I gritted my teeth and encouraged him to travel the world, but every time he set off I shed secret tears at night. My child started to go and see the world on his own at the age of seventeen. Every time I heard him talking freely and happily of his experiences in some far-flung corner of the world, I would always feel caught between joy and sorrow. For the next few days, almost all his stories would reappear in my dreams, as vivid as the real thing, his every action, every move, catching at my heart strings. As a Chinese mother once said to me over the phone, 'When children fly the nest, mothers are shut up in a prison of terror! And when they grow into Sun Wukongs, striding like heavenly steeds across the heavens, is this when we become Xuanzangs, beset by demons and evil spirits?'

Using this analogy one could say that if Lily's university friend, Lotus (in chapter 4), was like Xuanzang, unable to defend herself on life's road towards the scriptures, then Shiny was one of the Sun Wukongs of her generation; nobody could withstand her.

Fate brought me and Shiny together at a talk I was giving at a London bookstore. In the question and answer session that followed, a Chinese girl stood up easily and confidently amid the packed crowd and asked me, 'Why do Western people know so little about China?' Her clothes and hairstyle had the air of a modern Eastern woman, her English was very good and her body language confident. By that time, I had already visited more than 200 cities in over twenty countries, but I had hardly ever seen a young Chinese person stand up and ask a question in a crowded hall. This left a very deep impression on me. After the talk, I noticed the same girl standing politely at the back of the crowd. She seemed to be waiting for an opportunity to speak to me. That day we got to know each other and in due course became friends. That young woman was Shiny.

Shiny was in England studying Western drama criticism. I guessed that at the time she was probably the only Chinese student studying this subject overseas. Most Chinese students I had come into contact with were studying law, commerce, economic management, accountancy and other such 'money-making' courses. Even in Shiny's own words, drama criticism was 'purely abstract, poverty-inducing art theory'. Her real knowledge and practical experience of art came from her undergraduate studies at Peking University. She told me all about its Theatre Society, cultural salons and performances she took part in at the People's Artistic Theatre. When speaking about the current state of Chinese theatre she would sigh, as she looked back at it from the perspective of being in Britain. 'Although China lacks Britain's comfortable and relaxed theatre scene, and there is little public support for the performing arts, there are plenty of people who still keep the faith,' she said. 'In spite of strict government controls, political checks and mainstream commercial appetites, all of which lead to the tendency for artistic development to become diminished and rather bland in both quality and quantity, in every generation there have always been hot-blooded youngsters with a burning loyalty to theatre. Unfortunately, their ardour and pioneering creativity tended either to be stifled by politics and power, or used by a few theatre moguls as a ploy to sell tickets. Eagerness for instant success and quick profits are tempting an increasing number of theatrical people into abandoning their artistic spirit and respect for drama. But I'm just not willing to do that. I'm not prepared to let a long history of theatre like China's flow away and get lost while I'm alive.'

When I heard Shiny's words, I thought about how upset and frustrated I had been thirty years ago when old houses and city walls were being pulled down across the country. I felt like a mantis raising its legs to stop an oncoming chariot* which, heavily laden with 'smash the old and raise the new' slogans, rolled right over my spirit and passion. I sometimes see postcards in the West of those old buildings, those plain, simple, elegant courtyard houses, and every time I feel a pang. I ask myself why I have had to live in this stormy age that has eroded 5,000 years of civilisation.

Shiny came from a long line of high-up government officials. Her grandfather was one of the founders of modern China, a man of considerable fame, and both her parents had devoted themselves to the army for over thirty years. Shiny grew up in the army compound and was full of youthful vigour, brains and drive. Just watching her

---

* The mantis chariot is a classical story from the philosopher Zhuangzi. A mantis sees a chariot coming towards him along the road, and lifts his front legs in an attempt to hinder the chariot's approach. The story is often used as a metaphor for situations where one overestimates one's strength.

at the dinner table was enough to see that she 'swept away all before her'. However, I think her forcefulness came from growing up in a big family, rather than from some innate personal quality. She had all the hallmarks of a person trained in how to deal with life, who knows how to take life as it comes and to make the best of situations. In modern China, with its fast-paced enterprises and urbanisation, or perhaps one could also say desertification of culture, fussiness and arrogance have been taken by many people lacking in education as 'nobility', and copied accordingly. All the while, true nobility of spirit and strength of character are overlooked or even forgotten. Still more tragically, many university-educated only children are not even ashamed of their fussiness and arrogance, but rather believe them to be glorious. All their values seem to come with a price tag attached.

In Shiny, I could see shadows of three generations of Chinese women. Her values were like those of her grandmothers who had survived the chaos of war. Of all the only children I have met, she was the most unspoiled. As her grandmothers would have put it: 'To stay alive is a success in itself, good health is happiness, and family is more important than the nation.'

Shiny's personality was in some respects like those Chinese mothers who stand fearfully between the generations behind and in front of them, with their notions of right and wrong so starkly and painfully defined. They are afraid of making mistakes, afraid of losing face, afraid their husbands will take to drink, afraid their children will fall into bad ways. As far as they are concerned, right is right and wrong is wrong. They will happily go without food or sleep, but will argue with you every step of the way, because no ambiguity can be permitted in the rules.

Yet, in spite of her sense of propriety, Shiny's passions were more like those of these other daughters, who grew up surrounded by dizzyingly fast-paced development. They seem almost able to command the gods. They are more than a match for any task thrown at them in the daily changes and excitements of their lives, until you are left wondering if even the wind and rain respond to their beck and call.

Shiny's arrival in my life came as a delightful surprise, and a challenge to my research into her generation of only children. It was a big treat for me to discuss Chinese and Western cultural phenomena with her. We came from different generations and backgrounds, and these disparities were a novelty that actually drew us closer together. The variations in our personalities and fields of expertise meant that we always ended up arguing over the same issue from divergent viewpoints, and never agreed with each other without giving the matter serious thought. Our biggest difference of opinion was over only children, and their relationships to people, events and objects.

With regard to this phenomenon, our views were almost diametrically opposed. Shiny thought that the only-child issue was not a social, but a family problem. She said that the family is the smallest cell in the body of society, and if the cells become diseased then large areas of the organism will die off. She believed that modern Chinese society had effectively rejected family values. Parents pushed their children towards school, husbands and wives transferred their marital affections to restaurants and shopping malls, and children were left feeling that home was a cage or gaming room. On the other hand, she believed that the home was the petri dish where parents should train their children in survival skills and moral outlook, and to this they were duty bound. 'If Chinese people carry on like this, with the wife gone and children scattered or with no home to call their own, China will soon perish as a nation!' she said.

I admired her insight, but maintained my view that society was the source of life and support for the family, a buffering system and also the sky above it. Especially now, as China is transforming from an agricultural to urban society, most sons' and daughters' awareness of new things and their ability to take them on board surpasses their parents'. At this crucial time, if social mechanisms are slow or insufficiently sound, it will lead to excessive burdens on families. The sons and daughters who grow up in these changing times will be led astray and lose their direction in life. Ever since the one-child policy was implemented, China has been dragging itself along in pursuit of the trends formed by these only children, and parents have been worn out by their children's social needs, until they are exhausted and at their wits' end.

Shiny was of the opinion that global events are predicated on people and objects. When setting up a market or project, one first must have people and capital. I, on the other hand, hold to the philosophy that something can be created from nothing. I believe that things happen, and people find themselves getting involved. New things arise, and a simple idea can attract people and capital. Shiny would offer me no quarter in our endless debates, and at intervals would produce all kinds of details to challenge my views. Mobile phones, email, newspapers and books all became tools for the eloquent debates that she was liable to start up anywhere, any time. I would often tease her, 'In you, I have once again seen the power of communism. Always demanding that the people follow one voice, one direction, one political line!'

One thing I had to credit Shiny with was her dogged persistence. She set two records while in London working at my charity, Mothers' Bridge of Love.

In summer 2006, in order to increase contact between British families who wanted to adopt and Chinese children, MBL teamed up with the visiting Little Angels Song and Dance Troupe to organise a Chinese music and dance charity performance in Hyde Park. The ideal location was the big grassy space next to the children's playground. However, the park management told us that Hyde Park was a common space for all Londoners to use. With the exception of large-scale concerts approved by the local council, no organisations were permitted to use the space, and this was the law. In our next MBL meeting we decided to change our plan. As we were discussing the changes, Shiny, who was in charge of the event, suddenly jumped to her feet shouting, 'We can't change! Just because they've never done it before, that means we can't either, is that what you're all saying? If that were true the world would have stagnated long ago. No, no, I've made up my mind to get it done!'

We eyed each other in puzzlement. 'Has she lost her mind?' we asked each other. 'No matter how bull-headed she is, she can't take on the regulations of an entire city!'

However, one week later Shiny, through who knows what magical powers, brought back an official document from Hyde Park. It was a permit for the performance! To this day, I still have no idea how she got around the local council's rules.

London had just suffered a succession of dark and rainy days, but that day the sun shone brightly. MBL marked out a performance area on the grassy space next to the playground with several hundred balloons in vivid colours and flags printed with the MBL logo. The delightful performance by dozens of the Little Angels, with their brightly coloured costumes and props, attracted over a hundred families. During the interval we invited children of Chinese descent to come through the ring of balloons for a closer look, but politely asked the remaining spectators to remain outside. Our volunteers in the crowd heard children saying to their mothers, 'Mummy, I want to be Chinese!' Their mothers replied, 'Oh darling, sweetheart, we can't change that!' At that moment many of our volunteers were stirred by a powerful emotion. We had laid on VIP treatment for Chinese children on Western soil! Moreover, we had started off with twenty volunteers helping us organise and look after the safety of the event, but by the time the performance was over fifty or sixty passers-by had spontaneously joined us. Among them were electricians, lecturers, professors and architects, all Westerners, and all drawn to the Chinese spectacle, showing their love for Chinese culture.

Shiny gave the welcoming speech, infecting us all with her belief and determination. This girl was a true winner, to have succeeded in putting on such a lavish pageant for the Chinese children in Hyde Park, a royal park no less!

Following the success of this event, MBL and London's Chopstick Club banded together to organise a fund-raising Mid-Autumn Festival party in the Shanghai Blues Restaurant. We sent Shiny to organise the event, which both sides hoped would attract a hundred people. However, thanks to her skill in publicity and organisation, over 180 people showed up. Yet we ended up not having any money left over to donate, because Shiny refused to let the additional eighty guests pay, so the money made for charity from the first one hundred was spent on the cost of meals for the extra people. Shiny explained, 'We can't do anything that will make Chinese people lose face. We have to let Westerners know that we are givers not takers!'

'Championing Chinese face' in the way Shiny did is extremely common among Chinese people, even among little emperors and princesses. This comes from what their parents and society in general consider to be a good upbringing.

In the same way, many Westerners who have worked and studied in China have asked me, 'Why, while China is developing so swiftly and powerfully, even violently, is social awareness still stuck in the fields of agrarian culture?' They often tell me that the Chinese they know generally think they need to have good qualifications to ensure a prosperous future. That without an excellent job there can be no good life, and that without a superior flat and car there can be no happy family. No money means no success in any aspect of life. However, the characteristic that causes the strongest reaction in foreigners is Chinese people's 'peculiar international knowledge'. For example, China is the global leader, Americans are the most cultured, Persians the most artistic, Europeans the most small-minded, the Middle East is the poorest, white people are all bosses, black people are all refugees, Korea makes the best beauty products, Japanese buildings are the most modern, etc.

In some Chinese-Western families, the Chinese side constantly warn their Western relatives, 'If you don't wear designer clothes you have no status. It's inappropriate for you to appear like that in public, you'll lose face.' My Western friends often ask me, 'Why do Chinese people put so much emphasis on face? Isn't it, at best, a cultured way of polite interaction but, at worst, without refinement or civilised behaviour, just a fake mask?' What they say is quite true, but I do not know how to answer their doubts. The fact remains that 'never lose face' is by far the most important standard of behaviour. At all costs one must avoid losing face for one's self, parents, school, work unit, even country. This is a warning that we hear continually, from our earliest youth until old age. Face has become part of Chinese people's cultural character that is more important than body or soul. Even if we do not know what true face really is, or if the lives we live are inadequate to support our ideas of face, as Chinese, we must still drive ourselves to the brink of bankruptcy and beyond, to dress ourselves up and protect our face. After I left China in 1997 I cast off my old self and remade myself anew several times over. The hardest part of this, and one that to this day I have not yet achieved, is leaving behind the 'shackles of face'.

Although Shiny had been exposed to more international things, and was generally more grounded and well-travelled than many Chinese people, the 'face gene' was something beyond her control. It heavily influenced how she dealt with situations and people. If I am honest, I am exactly the same. Time and again, both of us have been roused to anger by Western media's criticism and condemnation of Chinese face and national self-respect. However, the more we experienced in this international space, the more we came to understand why people do not respect our face. It is because a face without soul or spirit is indeed like a mask. However, this is a notion that baffles many young Chinese people, who think of the spirit and soul as childish concepts, or just a big joke.

Shiny was a girl who was dismayed by the Western misunderstanding of her race, and we would often debate these matters until both of us were ablaze with righteous indignation. 'We must do something to help Westerners understand the values and spirit of China, with its ancient culture, huge population and immense territory. We should be guiding the world's thinking. Is the impression that China will leave on the world nothing more than a few political and economic statistics, or is it in fact our spirit as Chinese people?' she would say. Each one of my discussions with Shiny left me feeling moved and comforted. I could see in her generation the Chinese people's innate ability for continual self-improvement. This was a source of energy and nourishment for my writing and charitable work.

Two years later, when Shiny was about to go back to China, we went for a stroll around Hyde Park. She told me that she had been to see a retired relative who used to work in a Chinese embassy. She felt that in only a few days her knowledge of America had come on by leaps and bounds.

'America was such a disappointment to me, Xinran.' Shiny barged in front of me, forcing me to a halt.

'Why?' I tried to get past her and carry on walking, but she matched me step for step. Clearly she wanted me to stop where I was and listen to what she had to say. This was the signal that Shiny was about to embark on one of her monologues, a signal I had been trained to recognise from our previous time together.

'Now I know where all the ugly customs in Chinese society come from. It's all the Americans dumping their rubbish culture all over the world. Damaging the root systems of other civilisations, so the rest of the world is forced to wait for their culture to grow up!' Shiny said savagely.

'That's rather an extreme way of putting it, isn't it? Even if they have dumped their rubbish on us, we could have refused it. Communication and infection cut both ways.' I was hoping to placate her.

'How could it not be? I used to think that playing power games, falseness, talking big, cheating the poor and racial prejudice all came from China. That they were just the side effects of Reform and Opening-up. But it was only after arriving in America that I realised that this is bread and butter for the Americans. I'd even go so far as to say these are the special things about their culture.' Shiny started to stick her neck out towards me; her bull-headed spirit had arrived!

'Penetrating insights are good to have, but they can also be a double door. By shutting yourself behind the doors of your own culture, you are unable to absorb the novelty and wisdom of other cultures.' I deliberately slowed my speech, in order to avoid another battle.

Shiny was not pleased at my delaying tactics, and said urgently, 'American wisdom was stolen from all over the world!'

'But isn't the skill that lets you recognise wisdom and then steal it also a kind of wisdom?' I was not teasing her now, the words came from my heart.

Shiny's eyes blazed. 'Do you know something? Even their election campaigns are a con. They hand out a few sops and small favours to get votes out of those poor people! Isn't that making a mockery of the will of the people, while at the same time raising the banner of democracy? Doesn't that mean that whoever has money can play the game of politics?'

'But that's the same everywhere, surely?' I always tried to balance out her extreme views.

Shiny glared at me. 'Stop trying to let them off the hook with all that diplomatic talk! A lot of American culture is machine language, it just responds to bar codes, not culture. Several of my old university classmates are in America on scholarships. After their MAs they had no time to read books, to watch the news or see their friends, as they spent every minute of every day trying to keep up with the Joneses, earning money and consuming. On weekends they either play video games or just have a long lie-in. "Cultural activities? Never mind them," they say. "Those are rich people's playthings, we Chinese haven't earned nearly enough for that!" However, once those Chinese students, groping ahead blindly and completely illiterate when it comes to world history and civilisation, once they return home, they use "Western culture this and Western culture that" as a placard to sell their discount goods. They use it to mislead people who are new to the cities into spending money, earned through the sweat and blood of generations, on luxuries and ornaments for their "nobility and face". Just listen to those young Chinese who've never had to support themselves through their own efforts, in China and abroad. They're reckless and thoughtless, bragging shamelessly about throwing their money about and consuming, without the least sense of shame!

'Xinran, just imagine for a moment, if you took high-class cosmetics and plastered them onto the face of a group of walking corpses, in a city that was created by civilisation, imagine the scene! But that is precisely the success we Chinese enjoy under the bright lights of America. Political hegemony, economic strength, cultural weakness, uncivilised attitudes and behaviour. Tell me, isn't that a cruel injury done to our civilisation by American culture? Isn't that polluting our society with American rubbish? American "slasher" movies have practically become a spiritual food for our children and young people. Can it really be that nobody sees the poisonous harm of all of this?'

My heart was pounding with emotion in my chest, because I regularly find myself filled with righteous rage on this very issue. American action movies are indeed stealing our children's soul and, in the face of this power, nobody can fight against the temptations and tyranny of the US dollar.

Shiny noticed that I had not said anything but, impatient to continue venting her spleen, she went on. 'Why do Chinese people still treat America as the emperor and god of wealth all rolled into one? Many American family fortunes were acquired through slavery, and they support their families on money stolen from others. Sooner or later they'll trap us into paying for their extravagances!' Shiny declared, chest heaving with indignation.

When in 2010 I heard that the Chinese government was buying up US government bonds on a big scale, I thought back to what Shiny had said in 2007: 'Sooner or later they'll trap us into paying for their extravagances.' But, at that time, how many Chinese people had Shiny's foresight or breadth of vision? To be honest, I had not considered the matter myself.

That day our walk lasted three and a half hours. We discussed all our impressions of the US and China, during the course of which Shiny had another lesson for me concerning Chinese diplomats. In her opinion, one of the reasons why China struggled to enter mainstream Western society was the poor quality and incompetence of China's diplomats. Apart from strict discipline and a supervisory system that left diplomats afraid to move a muscle without the most careful thought, many of them simply did not possess any diplomatic ability or awareness. Some viewed overseas postings as a perk of the job that allowed them to go abroad and enjoy themselves on rotation. Shiny's relative who worked in an embassy told her that apart from the ambassador, the attachés, the First Secretary and the military liaison, who had all worked their way step by step up the carefully set out career ladder of the diplomatic service, many of the others were allocated their positions through family connections or other forms of nepotism. She contrasted this with the Ministry of Foreign Affairs, where staff were promoted only through seniority, and had to wait their turn for a chance at an overseas posting. Moreover, she had observed that once the embassy workers arrived abroad, they spent all their time in their own rooms, talking Chinese, cooking Chinese food, and living like overseas students in a communal dormitory. They really let down the country and their fellow countrymen.

'Foreign affairs is a very particular field,' I said. 'People in this line of work often don't even know the full responsibilities of the person in the office next door. As for you, how could you hope to understand the ins and outs of an embassy in just a few days?' I have often felt that this new Chinese generation takes the concept of 'we know everything' to excess!

Shiny said to me, 'I know you parents are all convinced that children don't think before they act, that they don't look at questions from all sides. I know you always write us off as acting brashly, but I'll tell you some things that'll show you I'm not acting like a child.

'I might leave some expensive gifts for my friends before I go back to China. They are all "diplomatic gifts" that my relative's diplomat friends stationed abroad didn't give out before leaving their posts. They get them handed to them free by the state, and are meant to use them to oil the wheels and open doors, but most of the time they never do. I've got thirty Olympic Games T-shirts, thirty silk ties each worth over 1,000 yuan (over $160), twenty silk tops, five very expensive brocade pictures, and ten silver-bordered leather document cases. It's frightening the amount of stuff they have, each one of them has piles of it. Even though some of them have been there for four years, they never get to give them away as they're terrified of taking part in local cultural activities! They say they're scared to speak English! In that case, why bother becoming a diplomat? Isn't that just like being in the toilet but not going?'

The more Shiny spoke the angrier she became. Walking beside

her, I could almost feel her scorching breath. 'My relative was keen to get rid of any notions I might have of becoming a diplomat, so he made a point of showing me something. One day at nine o'clock in the morning, he took me to a reading room for embassy workers, where several dozen newspapers were neatly set out on three desks. He then said he'd bring me back at half past four to check on them. We returned to the reading room just after four, to find the papers still lying neatly in their piles, still in their original wrappers. Shortly after a cleaner came in and stuffed all the papers into a bin bag, dozens of them! Apparently this happened every day. This was how much our diplomats understood, this was what they were worth. "Why would you want to throw away your future into this cultural rubbish bin?" he said to me.

'Isn't this infuriating, Xinran? If this is how our Chinese diplomats communicate then God knows how many years we'll have to wait before we come in line with the rest of the world! Tell me, what other hope does our country have?' Shiny asked me in frustration.

'There is hope,' I told her. 'Where there's pain and anger, there is always hope! It only becomes truly frightening when you have no feelings at all. Aren't there more and more Angry Young Men* now? This is China's hope! Pain is not something that any god or spirit can dissolve away, and neither can money.' Actually, I often ask myself the question, What should China hope for? When I heard this story about our diplomats, I felt very put out. I wondered whether these

---

* In 1950s Britain, the term Angry Young Men was used to refer to a radical group of writers. In 1960s Europe and America the term referred to groups of rebellious left-wing youths who advocated overthrowing traditional social values. In 1970s Hong Kong it referred to young people who were dissatisfied with the state of society and anxious for change. In the 1990s the term was used to describe staunch nationalists, and particularly internet users with radical ideas. The term also spread to nationalist movements in Japan and Taiwan, which the Chinese media called Angry Young Japanese Men and Angry Young Taiwanese Men.

diplomats realised that they were losing more face for the people and government by not speaking a foreign language properly and being afraid of losing face.

I remember discussing her future that day. I teased her, 'Oh Shiny, you agonise about the state of the nation, you fret about the misunderstandings between China and the West, you're able to steamroller through council regulations in Hyde Park, how come you haven't got a boyfriend yet?'

When Shiny heard this she laughed heartily. 'You're as impatient as my mum! I'm not even thirty yet, what's the rush? It's not like I'm some peasant, all in a hurry to get married, have sons, and build my status as a housewife in the family. In developed countries don't all young people wait until thirty or even forty before they start to talk about marriage? I think that's a very rational way to go about it. It gives you both time to build up economic independence, a chance to experience life to the full, and gives you enough time to learn about men. Otherwise isn't it just like kids playing house? Still . . .'

Shiny gave me a cheeky look. 'To tell you the truth, all the men I've seen seem to make such a fuss over small matters, but when it comes to discussing the important things in life, none of them can get one over on me. I need to find a man who can win me over utterly, not just with words but also from the heart. Perhaps such a man hasn't yet been born.'

After Shiny went back to China we only had two more brief encounters. The first time was about a year after she left Britain. She made the effort to attend an event for MBL volunteers in Shanghai. That evening we arranged to meet for a chat. She told me that for the first hundred days of being home she felt like a fish who'd found water, with original ideas and opportunities coming hard on each other's heels. However, after three months all her hopes, plans and projects seemed to come tumbling down one after another. She realised that it was no longer possible for her to readapt to the Chinese system and management style.

'This is a system where knowledge is managed by ignorance, where money and power browbeat spirit and culture,' she said. Plainly the differences in ways of life and the ever changing Chinese cultural climate had not worn down this girl's determination to pursue her goals. As before, Shiny was giving full rein to her abilities. 'Xinran, China's not only surpassed all the norms in terms of economic development, but also in terms of how people's ideas and values have changed. This can no longer be measured in standard generations, as things are changing so fast that young people separated by only two or three years are like a generation apart, and within five or ten years their views are obsolete! The differences between China and the West are no longer simply to do with culture, language and traditions. We've already started to perceive even the most fundamental things in completely different ways. In Western developed countries, the years before thirty are for a person to amuse themselves and explore life, but in China these are the years you spend studying and setting yourself up in a profession. Before the age of thirty, Chinese men are fighting to buy a house and a car, and struggling their way up into six-figure salaries. If they don't do this they're considered failures, and not fit to get married and have a child.

'As for women, keeping up with the Joneses is their bread and butter. They're not even comparing themselves, but the men beside them! All the big cities in China are like this, and now other cities, towns and villages are copying them too. Xinran, do you realise that Chinese people are now getting into extravagance in a big way and with great fanfare. Luxury shops, luxury magazines, even luxury schools have become the gold standard for happiness and well-being. You know, since ancient times "luxury" has always been considered a derogatory term, to be held in contempt! In China and abroad, families have always taught their children to be wary of the allure of extravagance. However, to this day there's never been a religion or civilisation able to stand up to its destructive power. Sometimes I wonder whether fighting and power struggles help society progress, while democracy and technology hold us back. I won't lie to you, I often feel like I'm backed into a corner. All the roads I want to walk are shrouded in darkness, while all the ones I dislike seem resplendent and brightly lit!'

Shiny's emotional outburst made me uneasy about how her life would develop in China, but in the end it turned out that I had been worrying for nothing. Her indomitable personality, powers of speech and English language skills very quickly opened doors for her into foreign-capital cultural projects. Finally, after much research and careful consideration, she chose to work on the film *The Nanjing Massacre* about the massacre committed by Japanese troops in 1937–8. She told me that the German director of this film was a big fan of my books, *The Good Women of China* and *China Witness*, and was deeply moved by my ideas. He told Shiny, 'Why have Chinese people not given the weak sufficient voice? The majority of the Chinese population has at some stage in history belonged to a downtrodden group. If one only records the history of successes and victories, is that an accurate capturing of Chinese history? Xinran's two books provided me with a lot of information about Chinese women's culture and the details of their lives, and an understanding of the humiliations and heavy burdens under which they laboured.'

In my heart I replied, 'And not just China. Throughout the wars and chaos of the human race, men have always used humiliation and mistreatment of women to take revenge on their enemies. But these women, who endure extremes of cold, hunger, unfairness and humiliation, always silently let themselves melt away, becoming the fertiliser that nourishes family after family, becoming the pulse of history and the strength of their menfolk.'

Shiny said suddenly, 'Do you know, Xinran, I used to be a little bit suspicious that your books might be showing China in a bad light, and losing face for Chinese women. It wasn't until I worked with Westerners that I fully understood how your books, far from losing face for Chinese women, have actually won them and the country a lot of respect. The director said that Germans understand your books better than other people, because after the Second World War Germany was a defeated nation. At least two generations of Germans struggled to hold their heads up in the world. As a German, he said that one always had to be careful, even when making jokes, as they were afraid of touching a nerve or provoking anger. Even when discussing fairness, people don't give defeated countries and the weak a reasonable or equal share in historical space. He said that only a very small minority of writers, like Xinran, discuss these feelings in their books, and suggest that the losers should also have self-respect and the right to speak. I really hope you can meet him, Xinran. Thanks to you, the director and I have become good friends.'

I told Shiny, 'It's not because of me. Wherever you go you will always find the job you want. You'll always find friends who appreciate character, because you have already laid good preparations for your future. Although you're fond of winning and always have to come out on top, you're thinking too. I believe that if you can extend your sight and hearing into more spaces, and learn to put up with those unclear things that are both black and white, even if they are as murky as a *bagua* Daoist picture, then tolerance will bring you peace to accompany your success. What do you say to that?'

Shiny smiled, and did not argue with me. Perhaps she had already come to understand the full implications of those shades of grey between black and white.

The second time I saw Shiny was a year and a half later, when we met in the bar of my hotel.

Before I had the chance to get a word in, Shiny burst out, 'Xinran,

I'm sorry but there's something I must tell you. I've finished filming *The Nanjing Massacre*, but it is still dragging me along in its wake. I feel as if I've lost all my peace of mind!' As she spoke, Shiny, who had never cried in front of me, was shedding tears.

I asked hurriedly, 'What's the matter?'

'That project shook me up terribly By the time the project ended, none of us involved in the film could escape from it. It was shattering, so many lives cruelly snuffed out like a game. Was that slaughter of one race by another committed out of malice and revenge? Women and children, old and young, 300,000 of them. If our flashbacks from the film left us unable to live normal lives, then how did the actual survivors and witnesses endure it?'

I nodded. 'Yes, why do we need war? Is the righteousness of the powerful the same as that of the weak? Humankind has arrived at the twenty-first century, but we still judge right and wrong using methods from the distant past, and we still glorify heroes whose past is steeped in blood.'

Two or three years later, very late one evening, an email from Shiny with a string of exclamation marks arrived in my in-box. *I'm in love, very deeply in love!!!!!!!!!!!!!!*

Who the man was, she did not say. I guessed that any man who could make Shiny give herself to him must be very mature, and she must admire him greatly, both spiritually and in his career. I had come to understand that many girls with characters like Shiny's often choose much older men for their husbands. Many parents of only daughters find this desperately worrying, believing that their late-marrying children have been forced into these situations through lack of choice. It is very hard for them to understand that their daughters' spiritual needs are more important than the 'age of requirements' that typified their parents' family values.

I wrote Shiny a brief reply enquiring who the lucky man was; she was online at the time, and replied at once.

Xinran, he's twenty years older than me, but I admire his spirit, his qualities and his ambitions. He is not only an idealist, but uses his wisdom and spirit to put his ambitions into practice. He is a director, but not of sensationalist films. His films make you think, you go back to savour them again and again. You once said that in life you should use both ears to listen, both eyes to see, and make different things come together in your brain to create something that is truly your own. He said something like this to me as well, that many people never in their whole life understand that you need two ears to listen to stories. They only listen with one ear, and only look at the world with one eye. When you can look at one aspect of things, but also deliberately seek out the other, and once you've combined all the different sides together, only then can you make a picture of your own. This is the true way to consider and think about things. I believe he will give me the family I've been longing for, a happy family. Do you believe me?

I believe you!!! I used these three words and three exclamation marks as my reply.

This symbolised our unspoken understanding about the Eastern and Western concepts of 'knowledge before understanding' and 'understanding before knowledge'.

A year and a half later, there was an addition to Shiny's happy family, a beautiful daughter. Shiny told me that she had spent her pregnancy under the 'direction and protection' of twelve relations from two generations above her. Her every move was linked to the fate of the family. She was now worrying about her child learning to walk, and what would happen when she took her to kowtow to the family at New Year. Would her child damage her little head with all that touching the floor?

Out of all the Chinese women I know, Shiny brings me the most comfort and happiness. She is the pride of the first generation of only children.

Her mother did not constrain her only daughter, but gave her ample trust. She did not force onto her cynicism about the world and its customs, nor did she force her to be perfect. She allowed her daughter to make mistakes, and permitted her beliefs and actions that went against society. All this gave Shiny opportunities to become aware of what was right and wrong in her own life, rather than living in the rights and wrongs of other people, or those defined by society or textbooks. In today's China, very many families are not complete. The parents are busy with their own struggles and with the accu mulation of material things for the home. Hurried and overworked, they simply and crudely define and correct the rights and wrongs of their children's development, without giving the child a chance to put together the fragments of life into a picture they can understand themselves. Very many parents do not allow children to use their two ears to listen to stories, or their two eyes to see the world.

The stories Shiny left for me are many, and every memory is a collection of happinesses to me. To this day I still treasure the only present she ever gave me, the first Christmas card she sent me. It contained seven pieces of card, each one a different colour.

Shiny had written on the first card, a red one: 'Xinran, have a happy Christmas! I am a poor student, forced to earn my own bread, so I don't have any present to give to you. These are the seven colours I like the best. I want to thank you with them, because you have made me understand the significance of these six other colours in a person's life. Each colour represents a daughter's feelings and thanks!'

The orange card was Shiny's thanks to me for guiding her two eyes and two ears to perceive the world.

The blue card was Shiny's thanks to me for the many insights and ideas I had given her in our discussions about China.

The purple card was her thanks for exploring with her the differences and similarities between men and women in sex, emotions and love.

The yellow card was thanking me for forgiving her for breaking a plate in my home.

The green card was her thanks for giving her the MBL project.

The grey card was thanking me for helping her to understand life and other people between the two poles of black and white.

Every card was covered in writing. When I look at those rainbow-coloured pieces of card, and read the elegant, beautiful handwriting, I can feel this young heart beating. Could there be any friendship in the world more moving than this?

Some time later, I looked over this present again, and to my surprise discovered that on the inside of the seal was also written in gnat-sized characters: 'Only children come in all colours of the rainbow too!'

How do you view the Yao Jiaxin incident? Why is Chinese society debating him (a post-80s man) so fiercely?

One clearly cannot understand Yao Jiaxin with normal people's logic of what is right and wrong, and I believe that to strip away another person's life in any way is inhumane. Of course, he was born into a white-collar household, and there was nothing abnormal about his family circumstances. His basic nature may not be utterly evil; first knocking over someone and then killing the injured party may have been the impulse of a moment, but he will not be the last. Before him we have the Qinghua University student who destroyed another person's face with sulphuric acid. After that there's the MA student from Peking University Law School who, having failed to find work, killed an innocent ten-year-old boy in an attempt to extort money from his family. These actions were perhaps a great mistake in a moment of weakness, but they are the result of an aberration in human nature. The result might be different in Yao Jiaxin's case, but there are certain to be a thousand other Ma Jiaxins or Zhang Jiaxins out there, who have committed similar crimes or others that are even more shocking.

I don't think this is just an only children problem, it's also a problem in Chinese education. The continual insistence on technique alone, on science alone, and the idea that only the strong flourish while the weak go to the wall. All this is bound to create more children and citizens of this kind. This is the tragic inevitability of Chinese education. We have practically no citizens with virtue in the real sense of the word, who are prepared to take on responsibility for society. We only have blinkered, ignorant people and mobs. The righteous love others, as it says in the classics, but our education, from family to school, simply fails to consider the inner worlds of those being educated. It eradicates their love and care, creating a numb emotional desert, where everything is regarded with total indifference.

Mr Yu Jie* said: 'Our education fails to give those on the receiving end a moral education informed by legal principles, a moral bottom line with ethical significance, a "moral sense" with cultural significance and the ability to love with spiritual significance.'

---

* Mr Yu Jie, born in 1973, is a contemporary author from Sichuan province in China. He writes on cultural and political themes. He was deputy head of the Independent Chinese PEN Centre from 2005 to 2007, and played an active role in Chinese human rights activities and openly expressed his own opinions. In January 2012 he and his family moved to America, where he is in the process of publishing *On Liu Xiaobo*.

7 | FIREWOOD

O NLY CHILDREN do come in all the colours of the rainbow. However, apart from dividing them into monochrome person-alities, it is very difficult to paint these children in colours according to time of birth, family background, social class, education or skills. Even the different hues within the first generation cannot easily be viewed through the three basic primary colours. They are a multi-coloured group, who span all the 256 colours of computer graphics. But my research shows that the cool colours greatly outnumber the warmer shades. From what I hear from friends and relatives, the media and internet, rumours and conversations overheard on the street, there are only limited examples that inspire and invigorate, but plenty that make one shudder and sigh. I used to steel myself with the Chinese saying: 'Good things never get past the front door, while the bad travel for a hundred miles.' Perhaps I had only seen and heard about the polluted dregs of society? As it turned out, what I was seeking (valuing the family, a knowledge of civilised society and a respect for a quality of life, such as I had learned in my youth from my family) did not exist, while there was a steady stream of things I did not want to know about.

In June 2011 a friend who knew I was writing this book emailed me with the following story.

A handsome and lively nine-year-old boy hated doing homework, and would think up all sorts of ploys to wriggle out of it. One time he soaked his exercise book under the cold tap, then took it to his teacher saying he couldn't do his exercises. He also hated it when other people did their homework. He once stole a classmate's exercise book and threw it down the toilet. When his classmate cried, he acted as if nothing had happened. One lunchtime, not long before the start of the summer holidays, he let out the air from all the bicycle and motorbike tyres while everybody's back was turned, then stood to one side enjoying their shouts and yells of alarm. Those around him finally had enough, and dragged him to the head teacher's office, whereupon he sat down calmly and unhurriedly, and waited for someone to deal with him.

'Why would you want to do something like this?' he was asked.

'For fun. It's fascinating watching the tyres deflate, and then there's that funny sound, peeeeeee . . .' the boy replied.

People commented, 'Is the child suffering from some sort of psychological problem? Why is he so unfeeling?'

His mother was a company owner and manager, so busy day and night. As soon as she was able she put her son into full-time nursery care, in order to develop her business. But while she earned more and more, his loneliness deepened every day.

Time passed, and each day he became more like a stranger to his parents. He became like the monkey Sun Wukong who, suddenly bursting from a stone, threw all his energy and feelings into making his mark through dirty tricks and hurting people for fun.

When the boy's father discovered that his precious son had been letting the air out of the neighbours' tyres, he first pleaded with him. 'You can't let down other people's tyres, if you have to let down someone's tyres then do it to your dad.' When the son heard this he was as pleased as Punch, and his misdeeds increased until his father could stand them no more. He unfastened his belt from around his waist and thrashed the boy savagely. But before long the son grew used to it, and told his teacher, 'I'm not scared any more, Dad's belt has gone soft from all the beatings!'

China's educational psychologists concluded: 'Because this nine-year-old child lacked sufficient care, and the softening influence of the family, problems surfaced in both his emotions and behaviour. He was unable to acclimatise to normal life, and became immersed in his personal interests and likes and dislikes. At first glance he is a cold and cruel child, but this only masks his great need for emotional warmth. It was because he could not satisfy this need that he strayed from the right path.

The story reminded me of a friend, Firewood, one of China's first generation of only children, who once told me about his rebellious childhood. I forwarded this story to him, asking for his thoughts, and he wrote back very quickly.

You're describing my childhood, aren't you? But I wasn't as lucky as him. My parents grew up in the countryside, but in order to get me a city residence permit they sold their house and land, and moved to the city. My father worked as a dock porter on five yuan a day, although this later rose to twenty yuan. My mother, who's totally illiterate, assembled cardboard boxes at a food production line on half a yuan a day, which later rose to all of five yuan a day. The family was always short of food and had to scrimp on clothes. I was the only one who got a bit of minced meat to eat every day. All their hard-earned cash went on my schooling, and they had to pay extra 'sponsorship fees' because I didn't live in the catchment area. I was very naughty and a bit of a tearaway, but my dad had no bike for me to let the tyres down, nor a leather belt to beat me with. When he beat me he used the sole of his shoe, straight off his foot! There was nothing at home for me to mess around with. We lived in an old storehouse my father's work unit allocated to us when we first came to the city, with a leaky roof and no glass in the windows. As soon as the wind blew or it rained our home was as loud as a concert hall. I didn't have anything to play with. My classmates all had

Transformers and computer games, but I didn't even have a rubber ball. I didn't go looking for games to play, who would play with me? I didn't get into trouble, I didn't even have anyone to talk to! I am an only child too, but I couldn't even afford to buy the snacks and stationery that other people had thrown away. I went to have it out with my dad and my mum, but they just sighed and wiped away tears, and what use was that? If I didn't set myself free, who was going help me?

Firewood set himself free by coming to the UK. He went behind his parents' back and contacted relatives on both sides of the family, managing to borrow well over 100,000 yuan (about $16,500). He then contacted an agency who sent him to study in Britain. When his parents discovered what he had done they kicked up the most almighty fuss, but by this time he had already landed at Heathrow airport.

I got to know Firewood in 2005, while my son Panpan and I were carrying out a research project. Our plan was to 'experience' the entire street of Queensway, where we lived in London. We discovered that there were restaurants from twenty-seven different countries operating in this profoundly international street. Panpan was about to take his A-levels, and I wanted to make use of this handy situation to teach him how to observe and analyse the process of globalisation that was going on outside our front door. Part of the project took the form of a simple meal in a different restaurant once a week.

That day, Panpan and I had chosen a Japanese restaurant in Whiteley's shopping centre. Sitting by the conveyor belt of dishes, we started to guess the nationalities of the Asian faces around us. Were they Japanese, Korean or Chinese? Actually, one seldom finds Japanese people working in Japanese restaurants. In those days, most Japanese people in London were relatively rich, and apart from a very small minority of bosses who might be Japanese, most of the staff were Korean, Vietnamese or Chinese. At the time there were not as many second-generation Chinese nouveaux riches as fill the streets nowadays, shopping and consuming. The majority of Chinese students had to earn their own spending money and travel expenses. As we talked quietly in Chinese, a waiter greeted us warmly in the same language, and asked us what we would like. Panpan took a look at the menu, and realised that egg fried rice was the only cheap option that would fill him up, so he ordered a portion of egg fried rice and a bowl of miso soup. Almost immediately, the waiter brought over a bowl piled high with fried rice. Panpan took a large mouthful. 'Try some of this, Mum!' he said. I tasted it, and it was incredibly salty! But Panpan was touched. 'That Chinese waiter was very kind, he added a bit extra of everything to the fried rice, not just eggs and rice, he even gave us extra salt!' However, if kindness is given without knowledge or a sense of proportion, a good deed can quickly become a disaster. Panpan and I ended up having to drink nine glasses of water with the meal, just in order to dilute it enough to force it down.

Before we left, the waiter came and introduced himself. He told us his name was Firewood, and that he had travelled from his home in north-east China three months ago to study English. We invited him to take part in an MBL event, to give him an opportunity to meet more Chinese students. Soon he started turning up at the MBL office and became one of our volunteers. He worked on several projects and became popular among other volunteers for not being afraid of hard work, and being outgoing and ambitious.

Firewood's big ambition was to take photos of himself with the world's hundred greatest celebrities. Everybody asked him how he was going to pull it off. He said, 'If I have a good camera and find a good opportunity then it can be done! If others can be Super Boy and Super Girl,* why can't I be Famous Boy?'

One day Firewood heard that a company had asked me to do a target market analysis for China, so he asked me, 'Xinran, can I have a word with you about my future? Can you do a target analysis for me?' I said of course I could. Helping volunteers analyse themselves, and firming up the direction their future will take is a charitable activity that I have been actively involved in for years. Many young people in China have little opportunity or time to mix with society and think about the future. Many never have the chance to discuss their lives with teachers or parents. Because of this, there is often a wide gap between their dreams and reality.

That day we had barely sat down to chat about things when Firewood burst out with, 'I don't know what to do. Should I be studying now, or paying off my debts, or struggling to realise my dreams?'

'Paying off your debts?' I said. I had never heard a Chinese student mention paying off their debts before.

'I'm different from other Chinese students. All the others live off their parents' surplus fat while studying abroad, and thoroughly enjoy themselves. In my case, I was the one who liberated myself, but now I'm weighed down by a debt that's bigger than I am!' Firewood's features were an odd mixture of pride and pained bitterness. He went on to tell me how his family had eked their way from the countryside to the city, how they had struggled in the city, how he had fought to

---

* Super Girl, or Super Voice Girl, was an annual talent contest on Hunan TV between 2004 and 2006, where female singers were chosen by the audience. It was based on the idea that you should 'sing if you want to sing', and overturned several of the traditional rules for music programmes. It became a huge favourite with viewers, and was one of the most popular entertainment programmes in mainland China.

get himself a footing in the world of city kids, and how he had fled from China. 'I have to turn my life around, both in terms of money and of status, otherwise won't my family have gone through all that hardship for nothing? In any case, I'm going to make sure that I didn't go through all that humiliation for nothing!' Firewood said fiercely.

I had not heard such a tone of voice for a long time. It took me back to working in China, where I frequently heard such grandiose statements from people around me and in letters from listeners. They were uttered with deep feeling by young people who had left the countryside, only to find themselves faced with the big bad city and the contempt of its inhabitants. But here was Firewood, faced not with the difference between city and countryside, but with a world as different from his as fire from water. Language, culture, customs, knowledge, terrain, each of these was a roadblock, and there were obstacles every step of the way. To be able to live a life of ease was hard enough, but to turn his life around and return home wreathed in glory? That would be easier said than done! However, I could not say that to his face because that was just where he had come from: an upbringing without guidance, without the care and protection of his family, even without the basic joys of life. What he needed was encouragement, empathy and a certain degree of family support and care. Otherwise he might lose hope in the world completely, and give up on himself utterly, bringing ruin to others at the same time. I planned to follow the vine to get to the fruit, to help him find a road he could follow, and a light to lead him. He needed an aim, to know how success felt, and gradually come to understand himself and what he would need to do to succeed.

'OK,' I said, 'there are three levels in target analysis. You're a student in your early twenties, so we'll start at the most basic level. Target analysis, put simply, is an analysis of your goals, their practicality and the necessary conditions for achieving them.

'Many people have lots of ideas, but are unclear about which are their inner dreams, which are influenced by other people and their environment, and which are needs of the moment but not long-term goals. Their goals can be split into three types: lifelong ultimate goals, intermediate ones and basic practical goals. All three are interlinked and rely on each other for support, the great and the small working together,' I told Firewood.

'The difference between these three types of goal is timing, when they're achievable and when they're not. Whether or not something is doable changes with the people involved and the time and place. The impossible can suddenly become possible, and vice versa. But first you have to confirm the basic reasons why something is realisable, and at the same time predict as far as possible any obstacles to success. This way you can take precautions to avoid trouble, and keep the goal reachable.

'The essential factor in achieving a goal is to analyse your everyday life, and to make choices based upon available time and energy. This will let you know if the goal is really necessary, something you should do, or just something you would like. Then you can work hard to maximise those things that make the goal attainable.

'Target analysis is about working out a path from the future back to the present day. Firewood, consider your situation for a moment. Between paying off your debts, your studies and taking photos with a hundred celebrities, what is the relative weighting and urgency of these three goals?'

'Taking photos with a hundred celebrities comes first. Once I'm famous then I'll have money. Once I've got money, I'll be able to go to school and pay off my debts,' Firewood said, with an air of having thought about this plan very carefully.

I thought this was a rather childish and opportunistic way of thinking, but wanted him to know that I accepted and respected his views. 'So who are these hundred celebrities? Where are they?' I was actually quite curious about who he had his heart set upon. Politicians, actors, experts or scholars?

'I haven't come up with a definitive list yet. One from each country I should think. I don't just want photos of European and American celebrities,' Firewood said very definitely.

'Well, that sounds good. Let's think about what you're going to need to take photographs with a hundred celebrities.' I was trying to get him to carry his ideas a stage further.

'I'm going to need a camera, money and visas,' Firewood replied without pausing for thought.

'Where are the camera and money going to come from? And why would those countries give you a visa?' I was becoming interested in how he planned to carry out this very singular fixation.

'Er, for the camera, I can get sponsorship. The money I can earn through part-time work. But the visas? I'll have to think up ways of getting to know a few journalists, and getting information out of them. Then I can write to the celebrities, or somehow get myself invited to their receptions, or follow them around on holiday. Or maybe I could write to their relatives and dig up some information from them . . .' Firewood was becoming more and more cheerful as he spoke, while I found myself increasingly unsure whether to laugh or cry.

'But how are you going to get to know the journalists?' I asked. 'None of them speaks Chinese! How are you going to write to these famous men and women? Do you think they'll be able to understand what you want when you've only been learning English for a few months? How good are you at reading newspapers? If you can't read the news, how will you track down your celebrities?' I was not trying to wind him up, but attempting to get him to take a serious look at the feasibility of his goals.

'Good point, I hadn't thought of that. My English isn't really good for anything right now, but I can learn,' Firewood said, showing at least a little self-awareness.

'While we're on the subject, let me ask you, what models of camera can you use? And what sort of camera will you use to take these pictures?' I asked him, pretty sure of the answer.

'I've never had a camera, never even touched one, but I can learn!' Firewood's tone was clearly getting more practical.

I took my next step in enlightening him. 'So you're saying that in order to achieve your goal you first need to get a basic grounding in the English language, so you can get on the trail of your celebrities. Then you need to learn something about cameras, and pick up a basic understanding of photography. And finally, you need to save up enough money to buy a camera and travel, right?'

'That sounds about right.' It seemed that the cogs of Firewood's mind were beginning to turn, he was no longer replying without thinking.

'In that case, Firewood, given these three conditions, what do you need to organise before you can move towards your goal?'

'Language, knowledge, money.' Firewood's eyes were no longer so vacant.

'OK, so you've seen what is a necessity and what you should do in order to achieve your goal. Every day each of us makes choices about the details of our lives based on these necessities, shoulds and likes. Things we like tend to give way to things we should do, while things we should do tend to give way to necessities. In this way, our lives have goals, every stage of our development has direction, and every day of our life has order. Having clear goals, clear direction and a definite order to your life will help you attain tranquillity, inner peace and emotional health.

'I also think there's something else you should consider as an only son, indeed as your parents' only child, and that is that you should live a healthy life, so they don't need to worry about you. This should be your first step in turning your life around and self-liberation. Otherwise you'll always be surrounded by the cage of your parents' worries! Am I right?'

Firewood nodded wordlessly, apparently deep in thought. This was a typical only-child reaction: as soon as the conversation turns to their parents they have nothing to say.

'You really believe you're going to return the money you borrowed, don't you? You know, your parents have hardly any education. I imagine all they know about Britain is that there's a clock called the Big Stupid Clock.* They gave up everything to move to the city, so that you could enjoy the same status as city people. However, instead of studying hard, you went behind their backs to borrow money from their brothers and sisters, then ran off to a far-flung corner of the earth they'd barely heard of. How do you think they must be feeling? Won't their relatives be after them about the money you borrowed? Just because you have ambitions, does that means that you should throw your parents into a world of fear and anxiety, even guilt and crime? If those journalists and celebrities knew what you had done, do you think they'd consider you trustworthy or responsible?'

Firewood hung his head. It looked like his heart was sinking too, but at least his ambition was beginning to reach solid ground. That day, I helped him put together a plan. In his first year in Britain, he would go to class and study hard in the week, and work on weekends and holidays to earn money. In the second year, he would try to get himself onto a good photography course, and continue to work part-time to support himself. He would use his third year to try to pay off the debts to his family.

Two weeks after our talk, Firewood called me to say that he had finally got round to phoning his parents to tell them not to worry

* This is a pun on Big Ben. *Ben* means 'stupid' in Chinese.

about him. The old couple sobbed so hard that they could hardly get their words out. They told him how their relatives had turned hostile and kept coming to the house demanding their money back, and cursing them for raising a conman son. Firewood said with a heavy heart, 'I've never felt like this about my parents before. Xinran, it's just like you said, I threw my father and mother into a world of fear and unease, even guilt for my wrongs. I have to pay back the debt as quickly as I can, so that my parents can return to a decent life. I want to clear my name with my relations, I want them to know that I'm not a double-crosser, that I'm not an ungrateful son! My mum and dad have never lived a day of the good life in their entire lives. I've got to help them turn their lives around.'

Firewood dropped off the radar after our phone call. He did not answer his phone or respond to emails, but he did send us greetings at festivals and New Year, so we knew he was all right. But why would he disappear like that? I could not think of a reason.

About eighteen months later, a message from Firewood popped up on my phone from an unknown number. 'Xinran, Happy Birthday! Do you have time to meet up? I've got three bits of good news for you.'

We arranged to meet in the coffee shop underneath the MBL office. Firewood had bulked out a lot, and his body language had become much more confident. Without saying a word he handed me a present, a Chinese silk scarf.

'You know I don't accept gifts from volunteers,' I said.

'Take another look,' he replied, 'it's your birthday card, I've written a birthday message on it!'

I looked again; he was right, the scarf was covered with words, all about ambition and parents. The final line was: 'Before I go haring off to visit the rich and famous, allow me first to be a good son!' The biggest and most pleasant surprise was that in just a year and a half he had paid off all his debts, reimbursing every relative he had borrowed from at a high rate of interest.

He leaned back casually against the chair, saying, 'I've turned my life around! Actually, self-respect is something you earn for yourself, there's no need to depend on famous people to get it for you.'

'What about the other two bits of news you had for me?' I was eager to know all his good news.

'It took me a year to become certified as a Japanese chef. After that I found a job as an assistant in the Harrods food hall sushi bar. It's the most expensive shop in the world, so my wages are much higher!' His face shone with happiness and excitement.

I looked at Firewood, imagining those eighteen months of struggle as he toiled night and day to get on in his new profession. I was deeply moved. The Chinese say that a reformed sinner is more precious than gold, and they are absolutely right! 'So what's your next move? Your ambition hasn't been exhausted yet, has it?' I asked him.

'My ambition's still there, it's just a bit further away. I've lived like a machine each day over the past eighteen months. I've been at the Japanese restaurant every day from noon till one or two in the morning, learning how to do odd jobs and cook. Because I was the odd-job man, I had to do any manual work that was going, and was always the last one to pack up for the day. By the time I got home I was exhausted and fell asleep as soon as my head hit the pillow. Then there was the next day and the day after that, every day just the same. Almost each day during those eighteen months I thought, Why do I have to live like this? I'm turning my life around! Since I can't rely on luck to change my fate, I'm just going to have to get myself out of this on my own. But at night, in my dreams, I would still go to see my celebrities!' Firewood laughed, mocking himself.

'You should take a break,' I told him. 'Go and see some of Europe. I know your goals seem far off, but you also need to soak up a bit of culture. This is an important part of your time in Europe.' I really wanted to help him make the most of this opportunity to rest and recuperate.

'Do you think I could do that? Perhaps I can earn a bit of money and then go? Could I go round Europe on a bicycle? It'd be a lot cheaper that way. Xinran, do you think I'm dreaming again?' Firewood thought I was joking with him.

'Things you can do under your own steam can never be called daydreams. Going to see Europe by bike is a great idea. Many Chinese people just skim the surface with a tour group, but if you go on your own on a bike, you'll see and experience a lot more than other people. I've heard that cycle tours are very common in Europe, with good, comprehensive facilities and service. Arrange the visa yourself, and bring me a plan to visit five European countries, then we'll discuss the matter. If it looks feasible, I'll help you finance it.' I thought that this experience would not only make a nice change from his hard and boring life of the last eighteen months, but also give him an opportunity to learn about Europe and his own abilities.

Before long, Firewood had arranged his visas. I gave him 500 euros for his planned trip, and bought him a return ticket to France and an all-weather sleeping bag.

Firewood returned two weeks later, having only spent just over 300 euros cycling between ten European cities across five countries. He showed me a lot of photographs, taken with a cheap disposable camera. At every stop he had made a record with photographs and postcards, and kept a small diary. He said that the tourism system in Europe was first-rate, as you could rent a bike in Paris and drop it off in Lyon, and you could do this across the whole of western Europe. He lived very cheaply, sometimes sleeping outside bars, and because of this had not spent all the money. 'Xinran, give the hundred-odd euros left over to another student to use,' he told me. I took the money, feeling as if it were the baton in a relay race. Another Chinese child had grown up.

Afterwards, Firewood gave a talk to the MBL volunteers on Europe's rural culture, local customs, public service and welfare systems, student activities, his conversations with staff from tourist offices that criss-crossed the Continent, and all the rest. His talk left many volunteers wide-eyed with astonishment, but there was also no shortage of doubters. 'Europe is certainly no richer than America, so why are so many public services free? Don't people care that their hard-earned cash is being given away to others? Why do parents live in big houses, while their children don't even have enough money to stay in a proper hotel? Why do the powerful families care so little about their children, forcing them to do hard work?' they asked.

Listening to their discussion, I felt as if the entire contents of a spice rack had been poured over my heart, with all its clashing flavours and sensations. In the space of just twenty years, Chinese values had been overturned and transformed. I thought back to something a Harvard professor once told me: 'In the West, the rich spend their lives struggling over the self, this is a typical character-istic of modern civilisation. However, the rich in China spend their lives in fear and parasitism, which is a classic characteristic of agrarian societies. Chinese people, in their ignorance, take trashy Western adverts as real world trends, and copy them to create markets of their own. Just like American farmers in the 1930s, who thought that those driving big cars had more money than those driving small cars. China will only leave its agrarian past behind when there is respect for individuals' abilities and responsibilities, and when blind consumption and extravagance become objects of ridicule.'

At the time, being rather agrarian myself, I did not understand, and we ended up getting into an argument over it. It has only been in the last few years, as my views have matured through being a reporter, doing research and starting to become urbanised, that I have begun to have an inkling of what he was talking about. However, I had no idea how to explain this to the young Chinese people around me, and when I saw them mocked and held in contempt by Western civilisation my heart ached and I blushed for them.

One night, about six months later, Firewood turned up on my doorstep well after ten o'clock at night and begged, 'Xinran, can you lend me fifty pounds?'

'Why do you need fifty pounds?' I asked. I figured that he must be in some kind of trouble to visit so late.

'I got kicked out by my landlord as I couldn't pay the rent,' he said, looking thoroughly dejected.

I could not believe my ears. 'How can you have no money? You've just cleared your family debts, and had a bit of your own left over. Where did the rest of it go?'

'I had a thousand pounds in the bank, then I met this girl. She said she urgently needed money, so I gave her the thousand pounds. I'd just forgotten that my rent was due today,' Firewood said haltingly.

'Why did she need the money so badly? Did she tell you when she's going to pay you back?' I asked in concern, as I went to get my wallet.

'She wanted to buy a new designer handbag that's just come out. She was afraid she'd be too late and they'd all be sold out,' he explained in a rising voice.

My hand stopped dead, clutching the purse. 'What! You gave the money you need to live on to a girl to buy a designer handbag?'

'I felt so sorry for her. She was crying,' Firewood said, embarrassed.

I lost my temper. 'I don't feel sorry for her at all. She managed to borrow such a large sum of money to buy a handbag, what's to feel sorry for? Firewood, this isn't a good deed, you're just helping a bad person do bad things! It's also a total waste of others' labour.

I can't lend you fifty pounds. When you lent that money to her, you should have considered how you were going to live, you should have sorted this out yourself.'

Firewood was stunned to see me so angry. 'But why? Xinran, you gave me a whole five hundred euros, why can't you lend me fifty pounds?'

I told him, enunciating my words slowly and carefully, 'Those two sums of money mean completely different things! The five hundred euros were to send you, a worker's son from a small Chinese city, on a trip to experience the peak of international culture, to enable you to experience a world your mother and father have never had the chance to see. The fifty pounds I'm not giving you would be you subsidising extravagance, wasting your own sweat and blood, all because you don't know how to live. If I lend you this fifty pounds, you will make other, similar mistakes in the future! This isn't a natural disaster, it's a man-made one, and you're the one who made it!'

I will never forget the way Firewood said, tears in his eyes, as he was leaving, 'Xinran, I really never thought you could be so cold-hearted.'

I walked with him as far as the staircase then said, 'Firewood, I think I should be hard with you in this situation. But the reason I'm being hard with you is because I believe that you can survive it. I believe you can sort things out for yourself and, more importantly, I believe that you need to learn this lesson in life.'

The following day I phoned Firewood to ask where he had spent the previous night. He said that he had not dared go home, but stayed at a friend's place, because his landlord's wife was a very tough lady. The next morning he managed to borrow money from two friends to pay his rent. I said to him, 'Firewood, you have to remember, you've only just paid off your family debt, you've just started to free yourself, both in your heart and in your ordinary life. You've already managed to help your parents turn their lives around. However, before you go indulging your desires for luxury items, you have to be independent, stand on your own two feet, and be able to feed a family of your own.'

Not long afterwards, Firewood told me that the same girl had borrowed money from a lot of other people, and then disappeared into thin air. She even approached Firewood's family in China behind his back, and cheated the old couple out of 30,000 yuan from their pension. 'Where did she get their address? How could she be so dead to shame? How could she stoop so low to do such awful things?' he asked, bewildered.

In Firewood's third year in the UK, he met a girl from Singapore and they fell madly in love at first sight. Interestingly, Firewood, who had always been prone to wild flights of fancy, now became much calmer and phoned me far less often. By this time I had learned from watching other children grow up that if they do not call it means all is well.

About a year and a half later, towards the end of 2009, Firewood approached me again. 'Xinran, can we talk? My Singaporean girl-friend is very good to me. She never asks me for money, in fact she's often the one who gives me money and buys me things. I want to take her back to China to meet my parents, but I'm afraid that when my dad sees me he'll give me an almighty telling-off. He's a man of few words, but once he does open his mouth, it's all swear words and all directed at me. My mother's totally uneducated, so has nothing to say for herself. I'm afraid they'll frighten my girlfriend away. My girlfriend doesn't understand, and just thinks I don't want her to meet my parents. I don't have anyone to talk to about this, and there aren't any brothers or sisters back home to speak up for me. Xinran, can you help explain the situation to her? Oh, and can you also phone my parents and talk some sense into them? I think they'd listen to you.'

I settled it with Firewood that I would phone his parents that weekend, and meet the girl the following week. However, Firewood rang me again two days later in a complete panic. 'Xinran, yesterday she just took off and left without even saying goodbye. I haven't slept all night. It's clearer than ever to me now that I can't go on without her. I have to go to Singapore and find her. I've just quit my job today, and am on the way to the airport right now. I'll call you again when I get there, thanks.' He rang off without waiting for my response, and when I called back his phone was already switched off.

The next news I had from Firewood was three or four months later, at the start of 2010, in the form of a text message. 'Hi Xinran, Singapore is too small for us, and right now we're talking about moving to Australia to further our careers. We're going home soon to see my parents, and discuss wedding plans. If for any reason I need your help again, please forgive me in advance for the trouble!'

I did not have to wait long for another text from him. 'Please call me as soon as possible. Firewood.'

Because of the different phone systems in China and the West, it is very cheap to call China from abroad, but about twenty times more expensive to phone out. I quickly dialled the number. Firewood answered immediately, sounding so excited that I barely recognised his voice. 'Xinran, my mum and dad really like my girlfriend. I've never seen my dad so happy, and my mum gets on so well with her! My dad says that this time I've really won them face in front of their friends and family. Every day loads of relatives come to check out my girlfriend. My mum says that once we've verified the astrology and chosen a lucky date for the wedding, they'll invite you as well!'

I was truly happy for Firewood. He had turned his life around, found freedom, and won his parents pride and dignity. I could only imagine how happy they must be, after the countless hardships they had endured.

On his return to Singapore, Firewood sent me an email. The

wedding date had been set for spring 2011, a long time in advance, to give them enough time to sort out all the emigration paperwork. They planned to move to Australia as soon as the wedding ceremony was over.

However, as the wedding date drew near, I received another text message from Firewood. 'My father is dangerously ill. I'm at the airport on my way back to China.'

I called him as soon as I could. On the other end of the phone Firewood told me, in a voice hoarse from weeping, 'Dad's just passed away, I didn't get here in time to see him at the end. He never told us that he had cancer, it was only when he was rolling about on the floor in pain that he told my mum. He was afraid that because she'd never been to school the news would terrify her, so he just put up with it and suffered in silence. When they took him to hospital, the doctor said that liver cancer patients always die in a lot of pain. There's so much I regret, Xinran.

'Last year when I came home, he said to me, "I hear they're good at football in England, but we can't properly watch something that far away, so let's go to a match here, that way we'll be a real happy family." Ever since I was small, he'd told me that his wish was for me to study well, and then once I'd grown up, to watch football with me. After I went to the UK, he asked me if I'd been to see a match. He told me to go for him, but I didn't dare tell him that I couldn't afford a ticket. My dad hardly ever left the place where we lived; the only time he went anywhere was to visit my granddad and auntie, an hour's bus ride away. We never had any money, and everything he saved up over his whole life I frittered away. I regret so many things. I really wanted him to get to see a football match, but I failed. He was gone before I got to see him one last time. He was only fifty-two, he didn't even get to see me married . . . How could he just go like that?' Firewood sobbed uncontrollably.

I could feel Firewood's pain, and still more his regret; that was the cruellest memory in the world for him. But he had neither the opportunity to make up for it, nor anyone with whom to share the burden. Perhaps he would spend the rest of his life wandering, confused and bewildered, caught between the bitterness of regret and the goodness in his own heart.

One day shortly afterwards, I received a letter from him. He said he had been very lonely since his father's death, his Singapore girlfriend having left him when she discovered his family could not afford to pay for the wedding. Moreover, he did not know how he was going to support his illiterate mother, and help her live out the rest of her days. 'This only-child family stuff makes for a lonely world. When you have no money, no power, no culture and no longer both parents, does this still count as a family?'

I replied with the following Chinese poem.

Money can buy an expensive house, but not a happy family.
Money can buy a comfortable bed, but not sound sleep.
Money can buy a watch, but not time.
Money can buy books, but not knowledge.
Money can buy medicine, but not health.
Money can buy rank, but not respect.
Money can buy blood, but not life.
Money can buy employees, but not friends.
Money can buy other people's hard work, but not their true feelings.

How do you view the Yao Jiaxin incident? Why is Chinese society debating him (a post-80s man) so freely?

Xinran, you asked me what I think of the Yao Jiaxin incident. I know many people are discussing it these days, but I don't want to talk about it. I may be an only child too, but that's where the similarity ends!

I was born in the city, into the lowest possible class, a family of peasant migrant workers. All three of us were honest, simple folk. When my parents met with unfair treatment or things didn't go their way, they were always forgiving and conciliatory, always working away busily and in peace with the rest of the world. But now my father, who was the breadwinner and the one who could read and write, has gone, leaving behind my mother who has never so much as touched a hundred-yuan note and is now over sixty. When I was small, every time I was lazy at school or acted up, my mother would always sigh, her hands never pausing at their work, and say, 'If you don't study hard you won't get into university, and you won't have a good life. You'll end up doing hard labour all your days, and when the time comes you won't even be able to get yourself a wife!' I'm thirty-one now, but when I see my old mother straining her eyes as her hands work busily to earn her keep, her mouth still chattering about my future, how can I not feel sadness and regret? If Yao Jiaxin had had parents like mine, he would never have gone off and killed someone.

It was only last week that I heard about the regulations on family planning and pensions. 'If the parents of an only child are workers for a state-owned enterprise, on retirement their work unit shall provide a one-off retirement payment equal to 30 per cent of their average annual salary. The amount will vary according to the city they reside in . . .' But we never got a thing. Dad's work unit never told us anything. My mum can't read, and nobody told her anything about the state subsidy either. Where we're from, if you break family planning policy there's no way to get out of paying a harsh fine. In the countryside, if you have a second child and can't pay the fine, you get fined until the family is ruined. We've seen it happen so many times that nobody is surprised any more. The family planning committees, law courts and local governments all take it very seri-ously, and team up to dish out fines. But why is there no government office responsible for making sure the rewards are handed out?

My mother and father kept to the letter of the one-child policy, but my dad never got his basic pension, and after he died my mum was cast out by society. How could we not be bitterly disappointed? Recently, Mum's hand swelled up so badly that it was all red and shiny. The doctor said she needed an operation, but we couldn't afford it because she had no health insurance. And I've got no family to help share the burden of medical costs.

When I hear about the homes of our neighbours who disobeyed policy, full of children and grandchildren, happy laughter and jokes, and when I compare this to my lonely mother's bleak, solitary struggle with all her illness and pain, it's really hard for me to accept. We obeyed the law of the land, my father toiled away his whole life in order to carry out national policy, yet he got no help or support. Why is this? Yao Jiaxin used his piano-playing hands to kill, yet I can't even use my hands, which can cook Japanese food, to find a wife in China to keep and support my mother. All because I'm an only child from the bottom of society.

China's only children aren't divided by decade, but by class, power and money. The majority of voices on the internet come from only children with money to throw around and time to waste. Only children like me have no time to muck around on the internet! When people hear the voices of Chinese only children, all they hear are the suns and emperors, nobody thinks to listen to the voices of labouring ants like us.

GLITTERING | 8

I WILL never forget the first time fate led me to Glittering, who could not have been more different to Firewood in every respect. I met her through some family friends. She had the most enormous pair of eyes that seemed to take up half her round, rosy face, which shone like an apple ready to be picked. She had always been her grandmother's favourite topic of conversation, and the darling of her heart. So much so that her mother often had to bite her lip to keep the peace in the family, giving the grandmother full rein to bring up her 'little angel' as she saw fit.

Glittering was born into China's Red aristocracy. Her grand-father is related to Mao Zedong, and came from the same village. He is the only surviving founding member of the Communist Party, an old man who does not mince his words and who, for the last thirty years, has been judging the course of history. He often warns the Chinese people: 'Struggles in the upper echelons of politics cannot destroy friendship between people . . . The Soviet Union's technical guidance and selfless aid were good deeds that should never be forgotten. The same is true of the American army's support in the Anti-Japanese War. The Flying Tigers* were

---

* The Flying Tigers were a group of volunteer American airmen based in Burma during the Second World War, who fought the Japanese in China. Because of the political situation at the time, they worked with the nationalist Kuomintang government led by Chiang Kai-shek rather than the communists. Once the communists took over, the Tigers received little credit for their efforts because they had worked with the non-communist forces. (Translator's note)

not supporting Chiang Kai-shek [who was struggling with the communists for control of China], but all the people of China. The Civil War was two political parties fighting each other, in which compatriots treated each other cruelly. The victories and defeats of history are all a waste of life. China cannot live by big words alone, and developing the future does not mean the destruction of tradition.' I wonder how many of China's policy-makers have taken in this old man's wise words.

The two generations before Glittering are seen as treasures from China's national archive. Glittering grew up bathed in their radiance from above, and showered with envy from countless people below. Her pampered life included a special car to take her to and from school every day, from kindergarten all the way through to university. Her family were treated like royalty, constantly surrounded by cooks, drivers, guards, secretaries, PR managers and other staff. From kindergarten to middle school, her playmates were the grandchildren of central party leaders, all living in the world that ordinary Chinese people call the Big Red-walled Courtyard. From a young age, Glittering believed that every Chinese child lived in this kingdom. It was not until she graduated from university and went to America for further study that she came across a kitchen with no serving staff, and an environment where nobody would help her survive.

When Glittering first arrived in America, she went to live with one of her grandmother's brothers. He was an old man who had been in the US for more than sixty years, and was not about to pander to every whim of an only child who had been brought up by three generations of servants. Glittering thought her great-uncle very cruel, as nobody was there to make her breakfast or bring her warm milk when she got up. When she returned home in the evening, she had to find her own food. However, she eventually discovered that food could be found in the white box called a refrigerator!

It was only after surviving on her own for several days that she realised how different her life up to this point had been from ordinary people's everyday world. Her three meals a day, the basic rules of eating and drinking, ignorance of her own history and her superficial knowledge of life abroad, all became obstacles that she struggled to overcome in her new life in America. She initially lived off any supermarket ready-meals she thought might be edible, but after a few weeks she could not stand any more American microwave meals. She missed her mother's home-made dumplings and the extravagant delicacies from 'mountain top to sea floor' cooked by her grandmother's chef.

Glittering told me that the two years spent living independently in America forced her to grow up. Her true education about life had come not from China's top universities, nor the red-walled compound filled with officials. In fact, it had not come from China at all, despite its surging economy, but from those two years abroad where she had to learn to crawl and then walk! What other people might see as day-to-day reality, even a life of plenty with good food to eat and clothes to wear, seemed to Glittering a weary daily grind. 'Ever since I was tiny, I'd never for the blink of an eye had to think about how I would live that day. It wasn't just my three daily meals; whenever I left the house all I had to think about was what I wanted to do that day. But even at parties with classmates I had to watch their faces carefully to judge their moods, because I never understood the way they spoke or the things they talked about; everyone seemed to understand except me. Back in China, my family and teachers would tailor their words to my mood. But at my American university I had to learn how to suck up to people and earn their goodwill. The things I became aware of in those two years completely contradicted all I had learned in the previous twenty!'

Unlike the majority of Chinese students, Glittering did not stay in America to continue her career, but returned to China as soon as she graduated. Was it homesickness that made her so eager to return home? Was she too lonely to carry on? Or was it that in America she had no family to call up the clouds and summon rain on her behalf? Her friends and relatives debated the matter endlessly, as it would have been very easy for her to remain in America. However, she said that it was not because she yearned for the comfortable life of a high official, nor that she missed her family's influence, but that she wanted to build her future where her roots were. She wanted her parents to have a home where they could all be together as a family, since they were unable to leave China.

I do not know whether it was due to Glittering's open nature, or because her study of English was useful, but in any case, once she was back in China, she very quickly received job offers from several foreign media companies. At the time, students returning from abroad were known as seaweed, *haidai*, because of the difficulty in finding jobs.* They were also called sea turtles, meaning that they were either waiting for something to turn up, or their job search was progressing slower than a turtle! This did not apply to Glittering and in early 2011, after six years in China and a variety of jobs, she was posted to her company's London office. This gave us more opportunity to get to know each other, and I found that those big eyes hid a multitude of deep thoughts and feelings.

Our chats mostly took place in the evenings. The two of us could talk from ten o'clock at night right through to the next morning, just two women together. Although we came from different generations, we had a lot in common in terms of our attitudes to feelings and emotions. She did not realise it at the time, but most of her

---

* Seaweed, *haidai*, is a pun on words meaning to wait around for work when back from study abroad. *Hai* can mean 'sea' or 'overseas', while *dai* can mean 'weed' or 'to wait for work'.

conversation revolved around her grandmother, just as her grandmother could never stop talking about her. However, whenever her
grandmother cropped up in the conversation, Glittering's eyes
would fill with tears. No matter how I expressed my opinion, or
found reasons to explain, Glittering would always ask, 'Why is
Granny so incapable of respecting that I've grown up?'

If I were to collate the complaints of grandmother and grand-
daughter, the result would be a series of dialogues like this.

GRANDMOTHER: You're all we have in the family, one single sprout
for two generations. No matter how old you grow, you will always
be a child in the old people's eyes, and a constant source of worry
in our hearts. You should always be answerable to the family in
your dealings with others, otherwise how can your family rest
easy?

GLITTERING: I'm an only child, not a victim to be terrified over. I've
been through the education you wanted for me, and done well at
it. I have my own career where I can win face for myself. I've
become an adult, and should be able to choose things for myself.
Why should I have to report to my granny every day?

GRANDMOTHER: There's a whole number of reasons why you are not
independent in our eyes. When you think you understand everything, that is precisely the sign of not having grown up yet. Your
independence is selfish, because you haven't considered your
family. It's a sign of naïvety that you feel no responsibility towards
your family; this is a very childlike mentality. You can't even
organise your own living space, sometimes you have to get the
orderly to help you look for things; quite often, in fact. So how
can you take responsibility for us?

GLITTERING: My generation's principles and ways of living are quite
different from yours. Why do you insist on making demands on
me based on your own standards? We think and work between
two different languages, can you understand that intense mental

effort to switch between them? Our speed of life is a hundred times faster than yours, how can you use your ruler to measure our lives? You don't respect my personal space, and often make that teenage orderly go and clean up my room, rifling through all my personal secret girl stuff with his big boy hands. That's the tyranny of a feudal matriarch!

GRANDMOTHER: If a girl doesn't understand cleanliness or respect, or if she has no sense of responsibility, then she's been badly brought up.

GLITTERING: Cleanliness comes with growing up. I will have a clean house and a comfortable home when I have a husband and child. Before that what's wrong with just doing what I want? Responsibility is also my choice, nobody in my company calls me irresponsible, not my colleagues or the boss.

GRANDMOTHER: If you don't learn cleanliness now, how can you be clean in future? When we tidy your things, it isn't because we disrespect you, it's that you've made such a mess of the house, and is that respecting me? If you can be responsible with people around you who you aren't related to at all, why do you feel no responsibility towards the family who raised you?

GLITTERING: Some people say that treating your family casually is called 'Smelling sweet from afar, stinking up close', but I've never agreed with this. My whole family are in my heart day and night, you're the oxygen I live on, how would it be possible for me not to think of you? But why should it be constantly on my lips? We live in a multi-media age, I send you texts, you never read them, but does that mean there are no feelings between us? Besides, for only children like me, we grew up with so many constraints, always living for other people. All I want is to live the way I want, just for a bit, can't you allow me even that?

GRANDMOTHER: You're thinking about your family? If you don't say it, if you don't let us know, how are we meant to know? I can't use a mobile phone, how am I meant to know about your text messages? If you understood the age that we came from, without electronic communication, would you still look down your nose at us for being stupid? How many people are there in China who enjoy our standard of living? Didn't we win all this through our struggles? You were born into a family like ours, and still you think you can't do whatever you want? If you carry on any which way, won't your family always be fretting over you?

If I were to record all the disagreements I have heard from this pair over the last ten years, they would fill a 100,000-word 'Anthology of Debates Between Grandparent and Grandchild'.

I do not know whether they had these exact arguments, but I do know that their conflicts at times reached white hot, both of them living under the same roof but neither speaking to the other! In the end, Glittering could bear it no longer and rented a flat to live by herself.

Looking back over these bitter disputes, Glittering said she felt very conflicted. As a white-collar worker whose job brought her into contact with the world outside China, she encountered encouragement and hugs in the open Western work environment by day. However, when she returned home in the evening, it was like being back in the deep well of ancient Chinese culture, dark and cut off from the rest of the world. Back to the traditional regulations of her grandmother's generation, and the army camp with its clearly defined rights and wrongs of her father's generation. Glittering found it very difficult to live with one foot in each culture twenty-four hours a day. On one side lay her open life with Western languages, work and friends. On the other, China's closed-in traditions, ranks and regulations, so tightly controlled that it even affected the way she dressed. She was not allowed to wear clothes that revealed her bare shoulders. 'This daily chopping and changing between cultures is becoming impossible!' she eventually said to me.

I remember asking her once, 'You grew up for twenty-two years in China before you went to America, how come you've completely changed your cultural stripes after only two years of Western education?'

Glittering gazed at me, apparently deep in thought. 'How shall I put it? I like the encouragement in Western culture, the optimism, the forgiveness, it's a culture of sunshine. Too much of Chinese culture is negative, all about keeping up with the Joneses and complaining. It's a dark and rainy culture. In the West there is trust and respect between people, who all have the opportunity to think independently, and principles by which they treat one another. The way they communicate and cooperate is a bit like a tangram puzzle, in which every person contributes their own special style and abilities to complete a picture that they have all worked out together. That way of working is such a release, such a freedom, it really lets you take pleasure in being yourself. The managers in Western companies never looked down upon my ideas because I was young, and none of my colleagues felt that just because I was new I should join the queue for any opportunities that were going. I often made mistakes, but nobody came out and blamed me. One boss actually used to come up with excuses for me that I'd never even thought of. I was moved by their goodness and tolerance, and this made me want to exert every last ounce of my strength to repay their understanding and trust.

'But in the Chinese cultural world, from school and family to work, most of what I experienced was complaining, blame and envy. Every moment I was expected to search my feelings about whether what I had done was right or wrong, so as to avoid getting on the wrong side of people. The older generation, managers, even random people on the street wearing official armbands or uniform, they all act as if they're messengers from the gods. They wave their hands at me, yell about my words and actions, but there's no concept of respect or responsibility between people. It's become impossible for me to breathe freely in the culture where my roots are sunk. Did all this come from two years of study in America? I can't say for sure. I remember my first day back, I could almost feel it from the first step I took onto the soil of my motherland. As my career in foreign companies continued, it became ever more apparent. It feels like a tear in my culture, ripping apart the life and feelings of every single day; it's very painful.'

When discussing plans for her future family, Glittering often sketched her own love story for me. Her anxious friends and relatives sometimes wondered if she might be gay. After all, this was no longer something that made headlines in Chinese media.

At the start of the 1980s, China's economy was surging forward like a tidal wave. The whole population was up to their eyes in work, from villages to cities. It seemed that apart from babes in arms, nobody had a moment to spare. Children were busy with homework, academic achievements and qualifications. Men were hurrying to the cities, 'jumping the trough',* going into business and earning money. Women were busy with life in and outside the home, not to mention with their faces, which had to be regularly 'upgraded to the newest style' through surgery, if they could afford it. People were not only seeking a second chance to set up a career in this first period of freedom, they were also seeking rebirth in an age of struggle for opportunity. Rebirth of career, rebirth of family and rebirth of self. It sounds unbelievable, but for many that period of frantic activity left no time for raising children!

A fashion emerged in society that became so widespread it was accepted without comment. Many business people sent their children to be raised in the countryside, or in the homes of poor city folk.

---

* *Tiaocao*, literally 'to jump the feeding trough', means to change jobs or move to a new work unit. The phrase became popular in China because of its freshness and cheekiness.

However, in order to raise these extra children without spending too much on food, clothes and bedding, these foster families often treated them as the same sex as their own child, explaining it away as 'standardising their daily life'. These children spent their early childhood without their parents and in an environment where they were forced into a gender that was not always their own. This unsurprisingly led to much gender confusion when they were older.

Nobody noticed that while China was 'planning a new era' with great fanfare, it was also creating the most open age for homosexuality in Chinese history. Although homosexuality had existed in China since the dawn of time, it had never been discussed without slight misgivings, or taken as so familiar as to be normal as it is today. I remember when I was presenting my women's radio programme, if people heard the word 'homosexuality' it was as if the enemy were at the gates! Most people felt a deep-rooted aversion, and the government certainly did not permit gay clubs. At the time, nobody had the nerve to declare themselves openly gay. But today, gay clubs, restaurants and tour groups can be found everywhere, so much so that it seems like a fashion among only children.

Was Glittering part of this trend? I did not think so, but she was nonetheless part of the gay community. She once told me that in order to end a painful romantic experience, she had sought release in the gay community. Eventually, she found her feet in Beijing's gay clubs.

'To me, it's not somewhere where I can let loose with my feelings, but more of a space for letting them settle. They're gay men's clubs. When I see those men, the looks that pass between them, the way they are in themselves, the way they treat each other, and when I see the determination with which they cling to their love, I ask myself, "I'm straight, so why don't I have such deep feelings for men?" Everybody there is good to me, and although I'm not a lover in their eyes, the loving care they give me is precisely what I crave. I know that I can never win the love of a man in this community, but through them I've found friendship, a network, a rewarding one at that.

'And helping those gay men deal with family difficulties gives me a feeling of achievement. I don't know how many people feel the way I do, or share the same aspirations, to help gay only children deal with their family who are keen for them to carry on the family line. As a female friend of many gay men, every Spring Festival, Mid-Autumn Festival and other traditional Chinese holidays, it's a set routine for me to visit their parents at home, to show their friends, family and neighbours that at least there is a girlfriend on the scene. Their sons might not be married yet, but at least they come back home every year to spend time with the family. As the years have passed, I've seen more and more people whose full-time job is "pretending to be a partner". Some people say the Chinese have pioneered this job, creating another first in world history, but I'm not sure about that.'

'Do their families suspect anything?' I asked her. It was very hard for me to imagine that these Chinese mothers and fathers could accept gay children, as most of them devoutly believed that 'of all the sins of the world, being without descendants is the worst'. Moreover, thanks to the one-child policy they had no right to adopt either. For them, there was no second chance to keep the incense fires burning!

'Oh, I think most parents know. Some know and don't come right out and say it. Some of them . . . well, they're completely open about it at home, but still hush it up outside. Only a tiny minority of families cheerfully and freely announce it to the world. Otherwise, we fake girlfriends wouldn't get such good treatment!'

'Then how do those parents treat girls like you?' To me, this was like something out of the *Arabian Nights*. I had no idea how to react.

'Well, it all depends on the educational background and general cultural awareness of the family. From what I know, in the main, parents treat their sons' fake girlfriends pretty well. The more enlightened households thank us for ridding them of a source of anxiety (that their children might be lonely), while the more feudal ones still think we are encouraging wickedness. However, they're also afraid that we'll let the cat out of the bag, so it's quite difficult to know whether they like us or not. The family of the boy I help know that I'm acting a part, they also know that their son has been living with another man for more than ten years, but outsiders still think that man is a colleague. The family is desperate for their son to find a wife. Every time I visit they buy me rings, bracelets, earrings and things like that, and get very hurt if I don't accept them. We often exchange letters too, just like a real family . . . You don't believe me? For the last two years, all my friends have been boys, and ninety-nine per cent are gay. So Mid-Autumn Festival and Spring Festival have become my busiest times of year. Sometimes I have to go and act as girlfriend for two or three different boys!'

'But aren't you afraid people will get the wrong idea?' I asked. 'You're not worried that this will influence your future husband? Aren't you afraid that your grandmother will find out and go through the roof?' Seeing Glittering's earnest appearance, my brain churned with questions from several generations.

'To tell you the truth, I haven't given it much thought. Anyone who loves me should know who I am and how I deal with the world. In my experience, there are no longer any secrets or stories too shameful to be told in society. As for my grandmother? I can't let her find out, it'd be the end of her for sure! I've never had an opportunity to make her proud, so what would happen if I made her die of rage? After she crossed over to the next world, wouldn't she be on my heels every moment of the day and night? I'd never be able to grow up in her eyes for the rest of eternity, and that would never do! Every time I can't go home at New Year or a festival, I tell her I'm off to do some charitable work, and there's nothing she can say about that, as she taught me from a young age never to do anything for myself, but to work primarily for the benefit of others. Do you know, even in trying to find a boyfriend, she tells me that it's more important to consider his family. *Aiya*, Xinran, tell me, what kind of logic is that? I'm the apple of her eye, what are other people's family to her?'

I had heard Glittering's grandmother mention a boy Glittering liked, a friend of hers from university. However, eight years had passed and nothing had happened between them, though neither had married anyone else. The old lady kept pestering Glittering, 'What's wrong with that boy?' She even went so far as to rope in her friends and relatives, telling them, 'If anyone can talk Glittering round, I'll worship them as a god!' But even she knows that nowadays marriage is a life contract between the man and woman and cannot be imposed on others. I myself have never had the nerve to try.

One time, Glittering and I visited one of London's oldest and most famous pubs, the Dove. In order to avoid the crowds and make it easier to have a private chat, we arrived just after opening time at twelve o'clock. By the time the main customers of the day came trooping in, we had already polished off a bottle of red and were decidedly tipsy. I plucked up the courage to ask Glittering about her love life, and she, bolstered by some Dutch courage, dropped her usual defences and told me her true feelings.

'Xinran, I'm nearly thirty and still not married. In China they're already starting to call me a leftover woman or a nun. You say I'm in no hurry, but is that actually possible? At the same time, this isn't something that can be rushed. I remember when I was at middle school, boys would chase me and buy me ice creams. When I got to university, I would be in the student union and the little cockerels would strut around me all squawking in turn! But I didn't give a fig about any of them. They had none of my father's wisdom, let alone his spirit and energy. They all thought they could hit on me because of their good looks or some new electronic gadget, but how does that make any sense? Still, there was a boy who was very close to me, who did everything I wanted and listened to me in everything.

Our parents knew each other, and at one point they were setting out a timetable for our marriage, but I went to America instead, and that put everything on hold. After I came back to China, I began to realise that we were not the same type of people. I wanted to find a husband I could respect, not a meek, slavish pretty boy. But he didn't take my words seriously, saying that if he couldn't marry me he wouldn't marry anyone. It's been eight years now, and he's still waiting for me.

'The man who really made a woman of me was my lecturer from night school, more than ten years my senior. He used to introduce me to all sorts of new ideas, and we'd spend hours debating social trends. With him I allowed my fancies to roam free without fear of god or man, and I thought that I had met the match of my dreams. We debated truth and falsehood, right and wrong. I could yell at him till I was hoarse, but he never allowed me to give way to my temper. Gradually, being with this man made me feel safe and relaxed, up to a point. Perhaps that's what they mean when they speak of happiness? Maybe jealousy is also a side effect of love? When I found out that he was like this with other girls, I was very hurt. In order to show that I was different from the rest, I decided to move in with him. But after we started living together, I found out that he was still going around with other women. I was devastated, but he told me that before we had a family, what right did I have to prevent him from spending time with other people? I told him that we belonged to each other, but he said that wasn't the same as hogging another person's freedom! We started having fierce arguments, so I came up with a gutsy plan to see how many days I could survive without him and test the extent of his love for me. I moved back home. I never expected that just two months after our split he would actually be married to one of my colleagues!'

Glittering's face was streaming with tears, which mingled with her red wine. I thought to myself that the art of life is formed in this way, through a blending of joy, anger, grief and happiness, mingling and separating, with nothing certain, and its logic and principles murky and confused . . .

Glittering paid no attention to the wine in front of her. 'I just don't understand how a man who could swear such solemn vows to me, with such deep emotion and intense love, could, in the space of only a few weeks, switch it all off just like that. And that wasn't all: my friends heard him announce at his marriage that what his home needed was a wife not a lover! To him a lover was just seasoning for life. To be honest with you, there was a time when I spent more nights than I care to remember pacing back and forth underneath the window of his new home, spying on him and his new wife. The more I saw, the more convinced I became that there was no love between them. I never once saw them throw themselves into each other's arms or kiss passionately. They seemed to be a very cool, calm couple. Once I watched them for two weeks on the trot, until he sent me a text: "I know you're watching our new married life!"'

Glittering downed the remains of her wine in one gulp. 'When I saw that text, I felt a mixture of hate and regret. He did love me after all, but he was using another woman to get revenge! Without love, how can there be hate? If he hated me so much, it must be a very deep love that I had injured, for him to be hurting himself in order to get back at me! It's been two years, he's been married two years, but every time I have a birthday or an important festival comes around, he visits me with a big present. He's given me a ring, like for an engagement, and sometimes he gives me a night. It's happened so many times now, and is showing no signs of stopping. What should I do, Xinran? I don't have the courage or will to refuse him, and it makes it impossible for me to have feelings about other men. Luckily I have those gay guys, who've given me space to bury myself for a while. But, but . . .' Glittering paused. It looked like she was not drunk at all, for drunks do not hesitate.

'Do you know, I feel very conflicted. He often phones saying he wants to come and see me in London. A part of me wants to say, "Come on then, life's too short, there's no need for all those scruples." But another me says, "No, a love affair unbounded by any sense of morality will only lead to pain and regret."' Glittering's eyes burned with both longing and helplessness.

'He's coming to London to see you? How long is he going to stay? Is he still in his marriage?' I felt a bitter taste well up on my tongue.

Glittering nodded blankly, adding, 'He's just had a daughter.'

'Do you really believe that this man loves you?' I said. 'That his getting married was to get revenge on you? If that's so then why hasn't he got a divorce? And he's got a child? Have you tried to find out anything about him? Perhaps he has more than one girlfriend as well as his wife? Also, aren't the pair of you deceiving his wife, hurting her? And his daughter, aren't you worried that one day that little girl will come looking for you, to get revenge for her mother?'

By this time I had sobered up, but I still had no real idea what to say. Yet another sacrifice to a certain sort of man! Yet another girl giving herself willingly to their ravages. Most infuriating of all, they use sex to crush young love underfoot. The girls are left drowning in their own tears, unable to tear themselves away, while those men indulge their fantasies on another girl's body, directing scene after scene in a 'tragedy of love'. The real tragedy in this drama is that these girls believe it is true love.

Glittering ordered a glass of water and drained it in one gulp. 'Tell me, am I finding it so difficult to come to my senses because this was my first love? I've heard that first love is imprinted on the heart, and follows you to your death. But my grandmother says that her first love was my grandfather, which I don't believe. My mother says she's never had a first love, so what about my father? Has she never been in love with anyone, ever? I just don't get it, life is really hard!'

What was I supposed to say? Instead, that day, over British

afternoon tea, I told her about Turgenev's *First Love*, his story of passionate but fruitless love.

On the way home, Glittering said, very slowly, as if she were teasing out the threads of her ideas one strand at a time, 'I . . . think I have two selves that are in conflict. One wants to be a good daughter and granddaughter. The other says why should I care about being either of those things? Have you experienced love the way they do in my family, Xinran? In a space where there's nowhere without someone in army uniform . . . can you call that a home? My grandfather is always surrounded by crowds of attendants, inside and out of the house. You can't even go for a stroll with him alone. And not a day goes by without my grandmother giving every one of us a good telling-off. It's as if whatever she believes has to be right for the entire world. Dad seems to work at least fifty hours every day, even at mealtimes he's on the phone.

'And Mum lives in the shadow of my grandparents' power, always fitting in with whatever is going on. No one seems to realise, not even the staff, that she's from an eminent family too. She's the daughter of one of our national leaders, for heaven's sake. Sometimes I want to stick up for her, but she always stops me. She says what kind of family will we have left if everyone tries to go their own way, pursuing independence and freedom? She thinks the family is not a place to let oneself go, but a place where one should feel free from worry. She says our family has such powerful personalities that it's too crowded, so she doesn't want to take up too much space or limelight. She shrinks, or even loses herself, at home. When she comes back from working at the museum, she either sits quietly reading a book or keeps to herself in front of the TV. At weekends she makes her speciality noodle dish for everyone in the family, old and young. It's been like that for over twenty years, ever since I can remember, never changing! I often wonder whether she's ever noticed that times have changed?'

'Perhaps it's precisely your mother's immutability that brings stability to the thousands of other changes going on in the family?' This was a heartfelt belief of mine.

'Perhaps,' said Glittering, without much conviction.

'If you could make a plan for your latter years, what would it be?' I asked her, really wanting to know her ultimate goal.

'I've thought about this,' she said, waking up as if from a profound dream. 'Believe it or not, I really have thought about it. Recently my grandfather hasn't been well. Sometimes he doesn't recognise people, and one time he even asked who I was. I cried for a long time after that, as I thought I was the apple of his eye. The doctors and nurses told me he's never failed to recognise my grandmother. No matter how ill he is, she only has to go and take his hand and he will call her by her pet name. His eyes shine with happiness and sometimes he even sheds a tear. Sometimes he tries to stroke her hair, as if she's still the young girl he knew over sixty years ago. Xinran, they've spent sixty years of their lives together, and they're still so close, so loving. I think that's the picture I have for the last years of my life.'

How do you view the Yao Jiaxin incident? Why is Chinese society debating him (a post-80s man) so fiercely?

The reason why the Yao Jiaxin incident has become such a hot topic in China is not because there is anything representative or typical about it. To put it another way, it is because of today's social media and because the broadcasting power of the internet has far surpassed our imaginings. I believe that over the last few years there have been very many similar incidents all over China, it's just that this time loads of well-known figures in society have got involved, along with social media sites such as Weibo, and this is what has given rise to these debates.

As to why everyone is discussing this issue, first it's because the people born in the 1970s and 1980s now make up the mainstay of society. They are probably the people across all forms of media who take the strongest exception to the late post-80s and the post-90s generation. They're not so dissimilar in age, but they were brought up in very different circumstances, and this has formed a sharp contrast between them. Second, as social media opens up, people realise that society is not as peaceful and kind as they used to think, and this has given rise to a lot of fear and questioning. Over the last few years, so many people have been banging on about how today's young people lack faith and conviction, but in fact they are the ones who are suffering torments. They suspect and question, yet they cannot find the answers or a solution. Of course, it is also impossible to overlook China's present speed of development. Once you've opened up Pandora's box, all kinds of values flood in. Plus we now have increasing economic power, regardless of whether it's a bubble or true progress. In any case, people born in the 1970s, 1980s and 1990s are all coming under attack.

9 | FLYING FISH

I LEFT China in 1997 after a twenty-year career, and was one of the generation who helped push open the heavy door of China's history. In the 1980s we young people were full of enthusiasm. When we found out that we were being given the opportunity to reform Chinese media, we believed that the party was starting to allow us to use our brains, allowing us to think and talk. However, soon enough the ground was littered with the bodies of many of my intrepid, radical friends, who had become victims of their own political ignorance and daring. Some of them blundered their way into prison, some mysteriously found themselves without a job, while others never recovered from the setbacks and steered well clear of politics thereafter.

Because private meetings could be viewed as illegal, we survivors would often 'play cards' together in small groups. There were never any winners or losers. Instead, each card represented one sentence of complaint, and each game a topic. Before parting company, we would remind each other of what game we were supposed to have been playing, so as not to give ourselves away if questioned. Looking back, I suspect there were two reasons why our little group survived. One was connected to our work, the army with its merciless punishments, the police that was a law unto itself, and the ever changing system of government. These were like the magic amulet that monkey Sun Wukong wore on his head, which could be tightened painfully at his master's command. We all wore such amulets, which constantly rapped a warning on our overheated brains: Don't enter the minefield. It won't be just you who gets blown to bits, you'll also bring down a swathe of friends and family. We were all very aware of this minefield. The second reason we survived was the common 'defect' that drew us together. In order to keep an element of personal freedom, none of us was a member of the Communist Party. In those days, no matter how good your work, how popular your programmes or how moving your scripts, non-party members were always treated as 'backward elements'. Chinese people tend to shoot at the first bird to stick its head into danger, and nobody cared about the popular opinion we had worked so hard to cultivate.

There were four seats at our card table. Three of us managed to escape the minefield with our lives intact, but one very talented man remained. He was the only one of us still forging ahead after all the other heroes of media had fallen. In fact, he was appointed to clear up the battlefield as the gunpowder smoke cleared. He appeared like a Red Cross flag set up on the sidelines, showing the wounded that there was still hope. This man was Flying Fish's father.

By the time I left China, our little gang of four had collapsed. One had taken early retirement on medical grounds, one had 'jumped the trough' and gone into business, and I had cut my losses and gone swimming in bigger seas. Only Flying Fish's father kept the faith. 'Nothing is impossible, it's only people who lack the strength of will!' he used to say to us. 'I'm going to lay out a new road to prosperity for Chinese radio and give the people something they can enjoy, instead of this blind, benighted political tool!' Soon after this, thanks to his startling career successes, he was transferred to the north-east of the country, and put in charge of an organisation directly controlled by the provincial government.

Every time I went back to China I would always listen with respect and admiration to his opinions. 'You have to believe that there is a way out for China's media. If politics doesn't provide a door then we can take the road of culture and economics. The long and ancient

Silk Road was never cut off by the multitude of different religions along its length, nor blocked by different languages. Why don't we draw lessons from this? In the ten years you've been away, Xinran, we've not only entered the lives of the common people, but also gained a presence in public transport systems. We must follow this up, using economic necessity to brainwash those policy-makers. We have to make them see what ordinary people need to move their lives forward, and what China needs in order to grow culturally.'

To tell the truth, I can count on my fingers the number of people who, after twenty years, are still carrying on the struggle, still full of proud and lofty words and undiminished ardour. Age is generally the excuse for giving up halfway. Parents often worry that their children will never amount to anything, but they are seldom clear why their own abilities fell short of their youthful ambitions. Flying Fish's father walked his talk. This was truly admirable and made me feel ashamed. Why had I not believed that China's media could escape the grip of politics? Why had I not remained and thrown myself into the fight alongside him? Was I really one of those people who only delighted in riding the first wave of a new trend, all high ideals but no substance? After I came to this realisation, I dreamed of being able to do something for him and my remaining friends in the media, and longed for an opportunity to prove my respect for them. But what could I, a poor writer living a vagabond existence overseas, do to assist the meteoric rise of his career? Every time I went back to China to visit friends and family, I would always get caught up in an endless parade of gifts, big and small, from people concerned that I was struggling to make my way in foreign climes. They were afraid I was homesick, with no home cooking or familiar clothes to remind me of my hometown, and living in a place with no Chinese home comforts. For my part, I suppose I always looked a bit down and out and shabby. My gifts were always postage stamps, cards or bookmarks, or keepsakes collected from book-signing trips all over the world. 'A goose feather sent from a thousand *li*. The gift is light, the feelings sincere.' I would often use this old saying to assuage my feelings of shabbiness and of somehow being in the wrong.

At the end of 2007, there was a sudden shift in China's political climate. Even ordinary people who spent their lives 'hiding in a drum of ignorance' could smell gunpowder on the air. For a time, furious debates took place over whether the Princelings* and Communist Youth League† had finally put aside their differences and gained victory over the Shanghai Clique.‡ Would the country finally break old taboos and start stringing up corrupt officials and their unscrupulous subordinates, who had emptied the nation's storehouses and sent their rich pickings overseas? The Cultural Revolution ended thirty years ago, was now the time to settle old scores? Once the foreigners have earned all the money they want, would they close down the factories and take off home? The Chinese Olympic torch was meant to bring such glory, but has been put out several times by anti-Chinese demonstrators. Have we been cheated by our national media? Was the world paying any attention to China at all? Did we still need to cosy up to the West, licking their faces like dogs?

Throughout Chinese history, whether in Hong Kong, Taiwan, the mainland or Singapore, when political winds change, culture and the media are always the first to bear the brunt. Because of this, we have become very sensitive to political moods and our ears prick up far

---

* The Princelings are officials who obtained important government posts through their connections to the ruling elite. In post-1949 China, this term is mostly applied to the descendants of those who held power in the military sphere. Currently, it is used to refer to the children or dependants of high-ranking officials, and represented by President Xi Jinping.

† The Communist Youth League is the largest faction within the Communist Party to oppose the Princelings, and is headed by the previous president, Hu Jintao.

‡ The Shanghai Clique drew its support from former president Jiang Zemin, but its power is now on the wane.

earlier than our peers' in Western countries. According to inside information from my media colleagues, the Chinese government held a 'routine' clean-up operation in the run-up to the 2008 Beijing Olympics. Over 220 local radio stations were closed for 'rectification' after being deemed 'low and vulgar' and 'having lost the support of the people'; eighty-four of these are still in a permanent state of limbo. Out of the major national stations, North Star, was forced to undergo a full audit on the grounds that, 'The flag of individualism is too readily apparent, and there is a tendency to deviate from the principles of the party.' The audit concluded: 'This was the biggest case of economic corruption in the media since the founding of the People's Republic.' However, not one of the official newspapers reported on this issue, and even smaller local publications that often dare to question the government remained utterly silent. But why, if it was a national-level media rectification campaign, attacking corruption and criminals, was it not reported openly? The open secret clear to any Chinese person was that there must have been a political agenda. The chief criminal in this major case turned out to be none other than Flying Fish's father, who was sentenced to twenty years' imprisonment just as he was on the verge of retirement.

I discussed the case with several friends, but none who knew him believed the charges. 'He embezzled over ten million yuan from the station's budget, did he?' they said. 'Even if that were the case, how come it didn't come up in previous financial audits? There is no such thing as a perfect human being, and he probably did make mistakes sometimes, it's impossible to avoid, but committing a crime, for that you need proof. Where did all the evidence come from? I wonder.' In today's China, which still lacks an independent judicial system, when political power turns on an ordinary citizen, 'if a scapegoat is required, a pretext is never wanting'. But as people in the media, surely we should have had a relatively acute political sense of smell and reliable channels of information? If ordinary people could smell a whiff of political gunpowder, how could he, the president of a provincial-level radio and TV network, not have noticed? Maybe he was insufficiently experienced in politics and naïvely believed he could save his own skin on talent alone? Or had he been given guarantees of safety, and so went cheerfully and light-heartedly to meet the oncoming political storm? Perhaps it was simply his beliefs and zeal that condemned him?

However, I think he knew full well what was coming a long time before the storm hit.

One summer's day in 2007 I received a call out of the blue from Flying Fish's father. 'Xinran, I think you were right, I should send my daughter abroad to study and see the world.'

'How come you've suddenly seen the light?' I asked. I was a little surprised and unnerved, as many parents only sent their children away if the floodwaters were at the doorstep.

'When are you next back in China? Soon, I hope?' He sounded very anxious.

'You really are a leader, aren't you! As soon as an idea forms in your head, you expect your underlings to turn it into reality. I've got a family too, you know, and China's a lot of time zones away from here,' I said, deliberately teasing him.

'To tell you the truth, I'd like you to take Flying Fish away with you, and the sooner the better. She's just finished university, it's the perfect time.'

When I look back on it now, it was clear he was not telling me the true state of affairs.

Next time I returned to China, I asked him, 'Several years ago I tried to persuade you to let Flying Fish study overseas, but you said she was too small and weak. How come all of a sudden you can bear to let her go? Are you having trouble with your means of retreat?' I guessed that he might be in the same situation as Du Zhuang's father, with the government making things difficult for him.

'There're all kinds of reasons,' he said, plainly reluctant to tell me anything.

'Best be prepared, just in case something goes wrong, eh,' I hinted.

'Xinran, how come you're saying this as well? What could go wrong? My body's straight, I'm not afraid of my shadow being crooked. Maybe you've become too Westernised?' he said, rather self-righteously.

'But what if the sun is crooked?' My instincts from twenty years of working in China were resurfacing.

'What does that matter? Even if I get dragged off to prison on some trumped-up charge, I'll just end up brainwashing the people in prison and the judicial system to my way of thinking. They can't block off the sky with a single hand the way they used to, not in this day and age,' he said confidently.

'So why are you in such a hurry to get your daughter out?' I said.

'I'm not going to try to deceive you, it's not me I'm afraid for if things get a bit rocky, but my daughter; she isn't strong enough to bear it. Flying Fish has been what you might call autistic since she was small. She's done a few things that really put the family in a panic. She locked herself in the house once, and wouldn't open the door to anyone, not even to her mother and me. We shouted at her to open up, then looked through the window. There she was, cowering under the desk, shivering. It seems she's an amnesiac too, often forgetting where she's put her school bag. Sometimes she can't find her keys either; it's like she's not all there. This is why we were unwilling to let her leave, we were worried that she wouldn't be safe. But now we have to place our only daughter in your care, so please keep her safe. First, she has to come back. Whatever happens you can't let her marry a foreigner. Second, you must treat her with the same loving care as you would your own. Third, she's very weak, so you mustn't let her get too agitated.'

When I heard these three conditions my head reeled. As far as caring for Flying Fish as if she were my own daughter, I would do this to the best of my ability. But how could I provide any sort of guarantee that a twenty-three-year-old university graduate would refuse the love of a Western man? And what did he mean by not letting her get too agitated? 'If I have to treat her as if she's disabled then the deal's off. But if she's not disabled, I'll help her to have the same experiences as other overseas students.'

For the sake of my long-cherished hope, and to give back some of what I owed my friend, I took Flying Fish to Britain to study a Master's course. Flying Fish's mother and father brought her to Beijing so we could travel together. When we were about to board the plane, Flying Fish's mother told me that her daughter had spent three months packing her bags, right up until late the previous night. In the end, her parents had to do it for her at the hotel. When I heard these words, a question sprang up in my mind. Have I taken on another Du Zhuang? Another Golden Swallow? Another Firewood? I shuddered to think!

By the end of the twelve-hour flight, my worries and concerns had become reality. Flying Fish had virtually no English, she did not know how to wash her clothes or cook, and had zero basic survival skills. Wherever she went she 'filled the horizon' with her scattered belongings. It is said that this ability to transform one's possessions into a rubbish dump is a common feature of only children! However, she was also very kind-hearted and agreeable, and capable of a good level of understanding if interested. She had the gift for independent thought from her father, and a set of firm, unwavering, black and white beliefs. Once her mind was made up, nobody could talk her round. Flying Fish's amusements were confined to shopping, listening to music and surfing the internet. She said that her home in China had been an empty nest, often without her mother or father. Her world consisted of a little dog and an old lady who waited on her hand and foot. It was only when she went to university that she started to spend time with her parents. They had family weekends together, going on walks and eating at restaurants, discussing the rights and wrongs of human life. Flying Fish always took her father's side, and they had long, rambling discussions about the future. But her mother, who worked in politics, always took an extreme stance when discussing reality.

I have always believed that the biggest mistake China made with modern education was its frenzied focus on memorising information, to the detriment of basic survival skills and the ability to enjoy culture. Education has become a closed-off pipeline. A child spends twelve years crawling through it, and by the time they finally emerge, everything in front of their eyes is black. They have no sense of direction, and no knowledge of life based on their own senses and experiences. They do not know how to enjoy the gifts of nature, and have no idea of how to live, starting with making their three meals a day. I always encourage any girl who stays in my house to collect leaves from all four seasons and make little craft displays. I encourage them to pan-fry, stir-fry, steam and boil all manner of different foods, then tastefully arrange them on plates and in bowls to create a beautiful picture. I encourage them to tidy up after themselves and keep their rooms clean. Any girl who wants to be a mother should start to train herself in mothering skills from an early age, and this organisational ability is one of the mainstays of motherly love.

Flying Fish quickly entered into the small pleasures of our life, and before long autumn leaves had become her passion. She developed a tireless delight in cooking, and cleaning up the kitchen gave her a feeling of achievement. However, her English was still a mental and physical stumbling block that she struggled to overcome. Like the majority of Chinese people, she did not credit the importance of acquiring a feel for language, and believed that she could not open her mouth before memorising a sufficient number of words.

Her heavily accented 'Manchurian English' left people unable to follow what she was saying, which in turn made her nervous and fearful.

Unusually, Flying Fish's introverted personality made staying with us a waste of her time. In British homes, she would not utter a word, spending all day on Chinese websites chatting with friends. She said she did not know how to study by herself at home, she could only study in class, so we got her enrolled on an English course at the London International Palace language school. After a few weeks she moved into student accommodation, coming back to us for weekends and holidays. However, I soon discovered that all the friends she made were Japanese and Korean girls, whose English accents were also barely comprehensible. Every day they went window shopping at well-known stores and lunched at restaurants. Her clothes, handbags, even the hats she wore seemed to change every day. When I expressed my concern, Flying Fish said that theirs was the only English she could understand, as the non-standard English of the other European students made it very hard to communicate. Actually, many Chinese students use this as an excuse to hide behind, as the majority of European students are independent, take a pride in their knowledge, and base their world view on practical experience whereas Asian students tend to come from wealthy backgrounds and their conversations revolve around shopping and consuming.

One day, Flying Fish told me in Chinese that the Japanese and Korean girls had taken her to a place where all the lights were pink or light blue, with drawings of naked girls on the toilets. Every karaoke room had a bed, on which were laid out some peculiar objects. When Toby heard my translation his face darkened. 'They must have visited a sex club, what would she want to go there for? To do what? Does Flying Fish understand about safe sex?'

When I heard Toby's questions I felt the blood run cold in my veins. I knew nothing about sex clubs. What was the difference between them and places selling sexual services? Were they brothels? Why had she gone there? What had she done? I could already see her parents' reproaches and the hurt in their eyes.

Toby said, 'Well, does Flying Fish understand about safe sex or doesn't she? It's a lot more important to know about that than language. She's a Chinese only child, and from what I've seen of her parents they're no *baofahu* [nouveaux riches]. For all we know, face could be more important than life itself in her family. Does she know how to use contraceptives?'

'How . . . how should I know?' My face had gone scarlet, but it seemed like this was a question I should be able to answer.

Later that day, I found a pretext to take Flying Fish out food shopping. When I mentioned the sex club, she said in great surprise, 'But we didn't do anything! The Japanese and Korean girls stayed very late, but I left long before that.'

'Toby asked me if you understood the basics about sex and safe sex? Do you know where to get the things you need for sex?'

Flying Fish burst out laughing. Oh, Xinran, is there anything you can't find on the internet? I know all about *that*!'

'What you see on the internet are just material, physical things. Sexual feelings don't always equate solely with the physical. Besides, there are people out there who'll give you a soft drink spiked with some drug, and your "I knows" will soon turn into "don't knows"!'

Flying Fish gave me one of her looks. 'How come you're talking just like my mother? Actually, all Japanese and Koreans have a lot of money, and that wealth gives them a lot of cultural refinement.'

'Is there a direct correspondence between being rich and cultural refinement?' I replied. 'I don't think so. Think of all those wealthy Chinese people, dressed from head to foot in designer clothes, who you see bellowing and screeching at each other on the street, or bawling out shop assistants. How many people from other countries look down their noses at us because of them? Spending money like water at such a young age, using their elders' wealth to satisfy their own extravagance, how does that count as refinement?'

'Are you prejudiced against Korea? Everyone back home knows that Korea and Japan are the centres of world culture,' Flying Fish said disapprovingly.

I fell silent. I no longer had any desire to reason with Chinese children on this issue. Korean adverts and Japanese entertainment products are undermining Chinese people's belief in their own 5,000 years of civilisation, with the childish notion that other people's things are better than our own. It is like a tiny leaf in front of our eyes that has blocked out much of what is in front of us, limiting our ability to see how a foreign culture has invaded our cultural space, and leaving us even less able to be aware of our ignorance of global culture.

Flying Fish's father would call me about twice a week to check on the latest developments with his daughter. When I indirectly raised my concerns about her studies and her circle of friends, he said, to my surprise, 'Xinran, you mustn't push her. A girl can't amount to much in life, it's enough that she marries well. So long as she's happy and healthy, that's fine. Our family has plenty of money and just the one daughter; if we don't give it to her to spend, who'll spend it? As for her English, if she spends three years in England she'll get the hang of it, even if she doesn't study.'

Since Flying Fish's father had such faith in his daughter, that she could master English without studying, who was I to go looking for trouble? Just as I was starting to let Flying Fish go her own way in her studies, her mother telephoned me one night in April 2008, her voice trembling. 'Flying Fish's father is in trouble. Please, whatever you do, don't tell my daughter anything.'

I immediately made some calls back to China, where it was very early in the morning. A friend of mine told me, 'Nobody knows anything. Someone at the station phoned me just as I was on my way out to say that Flying Fish's dad had been taken away, but nobody knew who took him.'

I hung up and woke another media friend who had just gone to sleep after a night shift. 'It can't be anything serious, can it?' he said. 'I heard that when they took him away yesterday afternoon they were just checking the accounts. It's hardly going to be anything major, is it? Besides, even if they want to get to him, they can't let it go too far, can they? It's not the Cultural Revolution any more, don't be so neurotic. I'll ask around tomorrow when I get into work.'

The following day I brought Flying Fish home with me, in an attempt to ensure she did not get wind of what was happening. I phoned China every morning while she was still asleep. However, nobody from the radio station could say with any certainty who had taken him away. Only the soldier on sentry duty and Flying Fish's father had seen their credentials, and the soldier was not about to say anything. Their guess was that Flying Fish's father had been taken in for allegations of corruption. Her mother sent me a steady stream of text messages, saying that several waves of people had searched their home, all wearing uniform. Where they came from she couldn't say, as she was very alarmed and upset, and had not asked to see their identification. She worked in the city government, organising the party hierarchy, and if she could not identify their uniforms then other people would have no chance.

About two weeks later, the Public Prosecutor's office informed Flying Fish's mother that her husband had been officially taken in for questioning. But what about the previous two weeks' detention? It is called *shuanggui* by the Central Commission for Discipline Inspection. According to an inside source, *shuanggui* is a kind of enquiry process or interrogation. Those responsible for the interrogation work in three rotating shifts, to ensure that the person being grilled has no opportunity to sleep in any twenty-four-hour period, the theory being to wear down a person's defences until they reveal the truth. I do not know how this method of 'interrogation through torture' prior to judicial process squares with China's legal procedures, but it is clearly an inhumane method and a breach of human rights. I was also concerned that Flying Fish's father, after having declared so boldly that he was going to give the central court and the judiciary a good brainwashing, would not be able to withstand days and nights of questioning without respite. Would he end up confessing to all his 'crimes'? Two months later, Flying Fish's father was 'without delay' formally arrested.

When Flying Fish's mother came to visit her daughter in Britain, she told me about her husband's disappearance. In the beginning, her mobile phone had been a source of information for her. Some calls were from acquaintances sounding her out, wondering whether they were about to be implicated. Some callers, though, tried to trick her into revealing whether her husband had hidden large sums of money at home. Then there were three to five phone calls each day, recommending lawyers with professional legal expertise. However, once her husband had been officially taken in for questioning, her mobile phone became no more than an ornament. All calls ceased, and when she made calls nobody would pick up. People who had previously claimed to be great friends all of a sudden avoided her like the plague, with excuses about business trips or work pressures. Nobody was prepared to stand up and help this isolated wife and daughter. 'Chinese society, which at one time put so much emphasis on human relations, has been transformed beyond recognition by money, power and personal advancement. Every moment is ruled by the market, it's a battleground where the victors are kings and losers are bandits,' she said miserably.

Despite her mother's opposition, I was determined that Flying Fish should know about her father. She was no longer a child and, besides, I could not keep her in the dark for ever, as rumours and speculation had begun on the internet. The internet is China's only free media, and words you do not dare speak aloud can be written on the net under a false name. However, in this fractured society, where the legal system is neither healthy nor complete, where morals and culture are in disorder and where dramatic changes take place daily, there is also a saying, 'The net is a knife that can kill!' Unsubstantiated rumours can become 'historical fact', as the net enters ever deeper into the hearts of the people. Nobody is entirely innocent or able to completely wash clean their 'internet crimes'. However, I still believe that treating children with honesty is very important.

When we told Flying Fish, she was stunned. 'It can't be true, can it? How come nobody told me? I was just saying how come he hasn't called me for days on end. I want to phone my daddy! Will he have air conditioning? He hates being too hot.'

Her questions left me speechless. Chinese prisoners receiving overseas phone calls in air-conditioned cells? It sounded like her concept of Chinese prisons came from Hollywood movies. I once asked a Chinese police officer about conditions in prisons in 2006. 'Even today, thirty years after the start of Reform and Opening-up, 80 per cent of Chinese prisons are still places designed to make you feel you'd be better off dead. Otherwise, wouldn't career criminals, with no other means of support, treat prison as a free hotel?' he told me.

Flying Fish spent the next few weeks in floods of tears. She was passionately devoted to her father, and had told me on more than one occasion that she wanted to find someone just like him for a husband. She had grown up wrapped in her father's unfailing protection. She told me of a time when she fell out with some girls in her university dormitory. Her father paid a visit to her head of department to support her, demanding that they put in a personal appearance to 'ensure fair play' for his daughter. 'But now this; has

Daddy really committed a crime? Has he let down the country or done something bad to other people?' she asked.

I told Flying Fish, 'You must believe in your father, no matter what he has done, whether it's a crime or a mistake. Your father is a good father, and that is what you should believe in your heart. He has been a good husband to your mother, and has never let your family down in any way. If he has committed some crime against society, that's in the past now. If he really has wronged other people, that too is also behind him. Your faith in your father is crucial to him and all your family. Moreover, you need to prove yourself a good daughter by helping him stay strong in prison, and helping your mother through this man-made disaster. You must work hard to pass your exams and get onto a Master's course. You have to prove to the world that you didn't let yourself go to rack and ruin because of your daddy. You are your father's daughter, and you must live an honourable and triumphant life for his sake!'

From this point on, Flying Fish's life was transformed. The harsh reality of the situation dawned upon the once carefree Flying Fish, that in the eyes of other people she had fallen from being a rich family's little princess to a jailbird's daughter. Because her family's assets had been frozen, even money for food began to be tight, and she was forced to change her former lavish spending into frugality. However, English was still her biggest stumbling block. After six months of desperate struggle, she finally got onto a media studies course at Royal Holloway University. But she still believed naïvely that she could master English after only a year-long Master's degree. She studied very hard, but because of her lack of even basic English, and the fact that her first degree was in Chinese law, a subject very far removed from Western media studies, she could only understand about 30 per cent of what the teachers were saying.

One of her teachers later told me that when he asked her if she understood, she would always nod her head, but when she went on to film or write she never did what she had been asked to do. When the teachers told her to film, she thought it was enough to take the video camera onto the street and film away at random. It took her teachers six months to realise that Flying Fish did not even understand key words like 'long shot', 'focus', 'composition' and 'frame'. But once she got to grips with the professional vocabulary of her field, she started to catch up with her classmates. I took her to our little cottage in south-west England to help her think about and discuss media topics. I drilled her each day, one shot and one topic at a time. Until finally, she made a very moving short film about mentally handicapped children in Britain.

When her graduation certificate arrived in the post, she wept and I cried. 'Xinran, do you know, I worked so, so hard, but I never thought I'd make it. How many people were able to understand me? I don't know why, but I've got a mental and physical phobia of all those letters. As soon as I saw that ever present English I would panic. Whenever I heard people outside my door speaking English, I was afraid. Other students spent their time studying for the course, but I had to learn the basics of life too, starting with my three meals a day and how to live economically. I never escaped from lessons. Even in my dreams I was studying, studying, studying. I'll be thirty soon, but apart from buying things I wanted, everything else has always been arranged for me by my family. Daddy even used to get someone to do my university homework for me! This is the first major decision I have made by myself since I became an adult, and I did it all by myself. Now Daddy will know that I can live independently, and do things on my own. He won't be living in fear for me any more. And Mummy will no longer be able to complain that he's held me back from happiness.'

Her studies over, Flying Fish returned to China, hoping to spend more time with her mother who had endured the political storm alone. After she left, I received a letter from her mother.

Xinran, thank you for helping our family through its darkest hour. Flying Fish's father still has seventeen years of torment in prison to endure, it could be the rest of his life. I'm nearly sixty, and I don't know if I will live to see the day when I can sleep beside him again. Please aid us one more time by helping Flying Fish emigrate to Canada. Will you do this for us? It's enough that I'm here to stand by her father, but the child should be free. Our only daughter has already gone through three years of prison with us, she should not have to serve out the remaining seventeen years of her father's sentence alongside him. Only when our daughter is happy will her father and I have the strength to live on, waiting, waiting for the day when our whole family can be together once more.

Flying Fish emigrated to Vancouver in early 2011. Soon after, a very thick letter arrived for me in London. The words were written by Flying Fish, who had still not escaped from her fear of English.

My dear Xinran,

Yesterday night I did not sleep a wink. Are you willing to share in my Canadian life and the little world I have just settled into?

Last night after a sleepless night, I recalled the first time I stayed up all night at university in England. I can still remember, I phoned you the next day, I was so excited to have burned the midnight oil! At that time, I had not yet started to think about how many children in China's countryside lie awake at night because they don't have enough to eat or clothes to wear. In those schools where there is no place for childhood, how many children stay awake all night for the sake of exams? And how many children of migrant workers stay up all night waiting for a job? I have started to consider these questions now.

I remember you said to me that once I start to think about others, and about whether I have the ability to take responsibility for them, I will have grown up. So, on the flight to Canada, I kept thinking, have I truly grown up?

I once believed that I was one of the lucky ones in our generation of only children. I had my parents' power network and accumulated wealth. I had a healthy body and passable good looks. I knew about global designer labels and had the power to possess them. But now I know that I am not one of them at all. I have the same university diploma, but none of the knowledge it contains, because my father planned out and managed the entire process of my studies. The 'society' we only children live in is a three-channel world, but I only knew how to watch TV and play on my mobile phone, I didn't know how to use a computer for work or study. I have a loving heart and yearn for a family, yet I am powerless to share my father's burden or relieve him of his cares now his life has collapsed. I thought that we had no opportunities to be independent or free because we were only children. However, when I was faced with independent living, I realised that I lacked the most basic life skills. I thought that when I reached the right age, everything would fall naturally into place for me. I've studied for many years abroad, but to this day I still can't live independently in an English-speaking world. I spent over a thousand days 'sightseeing' in the West, but I didn't even know that a visa for a family visit requires a letter of invitation from a sponsor, and that it's not done based on my 'oral testimony' . . . It's all too much, I can't bear to look back on any of it.

Actually, being an only child has become an excuse for my generation, the excuse of spoiled children over-indulging their own egos. This excuse is like a poison, which sickens our values and our understanding of life. Is there a medicine to cure it? I don't know. I just hope it's not too late. This only-child society is already suffering from all kinds of sickness.

I stayed awake all night because it was my father's birthday. I set the table and filled it with dishes for dinner with him, everything made by my own hands. Not one dish was ready-made, a birthday banquet especially for him. I took pictures of it, and will make them into a birthday card to send to him. I hope to prove to him from this that I have grown up. I hope that when he gets it, my imprisoned father will no longer worry about my naïvety. I hope my mother in her loneliness will stop fretting about how I live once she sees my ability to cook.

I looked at what I had created, sniffed and tasted the dishes on the table, but all the time I was crying, thinking of the three years without my father's voice, over a thousand days and nights. How many of those nights did I get through without tears? Precious few. Do you still remember when you planned that project for me? You made me use everything in that tiny student dormitory, photos, shoes, the wardrobe, food and all the rest to tell a story in photographs, my father's story. I asked you, 'Can shoes be connected to Daddy?' You said, 'Of course they can. For example, buying shoes with your father? Have you done that? When he first saw those shoes what did your father say? You haven't been shoe-shopping with him? Then have a guess, what would he say? Choose three pairs of shoes and arrange them together, like a family out for a stroll, who's in front, who's behind, why?' Yesterday, I thought up another exercise, and that was when I realised that your system had helped me to put the memories of my family in order, to expand my understanding of my father and my awareness of the incompleteness of my life, for there are only two pairs of shoes in our family that are free to stroll together. Your system has helped me to escape the confusion and lost feeling of being without a father, and the fear that comes from a lack of self-confidence. Thank you!

I visited Daddy in prison when I went back to China. They'd shaved his head, so he had lost his old elegant style with his head of tousled, unruly hair. As he forced himself to gather his spirits to chat and laugh with me, I saw the pain he had been made to suffer. The faith and goals he spent his whole life chasing had led to him spending his old age in a world living cheek by jowl with hooligans, bandits and murderers. I know that both our hearts were weeping and bleeding, but we were sending each other strength and smiles.

When I was about to leave, my father's lawyer told me, 'Live well, child. Your father has paid with his own imprisonment so you and your mother can have security for the rest of your lives, as he secured the family home and savings for you. I urged him to liquidate everything in exchange for a reduced sentence, but your father said that if he could keep both you and your mother safe through his personal sacrifice then it would all be worth it, because you were his only reason to live.'

Xinran, the day Daddy comes out of prison will be my wedding day. No man who fails to understand this can ever become my husband. Can you understand this?

Could I understand? Yes. But the price of this wish is too high, the time too long and the pain too great.

———————

How do you view the Yao Jiaxin incident? Why is Chinese society debating him (a post-80s man) so fiercely?

Although I don't understand how he could bring himself to do such a vicious thing, I don't think there's anything bad about condemning what he did. At the end of the day it's two young lives, two families. One thing I do believe is that he must regret it very much. What I find harder to accept is that there seems to be a very strong sense of self-righteousness in our society now. People are indifferent to life most of the time, but then some issue comes up and as long as it touches a nerve everyone cries out, 'Let him die!' The law has its own rules. I'm not saying that he should get a reduced sentence or lenient treatment, but what I thought at the time was, this too is a young life, here too was once a complete family. While I do feel angry, I feel a much stronger sense of regret. When I see the way my contemporaries on the internet are not just cursing him, but wanting to shoot him dead on the spot, a shiver of fear goes through me. I really don't like it when one person is held responsible for everything when something goes wrong. They think he's guilty of every imaginable crime, but they don't stop for a moment to consider why he would do such a thing. Is it a problem of education? Is it a problem with public attitudes? Is it a failure of the social system? After all, he's so young, why would he do something so awful?

10 | MY 'TEACHERS'

I BEGAN collecting stories on the only children around me in 2000, as I did not think it possible to understand the causes and effects of this phenomenon through hearsay alone. As a mother, to accept these children's stories honestly and without prejudice was no mean feat. Over the last ten years I have had over twenty 'close encounters' like the ones described in this book, all of which took place outside China. As for more distant encounters, if I were to include all those I have come across at various times throughout China, and the only children I have met during my travels across twenty countries, I could add at least another hundred to the tally. As their numbers increase, questions pile up exponentially, and I find myself ever more lost in my search for answers.

Among the mass of questions, one in particular continues to raise its head. How has the birth-control policy affected Han Chinese in cities differently to those in the countryside? There is a difference of several decades, if not centuries, between urban and rural China. If you drive a car west from Beijing, Shanghai or one of the country's other metropolises, two hours after leaving the city you will see things that you are more used to thinking of as 'historical'. Everyone in China knows that the one-child policy is really a two-child policy in the countryside, mainly due to the persistence of pre-industrial, agrarian notions such as 'having no descendants is the greatest of all crimes' and 'more sons equals more wealth'. Not to mention land-tax policies still in place after 1,000 years, which perpetuate a higher status for men over women. The birth-control policy was meant to be 'beneficial to the nation and its people', but often runs counter to rural people's beliefs, survival instincts and the well-being of their descendants, both male and female. Are rural people able to adapt to forcibly imposed changes as quickly as city dwellers? Years of research has shown me that plainly they are not. How do their sons and daughters grow up in this struggle of politics and culture?

The vast Chinese nation is developing in a kind of historical dislocation, with living conditions polarised between the distant past and ultra modernity. Five-thousand-year-old traditions living side by side with wholesale Westernisation. An era straddling slash-and-burn agriculture and cloud technology. Education differs vastly across the country, making me wonder about other differences, in upbringing, society, family, school, even the increasing trend in overseas education. How great are the differences among the first generation of only children, as they grow up in different regional sub-cultures and rapidly shifting social status? How do they feel about all these differences?

As questions lead to more questions, the answers become increasingly obscure. Perhaps this project will become a lifetime undertaking.

The vast majority of Chinese students who came pouring into Europe and America like a tidal wave at the turn of the millennium were the first generation not to need part-time jobs, live off instant noodles and stay awake all night worrying about the rent. Most of them came from China's 656 cities, with only a small minority, like Firewood, from the countryside or poor backgrounds. I was eager to hear about the experiences of students with lesser means and even keener to understand how their families in the countryside viewed their 'big-nose' overseas education that ran at a loss or at best broke even. However, before my first book, *The Good Women of China*, was published, opportunities for contact with overseas students from deprived backgrounds were few and far between.

I had much more opportunity to travel the world after my six books were published and translated widely; this included acting as visiting professor in universities across more than ten countries. According to local professors, not only were Chinese student numbers increasing every year, but their clothes were increasingly expensive and their study tools increasingly advanced. They had become both gods of wealth for universities and something of a headache, often believing that China was the world, that their parents were their personal property and teachers should be the same. They did not understand life outside the classroom, and had little practical experience of society, cultural differences or even basic day-to-day living. They did not realise that homework and thinking require an independent mind. Frugal and hard-working Chinese students were as rare as phoenix feathers and unicorn horns. Some university professors I met had yet to encounter a single one. This was mainly because China's deprived students could not afford costly Western tuition fees and living costs, and were not aware of the system of scholarships in Western universities.

I was finally fortunate to meet three groups of deprived Chinese students on scholarships, one group in America's Harvard University, one in Copenhagen in Denmark, and one in Cambridge in the UK. I have changed the times and locations in order to tell their stories freely and without cultural misgivings, and I regard them as my teachers. This is because they have helped me understand many parts of China I have never been to or even knew about.

In 2005 I gave a lecture at Trinity College, Cambridge, on the progress of Chinese women over the past few hundred years.

I noticed that the cavernous lecture theatre contained a large number of Chinese-looking students. But how could I tell whether they were Chinese, and not Japanese, Korean, British-born Chinese or American/Australian-born Chinese? Apart from body language and differences of expression typical of Asian people, I felt that what marked out Chinese students from the rest was that many were dressed in the latest designer clothes. A sense of bewilderment could be seen in their eyes, and they always kept their heads lowered, furiously taking notes on the main points. These habits had been conditioned over ten years in school, where they copied and memorised from one blackboard to the next. European and American students might occasionally jot down a few notes, but they generally pay more attention to eye contact with the lecturer. Probably all teachers have experienced the feeling when talking to a class that some students follow with their brains, some stare with minds far away and roaming free, and some couldn't care less what you are talking about, and can't wait to be saved by the bell! My judgements were also based upon the questions asked by students.

I always leave a third of lecture time for questions from overseas students, in order to find out whether they have grasped the content of the talk and encourage their thinking. I like challenges from inspired students, because they help me to think. But asking questions in class is a common difficulty for Chinese students. Teachers from universities all over the world have told me the same crude but classic joke. A tutor has four students, an American, a European, an African and a Chinese. She asks them, 'What is your personal opinion on the international food shortage issue?' The American student says, 'Before I answer the question, I'd like to ask, what's this "international" thing you talk about?' The European student says, 'Before I answer the question, what's a shortage?' The African student asks, 'What's food?' While the Chinese student asks, 'What's a personal opinion?'

That day at Trinity College, as soon as question time came around, and before I had even had time to pick anybody, to my surprise a Chinese student stood up. She was very petite, her face lacked the gloss that comes from being 'remade' by high-class cosmetics, her shoulders were drawn in and stiff, quite unlike the casual posture more typical of Chinese students, and she was skinny in a way that reminded me of some forlorn girls I had seen in the countryside. She was extremely tense, breathing heavily, barely capable of speech. I guessed that this might be the first time she had steeled herself to ask a question in public.

I tried to give her time to cool down, saying, 'This is great. I think you all know what a rare and precious thing it is for Chinese students to be so enthusiastic in class. By the looks of things, not only will China's economy lead the world, but Chinese students' questions will lead the world's thinking. For me, this is the best thing to come out of this class today! Thank you. Actually, you can sit down to ask your question, or you can come and stand next to me. This is a class, there's no hierarchy. Isn't that right? May I ask your name?'

'My name's Guihua, a real country bumpkin's name, isn't it?' she said, full of self-mockery.

'Why do you think that? Actually, awareness of the natural world in ancient Chinese culture is much broader and richer than in Western culture. In classical Chinese art, mountains, rivers and streams, birdsong and the scent of flowers all are present. Streets and villages, even our personal names, are mainly based upon a connection to mountains, rivers, flowers and fruit. Names remind us of a season or a landscape. Just like your name, which means Osmanthus Flower. Not only does it tell people that you were born in the autumn, it also tells us you come from a place that's full of the scent of osmanthus. Or at least your family enjoyed it, and that's why they gave their daughter the name Guihua, right? That's not country bumpkinism, it's beautiful. It helps make us aware of the beauty of nature.'

Guihua's face opened, gradually losing its expression of defensiveness and self-loathing. I asked her, 'What's your question, please?'

She smiled weakly and took a deep breath. 'Xinran, when you spoke about the plight of Chinese women, there's one issue you didn't touch upon. I would like to ask what you know of the phenomenon of infanticide?'

Infanticide? I thought. I wasn't sure I had correctly understood her English.

Guihua said urgently, without waiting for me to reply, 'Please don't tell me that even you don't know about this? I come from the Chinese countryside, where my father and mother forced my big brother to drown two of my nieces. They were determined to have a grandson. If you saw the bitterness on my sister-in-law's face, you'd understand how wretched it is to be a woman and all for nothing. It's just that, well, she, they were her daughters, and she was forced to . . .' Her voice was lost in sobs.

All the students were thunderstruck by her question. The entire lecture theatre held its breath. Clearly they had never heard of any such plight of Chinese women. The students looked at me anxiously, awaiting my response.

'Yes,' I said. 'What you say is quite correct. You have witnessed the cultural phenomenon of ignorance in the countryside. When I first became a journalist in 1989, I too was witness to more than a few of these "infant drownings". Many people in the remote countryside viewed drowning baby girls as just another woman's task and part of housekeeping skills. Even after more than twenty years of Reform and Opening-up, while one part of China is forging ahead, another is developing at a snail's pace, with some places still to pass key historical staging posts. I've spoken a lot in the past about how baby girls are abandoned because they are not valued as highly as boys. However, I don't feel strong enough to tackle this issue. It's not that I'm afraid Chinese people won't believe it, they will, it's a fact of life. It's just that I'm honestly afraid to open myself up to those scary, painful memories. The impact of those stories fades with the passage of time, but the pain of a true experience can wake you up in the middle of the night, isn't that right? I guess your brother was born in the only-child era, wasn't he?'

The girl nodded vehemently.

I continued: 'I'm sure that as far as your mother and father were concerned, their son was the lone sprout in the family. If he did not have a boy, there'd be no one to burn incense for them after they died, and the family line would be cut off, right? Has it ever occurred to you that it's only because your parents had your brother that you survived? Otherwise . . .' By this time she was crying again.

'I know,' said the girl. 'I had another two elder sisters who didn't get to live because they came before my brother. My mum wells up when talking about them, but why did she force my sister-in-law to go down the same old path? Why did she put herself through that unforgettable pain again? I studied as hard as I could to escape, as I was afraid they'd send me down the same road. But when I got into the county senior school and told the townspeople about all these poor babies, they thought I was exaggerating. When I made it to the teacher training college, the city people flat out refused to believe that what I said was true. I was angry and afraid. I wanted to find a place where I could speak my mind and get it off my chest. Now I'm at Cambridge on a scholarship. I thought that once I got to the world's best university people would understand me, but it turns out that my foreign classmates don't understand what I'm saying, and the Chinese ones just call me crazy and say I'm making China lose face. Xinran, why don't people believe me? If you went there and saw my sister-in-law's face, you'd know immediately how hard it's been for her and her two lost daughters . . . All because Mum and Dad forced her to have them drowned. They were my two sweet nieces, I even saw one of them and her pink little face . . . Why doesn't anyone believe me?' Guihua was desperate, weeping noisily, too choked with sobs to go on.

I walked over to her. 'Guihua, not only can I testify that your story is true, the facts speak for themselves: there are 30 million more males than females in China.* All over the internet you hear that rich families prefer girls, while poor countryside families have only boys. Have you heard about this? Why do you think this is happening? And then there's the 120,000 Chinese baby girls adopted every year by families from all over the world, which only adds weight to your story. I think you are right, I should write a book and tell the world.' (In 2010 I brought out a book on abandoned babies called *Message from an Unknown Chinese Mother*.) 'In fact, the world we live in is full of secrets hidden away by history because they are too humiliating and painful. I greatly admire your bravery and your respect for life. Many people now think that, with so many "facts" available on the internet, they can pick and choose between them. They are therefore unwilling to believe or understand that these ancient, ugly customs continue to survive. But you've experienced them, you've stood up and spoken out. And unlike many Chinese people, who believe it's a loss of face, you're calling out for people to work with you to put a stop to this as soon as possible. If we cannot stop the devastation caused by these appalling customs, after generations of us have gone through a modern education, and we still believe that we have made progress, then what was the point of all this education?'

By this time, hands were shooting up everywhere in the audience. I made a request: 'I hope you can understand my selfishness, but I very much want to give today's question time to Chinese students, because they don't get that many chances to speak the truth, OK? If you still have questions at the end, please leave them with me before you go.' Half the raised hands lowered, but a few Western students still kept their hands up.

---

* In 2009 the Population and Development Research Institute at Nankai University's School of Economics, and the Chinese National Committee on Population Planning, calculated a surplus of 33.31 million males compared to females in the population born between 1980 and 2000.

As I was hesitating, a young Chinese student got to his feet. He was tall and skinny. Like Guihua, he was in the grip of a powerful emotion, but expressed it differently. While she gasped loudly, he stood tall like a nail, a pillar, utterly immobile save for two streaks of tears pouring down his face. He made no move to wipe them away as they left dark watery trails on his blue shirt. 'My name's Li Jie, and I'm different from everyone else here today because I understand what that Chinese girl is talking about. I've never seen her before, but I want to say to her, I do understand you, because I come from the countryside in northern Hubei province. When I got into teacher training college, the whole family, no, the whole village was happy for me. I was the only person in the history of the village to get into university. Girls don't have a chance in the place I come from, only a few go to primary school, and only as far as their second or third year, then their families make them quit. Boys who finish middle school are rare, mostly they drop out to help in the fields. My university entrance marks were the third highest in the whole province, but I had no money to go to a good university, so I went to the teacher training college, which was free.

'When I said goodbye to the people back home, I raised a glass of cheap local spirit to thank my grandparents, my uncles and aunts. But the most important person to thank was my mother! I said to her in front of the whole village, "Mum, every day as far back as I can remember I have wanted to give you a present. Today, I finally have something to give you, the big bed at home. I'm twenty-two and off to college. Now at last you and Dad can have the big bed back. Mum, I know that you've never slept well. You leave me the lion's share of the bed, lying on your side against the wall." I also said to my father, "Dad, I'm sorry I haven't been able to give you back the big bed before this. You've never slept on that bed since the day I was born. Mum couldn't sleep on the floor because of her arthritis, so you gave up the only bed in the house for me and Mum. As I was growing up you said I had to sleep well in order to study well, and you wouldn't let me sleep on the damp floor. Mum, Dad, after twenty-two years you can now have a proper sleep, that's the only present I can give you." Xinran, do you believe me? When I got my acceptance papers from college, the thing that made me the happiest was that I could finally go to school without it costing them money, and I could give Mum the bed back at last.'

The lecture theatre was filled with sighs, and many of the students present shed tears.

Li Jie continued: 'My Chinese classmates don't believe my story. Now that I'm in Britain on a scholarship, I want to save money by sharing a room with another student, but no Chinese students will share with me. They think I'm just a country boy who doesn't understand their high civilisation. But the more I learn, the more I believe that the civilisation I hold in my heart is greater than theirs, because I was born from motherly love, the most precious thing in life. In twenty-two years I never once heard my mother snore at night, turn over, or heard even the tiniest sound from her. In order to help me sleep soundly, she slept with "extreme caution". If I spent twenty-two years aware of the trouble my mother went to even in her sleep, how could I fail to respect a room-mate? I'm from the countryside, so I must be a boor? Is that it? China has become big and powerful, but how many people understand those of us from the countryside? Or understand women like my mother? Do you know how good my mother is? She gave up her first daughter, my big sister, just so my father could pass on his family name through me! How can her heart not ache?'

Li Jie was unable to speak any further.

Before the lecture ended, I said to the students, who were all deeply moved, 'Over 70 per cent of China's population are peasants, and more than half of them don't get the chance to finish primary school. However, many of these people have taught me how to appreciate nature, how to experience life and how to struggle against hardship. Those illiterate peasant women might look dirty, speak crudely and not be too particular about their behaviour, but they've helped me to learn the steadfastness that comes from their mountains and wild places, they've taught me to reach out to nature and find peace in life wherever I am, how to give to my child and pursue nature and beauty while surrounded by poverty and deprivation. Village mothers have told me about the pains of being a woman, and of the beauty of a woman's spirit that neither time nor space can alter. As pebbles are worn into smooth egg-shapes by a river, so too is the inner heart of each pebble enriched. I give my heartfelt thanks to these two Chinese students and their mothers. I give my thanks to the land and water that raised you so wise and strong. I believe that your stories will be heard by many people, so that increasing numbers will understand how to respect life and the older generation, our parents by our side. We should love those who pass on such things, between cultures, between people. Those who pass on help and understanding between people and the environment in which they live.'

It was through these two young people that I got to know a group of Chinese students who were standing on their own two feet and making themselves strong. The majority were first-generation only children, but compared to their spoiled contemporaries, their lives and attitudes to responsibility were as different as heaven and earth. In May 2008 I received a letter from one of them.

Xinran,

I believe that you must be weeping for China's children, as we are. In the great earthquake on 12 May, over 1,000 school buildings in Sichuan's earthquake zone collapsed completely, killing approximately 9,000 schoolchildren. (In fact, nobody knows the true number of deaths from the Wenchuan earthquake, because the government has not released an accurate figure.)

We did some simple research and discovered that, after the great Kantō earthquake in 1923 in Japan, the Law for the Promotion of Earthquake-Proofing of Buildings ruled that all public school buildings must be extensively earthquake-proofed, and new schools had to be built in accordance with the newest rigorous earthquake-resistant standards. Existing schools had to undergo regular earthquake resistance testing, and those with problems were required to be reinforced or rebuilt. From that time on, Japanese schools became refuges from natural disasters and war.

On 10 April 1933 a 6.3-magnitude earthquake struck Long Beach, California, leaving 120 people dead and 50 million dollars' worth of damage. Seventy schools collapsed and 120 were badly damaged. The Field Act, sponsored by Californian congressman Charles Field, was passed a month later, and, once implemented, Californian schools and hospitals became some of the safest buildings in the world.

China's seismologists and architects must all know that much of China lies on the Pacific earthquake belt. There have been seventy-eight large earthquakes since records began, with more than ten in the last century alone. However, our notions of earthquake-proofing have not evolved with modern civilisation; still less have we drawn any kind of lessons on how to protect our children from the price paid by hundreds of thousands in the Tangshan earthquake of 1976. The schools of Wenchuan in Sichuan province became demons that devoured children's lives. Many of the buildings that collapsed in residential areas were schools. By approving shoddily built 'crumbly tofu' projects, corrupt officials and their unscrupulous lackeys cut off almost 10,000 lives in the bud, with countless families losing their only child.

We also learned that the majority of those buried in these paradises of learning were children from small countryside villages, while there was no major loss of life in city schools in the same area. Xinran, can it really be that the poverty gap makes the difference between life and death? Does poverty determine our chance of survival in random natural-disaster statistics? Do those parents of only children, who've never had a day's rest from toil, have to endure this agony all because of inequality? What's wrong with China? Is it an illness? Or has the country's conscience been totally eroded by money?

There is a sound basis for these questions. Thirty years ago I started to realise that Chinese people were so busy with internal struggles and politics that nobody had any time for science and day-to-day life. We've been preoccupied with making money for ourselves and our families for so long that nobody has stopped to think about the negative side effects of this frenetic activity. In another thirty years our children will be the victims of today's busyness. However, it never occurred to me that today's children would have to pay for our blind busyness with their actual lives. This should be a source of painful remorse and resentment, if we can still feel the pain of human nature, buried beneath all that money.

In 2009 I visited Denmark, where a group of scholarship students from China had invited me to speak at an academic conference. After the talk was over, a PhD student came and spoke to me. 'Teacher Xinran, I couldn't get in to your talk, but I sat outside listening all the way through. I was overcome with emotion. It's been years since I've felt so deeply moved. I just want to ask you two questions: when will I finally be *ready* (she used the English word), and when I'm *ready* what is the most valuable thing I can do for China?'

I asked her, 'What do you mean when you say *ready*?'

'I mean when I have enough knowledge and ability,' she said uncertainly. 'I'm studying charities, and want to make a contribution of my own by building up China's NGOs.'

'Well then,' I said. 'Why do you think that China to this day has no charity laws? Why does it not acknowledge the NGO system?' I wanted to learn more about this from her.

'I think it's probably because charities come from the principles of Christianity. Developed countries in Europe and America regard NGOs as one of the three pillars of government, economy and society. They support them in commercial law and give them appropriate government funding. However, in China, where there is no freedom of religion or an independent judiciary, NGOs might be misunderstood, exploited, or even get drawn into bribery and corruption. Apparently, a draft of the first charity law is being debated in China at the moment. But in reality, Chinese people are always several steps ahead of the government and the constitution. Chinese volunteers are already devoting themselves to charitable work, it's just that the safeguarding systems and training for charities are not up to much. On the one hand, there are many people already helping charities develop. On the other, they are hindered by the lack of results from charitable projects.'

I greatly admired her attitude. 'That's just how it is. China currently has a very primitive perception of charitable endeavours. Many people hold the simplistic belief that charitable cultural activity is just going to the countryside, herding children into a classroom and making them study something. But in many rural areas, parents need their children's help at home, so they are understandably strongly opposed to their children sitting down and studying. I often wonder why volunteers use city methods for countryside children? Does learning have to take place in a classroom? If these children spend all day carrying water and firewood, but have nothing to eat when they get home, why don't we set up classrooms on the road where they will pass by when carrying water? Why don't we help them carry water and scavenge for firewood, and teach them reading, maths and history at the same time? Then their parents might support the volunteers. I have to ask you though, why do you think you need to finish your studies before you can be *ready*?'

She looked at me thoughtfully for a while before answering. 'I belong to the first generation of only children. When I was growing up, both my parents were busy with their work, which took them away from home. My granny raised me from when I was very small, in an extremely poor, deprived village. I didn't go to the city to live with my parents until I reached middle-school age, but by then I'd already developed a phobia of the outside world. It felt like the only safe place was the classroom, and if I stuck my head out into society I'd fall into a deep abyss, so I just kept on studying. Now I'm about to finish my PhD, and I'm running out of things to study. Besides, I'll be thirty soon, so I think I must be *ready*, right?'

This is an opinion I often hear from Chinese students. They only feel *ready* at the very end, but miss so many chances while waiting for it. When learning English, they feel that they need all the vocabulary before they can open their mouths and speak. When looking for work, they feel they have to have a university diploma before they are up to scratch. Even in marriage, they think they must wait until they have a car and a flat before they can work on marriage itself . . .

I said to her, 'I don't know if I can say precisely whether or not you are *ready*. *Ready* is not the ability to summon the wind and rain, it isn't about whether you can build a whole new world by yourself. Being *ready* is a kind of faith that comes automatically to anyone alive. Take me, for example, I'm only one drop of water in the vast river of China. I'm not as fresh and lively as a spring, nor as wide as a river, but the drop of water I represent might be able to keep one blade of grass green, and someone a little bigger could perhaps water a tree. I believe I am already *ready*.

'Running an NGO and carrying out charitable work should follow the same reasoning. Take the example of helping children study. If the children in a family get an education because of your support and help, the whole family's faith in life gets a boost. So many of our people are educated now, and if each person helps one child then the whole family will benefit from the education, and all the happiness and good things that go with it. When the child has children of their own, still more people will reap the benefit. When will we be *ready*? I think that as long as we can manage the simplest things in life by ourselves, like finding food and shelter, then we're *ready*. Besides, just now you mentioned something very interesting. Why do you think the classroom is safe, but you'll fall into a pit if you stick your head outside into society?'

When she heard this question, her wise, thoughtful eyes darkened. 'My dad didn't like me because I'm a girl. He thought I'd made him lose face, and soon after I was born he packed me off to live with my grandmother in his home village, in the poorest part of Henan province. There were no toilets in the village, just two big cesspits about a metre and a half deep. Over 200 households, with only one pit for men and one for women, surrounded by maize stalks smeared in mud for a wall. There were two wobbly planks set over the big pits, where men and women, young and old, all squatted to relieve themselves. I was terrified of falling in when I was small.

'When I was about five I started to work in the fields and about the house, as Granny said that girls who don't work get no food. The jobs were so tiring that the cesspit became my refuge. I'd sneak off there, squat down and read. When Granny found out she took my books away, saying, "What's the use of a girl reading? If you were meant to study your dad wouldn't have sent you here." But there was nowhere else where I could get away from the back-breaking work, let alone find a place to play, so I would to squat on the two planks above the cesspit, and look down on the little maggots crawling about on the bottom. Those poor maggots, only the size of a couple of green beans, climbing up the wall of the pit. Arching their bodies with each wriggle, most got halfway up and fell back; hardly any of them made it all the way up. After struggling through extreme difficulty for half an hour, many of them would make a wrong turn and go tumbling back in! The ones lucky enough to escape were mostly trodden on or poisoned by farm chemicals, barely any lived out their natural lifespans. All because they were maggots, a lower form of life. How was this different to the fate of us country girls out in the wilds?

'After I returned to the city for middle school, every time I did my homework I would "see" those little maggots. I told myself, I'm climbing up just like them, I've got to get to the top, I've got to do well in my exams. If I blow my exams then I'll fall back down into that pit! Even after I got to university, and then to Denmark, I was still beset by this fear. Just like those little maggots, I was afraid that one moment of ignorance or a single mistake would bring a great foot down on my aspirations, crushing my faith to death. I've always been too embarrassed to tell anyone, but the truth is, my whole life's struggle was inspired by those little maggots in my granny's village cesspit!'

I have been to similar places in the countryside, and squatted above similar large cesspits. I too have been moved by the tireless perseverance of those maggots, but it never crossed my mind that they could become a source of culture and entertainment for a young girl. Still less that they could be transformed into the motive power behind her success. All this in the age of China's power and prosperity!

When the young woman I remember as 'Ready Girl' learned that I was writing a draft of this book, she sent me an essay from a report by journalist Cheng Ying, in the 37th issue of *Outlook Asia Weekly*.

It is estimated that there are currently over one hundred million only children in China. The issues and risks surrounding this enormous group, which are the result of exceptional historical circumstances, are attracting ever-increasing attention.

Since 2002, Professor Mu Guangzhong from the Centre for

Population Research at Beijing University has stated many times that 'one-child families are intrinsically risky families'.

The Five Risks of Only-child Families

Risks in growing up, in particular of dying young or serious illness. According to statistics, out of every thousand newborn babies approximately 54 die before they are twenty-five, and 121 die before the age of fifty-five. According to figures from the fifth population census in 2000, over 570,000 families in rural areas have been left without descendants after the death of a child. Moreover, the survival of only children directly influences the survival of their families. If problems arise in the early stages of life, they can be alleviated through remedial education, but if an older child dies early or suffers a serious or debilitating illness or injury, then the impact on the family is often disastrous.

Expectations that the child will be exceptionally talented. The saying goes, 'A single stick of firewood is hard to burn, and a single child is hard to teach.' A variety of factors including excessively focused parental love, excessively high hopes, and unscientific child-drearing and teaching methods have resulted in a number of only-child families overestimating the achievements that their children can realistically be expected to make. Moreover, if the parents become seriously ill, die or divorce, this also adversely influences the child's life, studies and work.

Provision for old age within the family. Along with the above two risks, there is also the risk of providing for old age. Even if the former two risks are avoided, provision for latter years is still a problem. The economic circumstances of a child's family, relations between the two generations, allocation of living space and many other factors may lead to problems in ageing parents' day-to-day care, emotional support and economic provision. Only-child families are less able than multiple-child families to look after their elderly relatives, as there is only one source of support, which leaves little room for manoeuvre.

If an only child moves away or suffers an unexpected accident, the parents will be left without alternative means of support in their old age, and no other forms of help currently exist.

Risk to social development. The aforementioned risks also affect the development of the whole society. Only children must enter society, and the question of whether they can adequately fulfil their roles as citizens is of vital importance.

Risk to national defence. If a war were to break out, or some other occasion requiring only children and their families to make sacrifices, risks to national defence would exist to a certain degree.

Professor Mu stated that from the point of view of life cycles, the only-child generation bears the heaviest burden. When only-child families come up against the challenges of only-child ageing or no-child ageing that come at the end of their life cycles, they will lack even the smallest room to manoeuvre. Only children have no experience in kinship between brothers and sisters, and growing up in an environment without companions has left them bereft of opportunities to learn from others, or the possibility of helping and being helped by others. This precious culture of close family feelings has been lost.

A few far-sighted people are aware of these risks to only-child families. But what can we do to minimise these risks?

By the summer of 2011, practically all the dangers that Professor Mu warned of in 2006 had come to pass. Families shattered after losing their only child in the Sichuan earthquake numbered in the hundreds of thousands. Cases of only children ruined by excessive wealth are no longer newsworthy events. The number of only-child families struggling under the burden of caring for their parents in old age is growing daily. Disturbances in society caused by only children appear one after another. Not only are rifts forming between different social classes, but the bitter struggle between city and countryside is becoming ever more heated. Experts and scholars are increasingly concerned that the exceptional nature of family structures and parent–child relationships in one-child families have affected this generation's physical and psychological health, and their scientific, cultural and moral education. These factors, among others, will affect recruitment into the army, and its strength, in ways that are hard to predict. This made me think of what German social scientist Ulrich Beck said in his book *Risk Society*, that, today, risks in general are greater and no longer only refer to the natural world but also to man-made ones that form part of the wider social environment. Are China's man-made risks increasing in severity because of the only-child phenomenon? Could it be that our thirty years of toil are similar to the little maggots in Ready Girl's memory? No sooner have we clambered to the edge of the pit than we go tumbling back in again because of a single mistake?

In the spring of 2010 I visited Harvard a second time with a group of Chinese students for a debate titled, 'Are we carrying out a globalisation movement, or are we just entering an anglicised world?' A fair number of Western students were also present. When the discussion turned to communication between nations, everybody thought that this should be multicultural in nature and for the mutual benefit of all, not just a uniform, simplistic strengthening of English-language culture.

A female student asked in a quiet voice, 'But Xinran, if there is no common language, how can races with no common culture communicate?'

I like talking with students because of their naked, unadorned questions, which often bring me back and force me to reconsider the basics. 'That's an excellent question!' I said. 'My husband's English, and every time I go back to China with him I feel sad, because it's my customs and native soil, but I have to speak to him in his language and respect his cultural practices. How is that fair? We account for a quarter of this huge world's population, but where can we hear the voices of Chinese people speaking out? I once told him that when he goes to China, he should speak our language and get used to our customs and life – you know, when in Rome do as the Romans do, right? My husband pulled a sour face and said to me, "I've learned Latin, a very difficult language, but that was at university. Isn't it a bit late for me to start learning Chinese now, at over sixty? Besides, in the past there were very few people who talked about China, and even fewer who dared to go there. I went when Chinese people's thoughts were still bright red and their clothes blue-grey, but when I came back to the Western world I couldn't find anyone in our society who was interested. When I first raised the idea of representing Chinese authors in the 1980s, everybody said I was crazy. Publishers even asked me, who cares about China?"

'He continued: "Although China has started to make its mark in today's world, everyone uses English to discuss China, because at the present time it's the international language of communication. This has led to a lot of unfairness, as people believe that global communication must be carried out according to the conventions of the English-speaking world. But the cultures and customs of English-speaking countries are often at odds with the majority of other countries in the world, and this is unfair to them. So what fair, commonly used method of communication *should* we use between different nationalities?

"'Over the course of human civilisation, these difficult issues have been tackled numerous times, such as Arabic numerals that are commonly used in every culture, and the system of picture warning signs for emergency and rescue, which have been in use since the First World War, and which are getting more comprehensive all the time. Then there's red, yellow and green traffic lights, which are not limited to language, region, technical know-how or anything of that sort. But we seem not to have drawn any lessons from these truths. In the process of globalisation, our knowledge of other cultures and customs should increase, instead of one side giving and the other receiving. But nowadays, all nations have come thronging to a cultural crossroads, pushing and shoving, complaining and blaming each other, because there is no traffic light system in our cultural communication that everybody can understand and where everybody is equal. So, what is this traffic light system? A system of government, economics or education? Or law, democracy and human rights?"'

Two or three voices disputed this. 'Then what exactly is democracy? A society with the family as the unit? If there's a family of a mum, dad and children, do the children have a right to free speech or a right to vote?'

One young man said, his face full of self-righteousness, 'Of course they do, otherwise it's a feudal family.'

'Not necessarily,' said a male voice from the corner, each syllable clearly enunciated and seemingly very sure of its own opinions. 'Most of us come from only-child families, and have no experience of a big family, but it's not hard to figure out if you use your head. In a "democratic family" with many children, if every child is able to exercise decision-making power, that family will never have a family holiday, or even a family dinner! It's the power of the mother and father in the family that brings family education and life together, and forms them into something meaningful. If human society has its roots in the family, why are we using so-called democracy to destroy the foundations of human life?'

The proud and self-righteous student replied, 'Well, perhaps the true importance of democracy has more to do with elections, human rights and freedom, not just freedom of speech?'

The voice from the corner came louder now, the tone a little heavier. 'Do citizens who have the right to vote necessarily have any concept of national security, or spare any thought for social fairness? If they lack these then their vote is led by the media and by whatever benefits them personally. Is there an impartial media anywhere in the world at present? Has humanity evolved away from selfishness and greed? If you've got a family with three children, and the children decide not to go to school and play computer games all day, should the parents, who are in the minority, go along with that "democratic decision"? Or should they force their children to go to school for their own good? This is a very big source of ambivalence in China's only-child society; we simplify democracy, the political system and the law into statistics and whatever benefits us. It's impossible for a couple with one child to have democratic education within the family, you either get a child mollycoddled with soppy love, or you get oppression. We have no brothers and sisters, so there's no possibility of equal communication inside the family!'

'That seems to be true,' said several girls, nodding their heads in agreement.

'I think,' continued the voice from the corner, 'that China lacks the ability to communicate with Western developed countries on a level playing field. Because of the differences between cities and countryside, the gap between rich and poor and between generations, it's impossible for us to communicate with them as a single, unified China. Only children who grow up in cities find it very hard to understand their classmates from the countryside. Country folk seem stingy and antisocial to them, but this is only because they've never had the material wealth to be consumers.'

'That's a bit strong, isn't it?' the other interrupted. 'It's not like we've never been to the countryside, and are we really unwilling to help our poverty-stricken classmates? The reason we don't get on so well is more down to cultural differences.' Clearly these students all came from the cities.

The debate had become like drops of water falling into a pot of boiling oil, where neither could exist alongside the other. I could barely distinguish who was saying what. It was plain that several of the Western students had never seen battle lines drawn up like this, and some were plainly lost. I thought that no matter how good their Chinese, they would not be able to follow a debate carried out in this tone and at such a speed! I raised my hand for silence. 'I'm sorry, I have a suggestion: in our "democratic discussion" shouldn't we respect each other's right to speak? If we Chinese people can't agree on a way of communicating between ourselves, how can other people taking part in the debate follow our train of thought? If we can't communicate properly then we're no more than a pile of fragments, which the world will have to try to piece together to form a concept of China. And whose mistake will that be?' I pointed to the voice in the corner, 'I believe you hadn't finished what you were saying before you were interrupted. Please continue, but keep it short so there's time for the other students.'

'I know that you city people all have good hearts,' he continued, 'and I know you've helped us poor students in the past. But what I'm trying to say is that you've never lived in poverty. You don't have a family who worries every day about keeping warm and putting food on the table, nor are you anxious about the possibility of returning to that poverty. Although we're all only children, we don't belong to the same class in society. It's like what we've just been saying about globalisation, the West's concern for China, their help, is perhaps like city people's attitude to country folk, a one-off giving, not living side by side for a generation. Equal communication just does not exist. What we need is not one-off gifts, but understanding and respect that lasts a generation.' The voice in the corner disappeared back into the shadows, but his words seemed to have pushed the whole classroom into a corner of silence.

After the talk, many of the students continued to debate internationalisation, China and family democracy. That was my hoped-for result, as I believe that stimulating young people's ideas into life is one of the most important principles in education. That one-and-a-half-hour lecture ran for three hours, right up until we had to call a halt for supper.

When I was leaving the lecture theatre, I noticed a very skinny, frail Chinese student standing at the back, who had not said a word the whole time. I guessed that he was either politely letting others go first, or else he was shy. Every time I give talks in the West, I always do what I can to give Chinese students a chance to speak, because they get so few opportunities to hear guest lectures from Chinese scholars. I took the initiative and approached him.

'Hello, you're waiting very politely for your turn, aren't you? Perhaps a bit too politely, even? Holding back in such a gentlemanly way,' I said to him.

'No, it's not like that,' he replied. 'I'm not at this college, so I don't want to take up their time. My old classmate, the one in the corner, has already said what I think. I'm not an arts student, so can't express myself that well. Besides, I only came here to see you because you remind me of my mother,' he said, with some embarrassment.

'Where is your mother?' I asked. Perhaps because I have a son of my own, I am always touched by sons who think of their mothers.

'She's at home, in the countryside outside Guiyang. A little village that isn't marked on any map. Look at the book I bought for her.' He waved an English hardback edition of *The Good Women of China*; the look in his eyes appeared to be coming from the bottom of a deep, dark well.

'Does your mother read English?' Several Guizhou women I had interviewed appeared in my mind, pickers of mushrooms in the wild mountains. Practically none of them could read.

'No, she can't even read Chinese. My mother only knows the character for woman, 女nǚ, and that's her name as well.'

'Then why would you buy her an English book?' I really could not think of any reason.

'Because the stories in your book are a lot like her experiences,' he said.

'How does your mother know about my book?' I asked.

'I often read your column in the *Guardian*, and I noticed that your photo looks a lot like her. My family isn't well off, and she's never had her picture taken, so I used your photo to stand in for hers, and stuck it over my bed in my dormitory,' he said awkwardly. 'At Chinese New Year, I borrowed my classmate's mobile phone and gave my uncle a call. They were all getting together for New Year, and I told my mum about some of the stories you've written. When she heard them she said it was like they were written about her. She said she never thought that there would actually be people who bothered their heads about small women like her. So I bought the book and kept it to give to her. She can't read it, but she can keep it at home anyway. It's full of Chinese women's stories, her stories.'

Tears were starting to well up in my eyes. 'Did you come abroad on a scholarship?' I asked.

'Yes, a full three-year scholarship for a doctorate in maths, with more money than I can use.'

More money than he could use? I thought. There's actually a Chinese student who doesn't know how to spend all his money?

His name was Zonghui, which means 'bringing glory to the ancestors', and he was in his second year at Harvard. I gradually got to know his group of poor Chinese students who had all come out together, including the voice in the corner. Their professor told me that they represented an alternative image of Chinese students at Harvard, owning only two or three sets of clothes for all the four seasons. They had no mobile phones or computers and never wasted food. They were always reading, and excelled at their studies. *These* were the pride of China! I later learned that Zonghui survived on a daily diet of fifty cent chips. He never used washing powder, but washed all his clothes by hand with a bar of soap. Whatever he could save from his scholarship he took home to his mother, because she had never felt able to spend money, and had never bought herself so much as a comb.

Zonghui told me that when he left to go abroad to study, his mother could only see him off as far as the end of the village because she had no money for a long-distance bus ticket. He would never forget the few words she spoke at their parting, which came chasing after his heart: 'My child, study well, live well! So many kids have never even touched a book. When you get on the plane, don't open the window, don't let yourself get blown by the wind!'

When I heard this story, I too could hear that mother calling out to her son: 'My child, study well, live well!'

That day, I sent myself an email.

Live well, my friend, for the sake of those ancestors who laboured in poverty. For the sake of those children who have never touched a book. For the sake of those mothers who have never been on a bus or plane. For the sake of those sisters who never had a chance to live. For the sake of former generations who gave us today. Every mother, every season, every stone, every leaf. Live well, live very well!

But what is living well? Do our children understand it? Why is it that children who grew up in poverty, who never had the chance of an education, are able to enjoy every crumb and morsel of what they do have, while children who grew up fed and clothed, educated and cherished, often end up sighing over their woes? Why do so many children from rich families regard their relatives as the enemy, and treat love as a source of resentment? Do we parents truly understand what it is to live well? We raised our children to adulthood, but did we nurture their faith and life skills?

As we approach a society of solely only children, these are questions that we all seek the answer to, including me.

How do you view the Yao Jiaxin incident? Why is Chinese society debating him (a past-80s man) so fiercely?

Zonghui's answer:
In my opinion, the Yao Jiaxin tragedy, and please allow me to call it a tragedy, is the very image of a tortured soul, and reflects the sadness that has infected society. His parents never taught him the basic moral principles of how to be a good citizen, or even a good human being. This kind of thing is happening all over China now, so stories like this and other less extreme ones are quite understandable.

However, as a relatively normal college student myself, I don't really understand how he could act like this. His inability to face up to the world and his lack of any sense of responsibility is really shocking. I know everyone's different, and that the young are always a bit self-obsessed, this is normal, but it shouldn't go as far as killing, it's unbelievably selfish. And all the arguments on the internet at the moment are just adding to everyone's fear. Everyone's thinking, What if some rich kid were to run over me or my family?

AFTERWORD

I RETURN to China once or twice a year but I always feel unable to keep pace with the changes in my motherland.

Since the 1980s China has brought about the most incredible era in human history. An era of only children that has transformed families and society. In the space of thirty years, China has taken a flying leap over ground that took the West more than 170 years of post-Industrial Revolution toil to cover. But the speed of development has varied greatly across different cities and towns, fluctuating and fragmenting like some frenzied computer game, while the remote countryside has been abandoned, left centuries behind in the wake of rapid city modernisation. So much so that any part of the country's 9.6 million square kilometres and its people are in constant danger of finding themselves consigned to the history books. I always sigh in amazement at the older people who have witnessed three or four generations of history. How can they face the world outside their window? A world where everything has been turned on its head. A world where their own children and grandchildren have changed so fast and so much.

Chinese author and painter Su Shi (1037–1101), who lived during the Northern Song dynasty, believed that a true hero is 'unafraid when suddenly attacked and not angry when criticised without reason'. Put another way, today's 1.3 billion Chinese people accept the overwhelming onslaught of politics and economics as something too commonplace to be worth thinking about, and allow the hundreds of reproaches from the West to waft past their ears without taking them in. There are heroes in every place, with courage and an imperturbable spirit forged from months and years of hardship. 'China is a sleeping lion,' Napoleon once warned. 'Let her sleep, for when she wakes she will shake the world.' The two previous generations woke that sleeping lion with their belief and toil, fed it its first meal on waking, gave it strength, and enabled it to roar its first roar to a world that had ignored it. These same old people are still leading their children by the hand, instructing them on how to 'buy the whole world outright' one step at a time. They have indeed done that: Asian companies, factories in Africa, even traditional leather-working villages in Italy and an entire French shopping street have been purchased. While the world struggles in a maelstrom of debt, three generations of Chinese have linked hands to snap up American and European companies. But, when they no longer have the strength to assist their children, will China's youth, these only children, be able to take on the heavy responsibility for which their parents fought? What will they do with the map of China, as it expands in ways that affect the whole world? Will these children be able to bring up this lion, which has waited so long for its chance to leap and run? If they can, will they have the energy to keep it alive? I long to know the answers to these questions, as this future China will belong to my son and grandchildren.

When I went back to China recently, apart from devouring interviews and articles, I also caught glimpses of the marks left on this era by the first generation of only children. They were everywhere. On elevated city metros, in the streets and alleys of towns, and in the villages discarded in their wake.

Everywhere I looked in big towns and cities I saw the main characters from this book. In the tide of expensive sports cars I saw countless Du Zhuangs and Glitterings, discussing international trade in English on their flashy mobile phones. On the road to and from work, I saw Moons rushing hither and thither, their minds pulled in all directions at once, thinking about work, missing their children, worrying about several generations of elderly family members. On the grass in parks at weekends, I saw Shiny's children laying down the law to several older generations clustered around them. In restaurants on main streets and narrow alleys, I saw Wing's lonely parents, wordlessly watching the cheery family meals at neighbouring tables. I saw postal companies booming, as they delivered messages and parcels for the Lilies and Flying Fishes, couriering concerns and assuaging thirsts between families in China and their children abroad. In the low, narrow farmhouses and dilapidated classrooms of the countryside, I saw my 'teachers' toiling over books by moonlight. I saw their peers, who didn't have a clue about books, counting the seasons and earning money. Their parents unable to resist converting every last cent into words and knowledge on sheets of paper. In the stream of people coming and going through China's 266 and more airports, I saw a new generation of countless Golden Swallows jumping for joy, along with dispirited and withdrawn Firewoods, all making their farewells, waiting in that space between dreams and reality.

But there is more to this first generation of only children than can be found in this book alone. There are taxi drivers with permits inherited from their parents, and extended again after twenty years, toiling day and night, ferrying important people no older than themselves to and from work. They wait through the night to whisk home children from nouveau riche families after their late-night revelries, and listen as other passengers sigh with emotion over their fate, unable to keep up with the country's ever increasing GDP. There are helicopter parents waiting to drop off or collect, guarding and watching, mollycoddling their only child on behalf of three generations, circling like helicopters over their precious child's life, ready to land at any moment, to pass the paper when their little darling needs the toilet at primary school, to dust down their precious treasures after playtime at secondary school, even to arrange ghost writers for their children who cannot cope with their university coursework. Behind the little shops and market stalls you find everywhere on the edges of towns, young mothers are scraping together their child's costly school fees from the minuscule profits from their stock of odds and ends. There are young fathers, construction workers, whose sweat falls like rain as they cling to scaffolding, whose talk and memories always turn back to their home villages that have neither wealth nor power, water nor electricity. Then there are the sons and daughters who never get a chance throughout childhood to see their frantically busy parents, have no time or space to play, toiling to build a future that leads to the white-collar class, aspiring to a life with what they deem 'basic standards' in modern China, to be able to buy a flat, drive a car and get married.

This is period in history that I struggle to see, imagine or learn about in its entirety. Like clouds, rain and wind, with drifting and unsettled shapes, it has the power to sweep things away as easily as breaking a branch from a dead tree.

When I left China in 1997 I had the first computer in our radio station. When I returned in 1999, only a few large radio stations were starting to lead the way with computer layout and control systems. In 2000 computers were moving from a fashion to a necessity in the life of the 400 big cities. By December 2010, China's netizens numbered 457 million.* This first generation of only children are pioneers of computer and internet education. Their curiosity and enthusiasm have given rise to a 'cultural revolution' in its truest sense in modern China, setting speech free and opposing political power online. This has led to the creation of a political space that neither politics nor the law can easily rein in, and all this in a nation

* Figure taken from the National Network Information Centre's 'Twenty-seventh Statistical Report on China's Internet Development'.

which over 5,000 years never once witnessed an age that dared to challenge the emperors or the ruling power. As my friend and translator of this book, Esther Tyldesley, says of translation from Chinese to English, 'Nobody can fit a cloud in a box! The system of political censorship, which has ruled absolutely in China's recent past, is having great difficulty in cutting down the freedom of the masses to shout out their thoughts.'

Around 2002, young Chinese university graduates began flooding onto the internet, under the banner of 郁闷 *yumen*, launching the first search for a symbol for China's first generation of only children. The word *yumen* means wishing to speak but struggling to find words, having trouble coping with events, and helplessness when dealing with other people. Around 2006, the post-80s generation, unwilling to be left behind, took the term 纠结 *jiujie* (tangled) as the special characteristic of their time. It represented living in diffi-cult circumstances, with hearts and minds in turmoil, and mentally and physically out of sorts. And the post-90s? It was only in my most recent visit to China that I learned the word that represents them, 囧 *jiong*. Originally, *jiong* meant 'bright', but from 2008 onwards it became a popular emoticon among Chinese netizens, and one of the most commonly used characters in chats, discussion boards and blogs. It means 'depressed, melancholy and helpless'. Some people say that *jiong* is the coolest character of the twenty-first century.

Yumen, jiujie, jiong? They reminded me of experiences in my own youth, dazed and perplexed, caught up in fantasies and desperately busy.

The 1970s were the dizzy days of my twenties. Thirty years of political turmoil were drawing to a close, but none of us knew it, and we were powerless to imagine what the future might hold, for the nation or for our family fortunes. The 1980s were the fantasy years of my thirties, a time when anybody could go into business and become a boss, but equally a time when anyone could become a criminal and find themselves in prison. The 1990s was the frantically busy decade of my forties, a time when many Chinese people woke up with a start to the truth. If they wanted to release their long-repressed selves they could give up following the party, turn their backs on the nation, even discard family members. They were ready to climb as high as the heavens and dig deep into the earth, stopping at nothing in their quest for opportunities to change their fate.

The generation before mine was, in many ways, a tragic one. The 1950s were full of hope for a new China, as well as high morale and a fighting spirit. But the frenzy of the 1960s split the country and drenched it in fresh blood. Then the 1970s brought a disconsolate melancholy, with its struggles against all the forces of nature. Families were broken and scattered, yet nobody was sure what it was all for.

People often gasp in amazement that these three generations of Chinese people had such unprecedentedly different experiences of youth. But I am not sure that this is completely the case. The generations from 1950 to 2010 have a great many genes in common, all inherited from Chinese history. Seeking a common voice in the midst of complaints, stirred by emotion in the midst of tragedy, with no shortage of resolve when in poverty, but oblivious to pitfalls ahead when wealthy. Class distinctions abound, with power and wealth holding equal status with dignity and honour. We were 'opening up' an age that was to be ours, but leaving behind the universe our ancestors knew. We tried to plan our own sun and moon, so it is no surprise that our children, our only children, take it as given that they can buy the stars!

Just as I was about to lay down my pen after yet another draft, a new tidal wave crashed into Chinese society, sparking off another post-Yao Jiaxin controversy over attitudes to morality, the understanding of law and the value of life, all of which took place far outside the realms of common sense.

At 5.30 p.m. on 13 October 2011, Yueyue, a little girl just two years old, was crushed twice by a minivan, then run over again by a small delivery vehicle several minutes later. In seven minutes, eighteen people walked past little Yueyue, who was crying and calling out weakly, lying in her own blood, but not one came to her aid. Eventually, a woman scavenging for rubbish picked up the girl, who by now was gasping her last breaths, carried her to the side of the road and handed her over to her mother, who had come looking for her. Three days later the little girl passed away, leaving behind a young father and mother in an agony of grief and also leaving behind a fierce debate on China's ethics and morals.

I imagine that if those eighteen bystanders were sitting around a table after a good dinner, discussing a similar case, the majority would express intense hatred and disgust towards the wickedness and hard-heartedness they had read about elsewhere and, if circumstances allowed, would too have posted bitter diatribes on the internet under assumed names against such heartless, unfeeling behaviour. However, when brought face to face with little Yueyue, they ignored their consciences without a backward glance, as having no connection to real life.

For several weeks the waves churned and broke on Chinese internet sites. People were scandalised at the callous indifference of society and thrown into a panic over the seeming extinction in China of any kindness or code of ethics. Through little Yueyue, they realised that it was not just eighteen people who walked past a dying girl, but that such people can be found all over China, in all locations. They exist across occupations, ages and educational backgrounds. Almost every day when I check the internet, I see reports that cause Chinese people to wring their hands and sigh deeply in pain, even pound the table in indignation and shock.

Why? Why has the traditional morality and humanitarian code at the core of the Chinese nation hit rock bottom at this time, when the economy is developing at such a pace and standards of living are improving daily? Why is it that this new generation, reared from the life blood of the two generations before it, has food to eat, clothes on their backs, money to spend, and yet has lost all feelings of kinship and compassion? Have money and power made them dismiss morality and conscience as something of no use? Have these traits only been passed on to those living on the lower rungs of society, in the wilds of the countryside and in poverty-stricken places?

Perhaps the grief and fury of the Chinese people might in fact awaken this nation to self-examination and self-respect. Perhaps we Chinese may reflect, and once again recognise, the existence of darkness and light. Perhaps our pain will become a source of strength, a strength forged from the death of a young innocent. Perhaps this strength will lay aside the clouds and fog of power and material desires, and allow our only children to see and enjoy the sun, moon and stars of civilisation and morality.

ACKNOWLEDGEMENTS
My Heartfelt Thanks

EACH TIME I write acknowledgements, I am reminded of the narrowness within words and between lines. Every expression of thanks feels like a new seed planted in my life, so that my writing and life are lived in a green forest of gratitude.

It was Toby, my husband, who first encouraged me to write this book. He said that the world needs to understand this age created by China's first generation of only children. An age highly vulnerable to storms within the family, with every member suffering from this pressure in isolation. It is an age when social awareness and values have mutated, and what is being passed on to these new lives has had to navigate a series of massively changing faults and dislocations. It is an age of power politics, but also one of constraint, as China will struggle to expand its supremacy in the outside world when its people are unwilling to send their only children off to be soldiers. Thank you, my Toby, for being the driving force behind my writing.

But it was my only son Panpan who really caused me to live within this book. I once longed for many children, and dreamed of their games, squabbles and noisy jokes. I dreamed of presiding over their debates, dreamed of my brood sharing the small responsibilities of the household, dreamed of taking them to the fields for picnics, tasting and enjoying the delicacies each child had produced, and I dreamed of them one by one creating families and careers for themselves and presenting me with a series of cherubic grandchildren! The one-child policy deprived me of the right to become a mother to a crowd of sons and daughters, but by a stroke of great good fortune, I did become Panpan's mother. From that day forth, I warned myself never to let Chinese parents' traditional power or social pressures destroy my only son.

Like the mothers of all the only children in this book, the price I paid for my child was my own life. I was turning myself into bricks and mortar for his happiness, even willingly letting myself rot away into compost so that he might grow well and thrive, but I myself was never free. I piled all my hopes on his lonely shoulders. It had never occurred to me that the dreams of parents weigh heavily on their children. It was only when I met the young people described in this book, my son's contemporaries, and saw their struggles and hardships that I became aware of Panpan's loneliness. I would like to thank my child, Panpan, for sharing the weighty burden of life with me for twenty-four years. For working hard and forging ahead to repay his mother for raising him, and for helping me to enter into the hearts and souls of only children.

No matter how limited the space, and regardless of the poverty of my language, the one thing I must not leave undone is to thank the young people in this book. Without them, I would have had no way to understand this unique age of only children in such detail. Without them, I could not possibly have had this multi-layered reading of the only-child phenomenon. Without them, it would have been impossible for me to understand as I do the direction in which China is developing. Without them, I would not have been able to write this book. Without them, I would perhaps never have experienced my own dear child's solitary happiness, anger, grief and joy.

Thank you, Du Zhuang, for the clashes you went through in your first taste of independence. You opened the door that led me towards the first generation of only children. Thank you, Golden Swallow. Your brave flight gave me more space to see your generation. Thank you, Wing, for your ability to change the channel of your life, and ease my anxieties as a mother of an only child. Thank you, Lily, for the honesty and candour with which you live your life. Your pursuit of your beliefs comforts and inspires me with the knowledge that there will always be people to carry on China's traditions. Thank you, Moon, for your wise and far-sighted views, your perceptive understanding of Chinese society and your pain at the changing world of family emotions that has led me to ponder China's only-child families. Thank you, Shiny, for your description of the many-coloured lives of only children. Your stubborn affirmation of China's rights and wrongs reawakened my passionate spirit, which age had come close to driving into hibernation. Thank you, Firewood, for your will to strive against your fate in this world of the new millennium. You confirmed for me Chinese people's strength of will, like a single spark that sets the plains ablaze. Thank you, Glittering, for your ethics and ideas on right and wrong founded on emotions. You left me deeply moved by the Chinese spirit living within you single sprouts, a spirit that is becoming more healthy and vigorous by the day. Thank you, Flying Fish, for your daughterly love that politics and society could not destroy. It was a balm for my pain when I heard of the fathers and mothers who abandoned their only children for personal gain. Thank you, my 'teachers'. With your boundless energy you have nurtured wings as wide as an eagle's in your insect-like living spaces. You have given humankind pride in, and hope for, the Chinese people!

I am certain that from today onwards, China will thank your generation and your parents' generation for your gifts. Because of the price you paid, the spirit and roots of Chinese people have not dried up. The painful experiences of two generations of Chinese have not been forgotten. China's future has not been cut off or lost its way from its history because of man-made politics, because you hold the generations together, forming a link between what has gone before with what will come after.

My thanks to all the volunteers at Mothers' Bridge of Love (MBL).* Without your knowledge, your confirmation of my ideas and your contribution to my collection of experiences, this book might have been no more than the far-distant image of a lonely sail in the flood-tide of only children, buffeted to and fro by the current in China's age of great collisions. The support of the MBL volunteers has made this book more like a member of a vast crew of only children on the same ship, observed and gazed at from afar by the skies and oceans of the world.

Thank to my office staff, Nicola Chen, whose wise and intelligent questions often inspire me, and Cui Zhe, who assisted my recording and typing with her thoughtful questions on behalf of her post-80s generation. My thanks to Esther Tyldesley and David Dobson. They are not only university teaching fellows and the translators of my other books, but also valued teachers of mine, who have done the most to teach me the wisdom that comes from self-knowledge, and from that to know today's China. Every time we have a conversation, the time flies by, our topics always tightly packed with a little bit of everything, sweet, sour, bitter and spicy! Whenever I send them the manuscript of a book, I always wait for their comments like a primary school student waiting for a mark, an experience of longing and terror. It is as if they hold a ruler across my heart, one that might at any moment rap me for my ignorance! Without their knowledge of China and understanding of me, without their feeling for and awareness of China's culture and language, few Westerners would know the China whose story I wish to tell, or my own complex feelings towards China. Without translators, people would never be

* See Appendix III: The Mothers' Bridge of Love (MBL)

able to understand each other, or have a common understanding of peace and democracy.

I do not know how many more opportunities I will get to thank my editors on the printed page. Over the years I have been writing, I have seen people excitedly put everything they see and hear, all their perceptions, into the world of video, without ever really considering the matter. While paper, pen and ink and printed books are disappearing from under our fingertips, and gradually becoming words and images from history, I know that my own writing will be read on a screen in the end. But I am one of the lucky ones, who the people of the future may look back upon with longing, because I often still drink tea with my editors, hug them and scrawl points from our discussions on paper. I am so grateful to my editor Judith Kendra and her team for sharing all this with me, for what may be the last time, and observing with me this epoch-making era of Chinese only children. Without Judith's wise choices and professional guidance, this book would exist only in my heart, and the best it could hope for would be to wait as scrap, longing to find a use.

The list of people I would like to thank seems to be growing much faster than the days and months of my life. The same applies to you, my reader, for getting to know me here. I cannot go without thanking you for your time and interest, and for your thoughts and feelings that have travelled alongside mine, and for sharing this book with me from the first page.

APPENDIX I
China's Birth-Control Policy

YU XUEJUN, spokesperson for the Chinese National Population and Family Planning Commission, told journalists on 10 July 2007 that in the vast majority of provinces, autonomous regions and directly controlled municipalities, only children were allowed to have a second child. However, he was clear to point out that this did not imply a change in the country's birth-control policy, nor was the birth-control policy itself a fundamental cause for the imbalance in gender ratios at birth.

'China's birth-control policy is certainly not a "one foetus" or "one child" policy, rather there are guidelines for different categories of people, and there are differences between them,' Yu said. He stated that at present between 30 and 40 per cent of the population could have two or more children. According to the briefing, social development and population growth are very uneven in China because of the country's vast territory. Each region is at a different stage of development and has different population issues, so the rules were developed in order to allow each region to set its own specific birth-control policies. For example, the policy in Beijing, Shanghai and Tianjin, as well as Jiangsu, Sichuan and other provinces and big cities, is that one married couple can have one child. Nineteen provinces have ruled that in rural areas, if the first child is a girl, a second child is permitted. In the countryside of Hainan, Yunnan, Qinghai, Ningxia and Xinjiang provinces, current policy allows married couples to have two children. In Tibet and other sparsely populated areas, more than two children are allowed. In the vast majority of the country, if a husband and wife are both only children, they are allowed to have two children. Six provinces allow a rural couple to have two children if one parent is an only child.

For full details of China's family planning policy see: *npfpc.gov. cn/policies.*

APPENDIX II
The Dizigui

Summary

The rules for students are the teachings of the Sage.
First you must be reverent to your parents and elders, then
be respectful and trustworthy.

Love everybody, and get close to benevolent people.
If you have energy left over, study from books.

Filial respect for parents at home

When your mother and father call, you must not be slow to respond.
When your mother and father give an order you must carry it
out, and not be lazy.

When your mother and father instruct you, listen respectfully.
When mother and father reprimand you, accept it.

In the winter be warm, in the summer be cool.
In the morning examine your conduct critically, in the
evening make yourself calm.

When you go out you must tell your parents, when you come
back you must see your parents face to face.
Have regular habits in daily life, and make no changes in your career.

Even in small matters, you cannot just follow your own will.
If you just follow your own will, you will deviate from the
correct way that a son should follow.

Even with small things, you should not selfishly keep them to yourself.
If you selfishly keep things to yourself, your father and mother will be sad.

What your parents like, work hard to possess.
What your parents detest, carefully eliminate.

If your body is injured, it will cause your parents anxiety.
If your moral character is damaged, it will cause your parents shame.

If my parents love me, treating them with filial respect will not be hard.
If my parents detest me, and I still treat them with filial respect,
this is true virtue.

If parents make mistakes, remonstrate with them and make
them change their ways.
Your expression should be pleasant, your voice soft and gentle.

If the remonstrance is not accepted, try again when the
parents are in a good mood.
The next step is wailing and crying, even if beaten with a
whip you should not complain.

If your parents are ill, try their medicine first to make sure it
has been correctly prepared.
Wait on them day and night, without leaving their bedside.

Observe the three years of mourning, often weeping sadly.
Your place of residence should change, and you should avoid
wine and women.

At the funeral observe all the proprieties as best you can, when
holding sacrifices be as sincere as possible.
Serve the dead as you served them when they were alive.

Respect for elders outside the family

Elder brothers should be friendly and kind, younger brothers should
be respectful.
When brothers are in harmony, that is in itself an act of filial duty
towards their parents.

If you look lightly on possessions, how can resentment arise?
If you tolerate words, anger will naturally die away.

Whether in eating or drinking, in sitting or walking,
Elders go first, juniors follow behind.

If an elder calls for someone, then immediately call that
person on their behalf.
If that person is not there, then go yourself in the meantime.

When addressing an elder or better, do not call them by name.
In front of an elder or better, do not show off.

If you meet an elder on the road, promptly approach them and bow.
If the elder has nothing to say, then withdraw, and stand
by respectfully.

When riding get off the horse, when in a carriage get
down from the carriage.
Wait once the elder has passed you, until he is a hundred
paces or more away.

When an elder stands, juniors should stand.
When an elder sits, juniors should only sit down once they
have been ordered to sit.

In front of elders and betters, you should speak in a low voice.
But it is not appropriate to speak in such a low voice that you
cannot be heard.

When going in to see an elder one should be quick, when leaving an
elder one should be slow.
When asked a question, stand to reply, without moving your gaze.

Serve the elders of your father's generation as if you were serving
your father.
Serve the elders of your elder brother's generation as if you were
serving your elder brother.

Reverence

Get up early in the morning, go to sleep late at night.
Old age will come very easily, treasure this time.

In the morning you must wash your hands and rinse out your mouth.
On returning from defecation and urination, you must wash
your hands clean.

The hat must be worn straight, the buttons must be fastened.
Socks and shoes must be neatly and securely fastened.

For hats and clothing, there should be a fixed place.
Do not leave things lying any old how, this will lead to a sweaty mess.

In clothing value cleanliness, do not value flamboyance.
First keep to your station in life, then act as appropriate to the
economic circumstances of your family.

With eating and drinking do not be fussy or picky.
Stop eating when you have had sufficient, do not eat to excess.

When you are still young, do not drink alcohol.
Drinking to intoxication is the most ugly thing.

When walking set a leisurely pace, when standing stand upright.
When bowing be deep and round, when kneeling to
kowtow be reverent.

Do not tread on the doorsill, do not lean on one leg when standing.
Do not sit on the ground with legs open in front of you, do not
wiggle your bottom.

Open curtains slowly, without making a noise.
Turn corners widely, do not bump into corners.

Carry an empty vessel as if you were carrying a full one.
Enter empty rooms as though you were entering a room of people.

Do not do things in a hurry, if you are hasty many mistakes will occur.
Do not be afraid of difficulties, do not ask frivolous questions.

Never go near places where there are fights and disturbances.
Wicked or twisted things should not ever be spoken.

When you are about to go through a door, ask who is inside.
When going into the main hall, announce your arrival
in a ringing voice.

When other people ask who you are, tell them your name.
Just saying *It's me* is not clear.

When using other people's things, one must clearly ask.
If you do not ask first, that is stealing.

Trustworthiness

When borrowing other people's things, be timely in returning them.
When other people borrow your things, do not hold back if you
have them.

When you speak, honesty should come first.
Telling lies and rash, wild talk, how can one do such things?

It is better to say too little than too much
Only speak the truth, do not speak flowery, spurious words that
are not true.

Unkind words and filthy speech
And a vulgar air, are all things to be eliminated.

When seeing something which you have not determined is true,
do not hastily speak on the matter.
If you do not know if something is true, do not lightly pass it on.

When circumstances are not right, do not make promises lightly.
If you make a promise lightly, both proceeding to fulfil it and backing
out of it are wrong.

When you speak, your words should be solemn and relaxed.
Do not be in a hurry, do not be obscure or unclear.

One person gossips about one thing, another about a different thing,
If it does not concern you personally, do not meddle in it.

When seeing others do good, think about how to bring yourself
up to their level.
Even if you are far behind them, you can gradually improve.

When seeing other people being wicked, examine yourself.
If you are like that then correct it, if you are not like that take
it as a warning.

In virtue and learning, in talent and skill,
If you cannot compare with others, you should encourage
yourself to do better.

With clothing, living space or for eating,
If you cannot compare with others, do not be sad over it.

If you get angry when hearing about your mistakes, and happy when
hearing yourself praised,
Dangerous friends will come, and beneficial friends will draw back.

If you hear praise and are afraid, and are pleased when you hear
about your mistakes,
People of integrity and honesty will gradually become closer to you.

Things done wrong unintentionally, are called mistakes.
Things done wrong deliberately are called evil deeds.

If you put right what you have done wrong, it is as if it
never happened.
If you cover up your misdoing, that is adding to the fault.

All-embracing love

All who are human, you must love.
Heaven covers us all in the same way, the earth holds us all up in the
same way.

For people of high moral conduct, their reputation is naturally high.
It is not lofty bearing that people admire.

For people of great talent, their reputation is naturally great.
It is not big words that people admire.

If you have talent, you should not be selfish.
If other people have talent, do not disparage them.

Do not flatter the rich, do not be arrogant with the poor.
Do not reject the old, do not favour the new.

If someone is not at leisure, do not disturb him with your business.
If a person is not at peace, do not disturb him with words.

If somebody has shortcomings, be sure not to expose them.
If people have secrets, be sure not to tell them.

Talking about other people's good works, is in itself a good work.
When other people know about them, they will feel encouraged.

To spread other people's shortcomings abroad, is in itself wicked.
People detest it extremely, and disaster will follow.

If everyone encourages each other to virtuous behaviour,
everybody's virtue will be built up.
Not dissuading others from wrongdoing damages the moral
character of both people.

When receiving and giving, the most valued thing is to
make everything clear.
It is better to give more and take less.

When doing something to another, you must first question yourself.
If you would not like that same thing to be done to you, then
stop it at once.

Kindnesses should be reciprocated, grievances should be forgotten.
Repaying grudges is short, repaying kindness is long.

When dealing with servants, you are of a higher station.
Although you are of higher station, you should be
charitable and forgiving.

If you use force to make people submit to you, they will not give in
to you in their hearts.
Only by using reason to make people give in to you, will there be
no words of resentment.

Getting close to the righteous

All are human, but the types are not the same.
Vulgar people are many, benevolent people are rare.

A truly benevolent person is feared by most people.
In his speech he is not afraid of causing offence, there is no flattery
in his countenance.

If you get close to a benevolent person, there will
be limitless benefits.
Your virtue will improve by the day, your mistakes will
lessen by the day.

Not getting close to the benevolent, will bring limitless harm.
Petty and despicable people will enter, and everything will go to
the bad.

If there is any energy left over, study books

If you do not work hard on your conduct, and just study from books,
You will gain a superficial flashiness, and what sort of person is that?

If you work hard on your conduct, but do not study from books,
Then you will rely entirely on your own opinions, and be ignorant
of true principles.

Three things are required to study from books,
The heart, eyes and mouth, all of these are necessary.

When you have just started reading one book, do not hanker after
another.
When you have not finished one book, do not start another one.

Set wide limits, control your efforts tightly.
If the effort is in the right place, stagnations and blockages will be
cleared away.

If there is a question in your mind, make a note of it at once,
In order to ask people, and seek out the correct meaning.

The room should be tidy, the walls should be clean.
The table should be clean, pens and inkstone should be neatly arranged.

If the ink is ground unevenly, the mind is not regular.
If the words are not respectful, it is because the mind has
become diseased.

When arranging books, they should have a fixed place.
When you have finished reading them, return them to their
original place.

Even if you have urgent business, you should arrange the
book-scrolls neatly.
If anything is missing or broken, mend it immediately.

Books that are not the works of the sages should be rejected
without a single look.
They will mask your intelligence, and damage your mind and will.

Do not treat yourself with violence or give up on yourself.
Gradually, you will attain saintliness and virtue.

APPENDIX III

The Mothers' Bridge of Love (MBL)

The Mothers' Bridge of Love (MBL) is a UK-registered charity (registration number 1105543), set up by Xinran and a group of volunteers in 2004. MBL's aim is to provide Chinese cultural support to children in all corners of the world, by creating a bridge of understanding between China and the West and between birth and adoptive cultures, as well as helping education in rural China.

After ten years MBL's achievements include providing assistance, advice and educational activities for adoptive families around the world, supporting a number of disaster relief projects and building 15 libraries for children of migrant workers and children living in China's rural countryside. Now MBL invites Xinran's readers and families from all over the world to support MBL in creating more reading opportunities for children in rural China.

For On-Line Charity Donations
Please use this link http://www.everyclick.com/mothersbridge

OR

To make a donation to MBL, please post your CHEQUE to
MBL, 9 ORME COURT, LONDON, W2 4RL, UK

OR

Please WIRE the money to The Mothers' Bridge of Love (MBL)
Sort Code: 400607, Account Number: 11453130,
SWIFT Code: MIDL GB2142E, IBAN No.: GB08MIDL40060711453130
HSBC Bank, 1 Woburn Place, Russell Square, London WC1H 0LQ

Your heartfelt support will improve the education of Chinese
children from country to country, village to village …

Thank You – XIE XIE NIN!

Also available by Xinran:

The Good Women of China

For eight ground-breaking years, Xinran presented a radio programme in China during which she invited women to call in and talk about themselves. Broadcast every evening, Words on the Night Breeze became famous for its unflinching portrayal of what it meant to be a woman in modern China. Centuries of obedience to their fathers, husbands and sons, followed by years of political turmoil had made women terrified of talking openly about their feelings, and Xinran became the first person to hear their true stories.

This unforgettable book is the story of how Xinran reached out to women across the country, changing her understanding of China forever.

ISBN 978 0099440789

Order direct from www.penguin.co.uk

Sky Burial

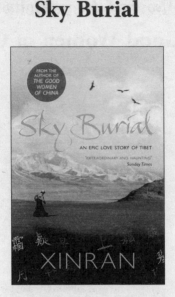

As a young girl in China, Xinran heard a rumour about a soldier in Tibet who had been brutally fed to the vultures in a ritual known as a sky burial. The tale frightened and fascinated her. Several decades later she met Shu Wan, a Chinese woman who had spent years searching for her missing husband. He had been serving as a doctor in Tibet, and her extraordinary story would unravel the legend of the sky burial.

In this haunting book, Xinran recreates Shu Wen's remarkable journey in an epic story of love, loss, loyalty and survival. Moving and ultimately uplifting, *Sky Burial* paints a unique portrait of a woman and a land, both at the mercy of fate and politics.

ISBN 978 0099461937

Order direct from www.penguin.co.uk

Miss Chopsticks

Xinran's first novel follows Sisters Three, Five and Six. They may not have much education, but they know two things for certain: their mother is a failure because she hasn't produced a son, and they only merit a number as a name. Women, their father tells them, are like chopsticks: utilitarian and easily broken.

But when they leave their home in the countryside to seek their fortune in the big city, their eyes are suddenly and shockingly opened. Together they find jobs, make new friends, and learn more than a few lessons about life...

ISBN 978 0099501534

Order direct from www.penguin.co.uk

Message from an Unknown Chinese Mother

Ten chapters, ten women and many stories of heartbreak, including her own: Xinran takes us right into the lives of Chinese women and their lost daughters. Whether as a consequence of the single-child policy, destructive age-old traditions or hideous economic necessity, these women had to give up their daughters for adoption, others were forced to abandon them, and others even had to watch their baby daughters being taken away at birth and drowned.

Personal, immediate, and full of sorrow, this book sends a heart-rending message to those girls who were adopted, showing them how things really were for their mothers and offering reassurance that they were always loved.

ISBN 978 0099535751

Order direct from www.penguin.co.uk

JOIN THE RIDER COMMUNITY

Visit us online for competitions, free books, special offers, film clips and interviews, author events and the latest news about our books and authors:

 www.riderbooks.co.uk

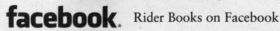 Rider Books on Facebook

@Rider_Books

 riderbooks.tumblr.com

RIDER BOOKS, 20 VAUXHALL BRIDGE ROAD, LONDON SW1V 2SA
E: INFO@RIDERBOOKS.CO.UK